The Eye of the Beholder

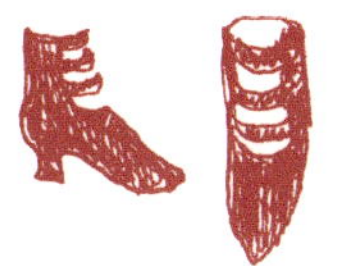

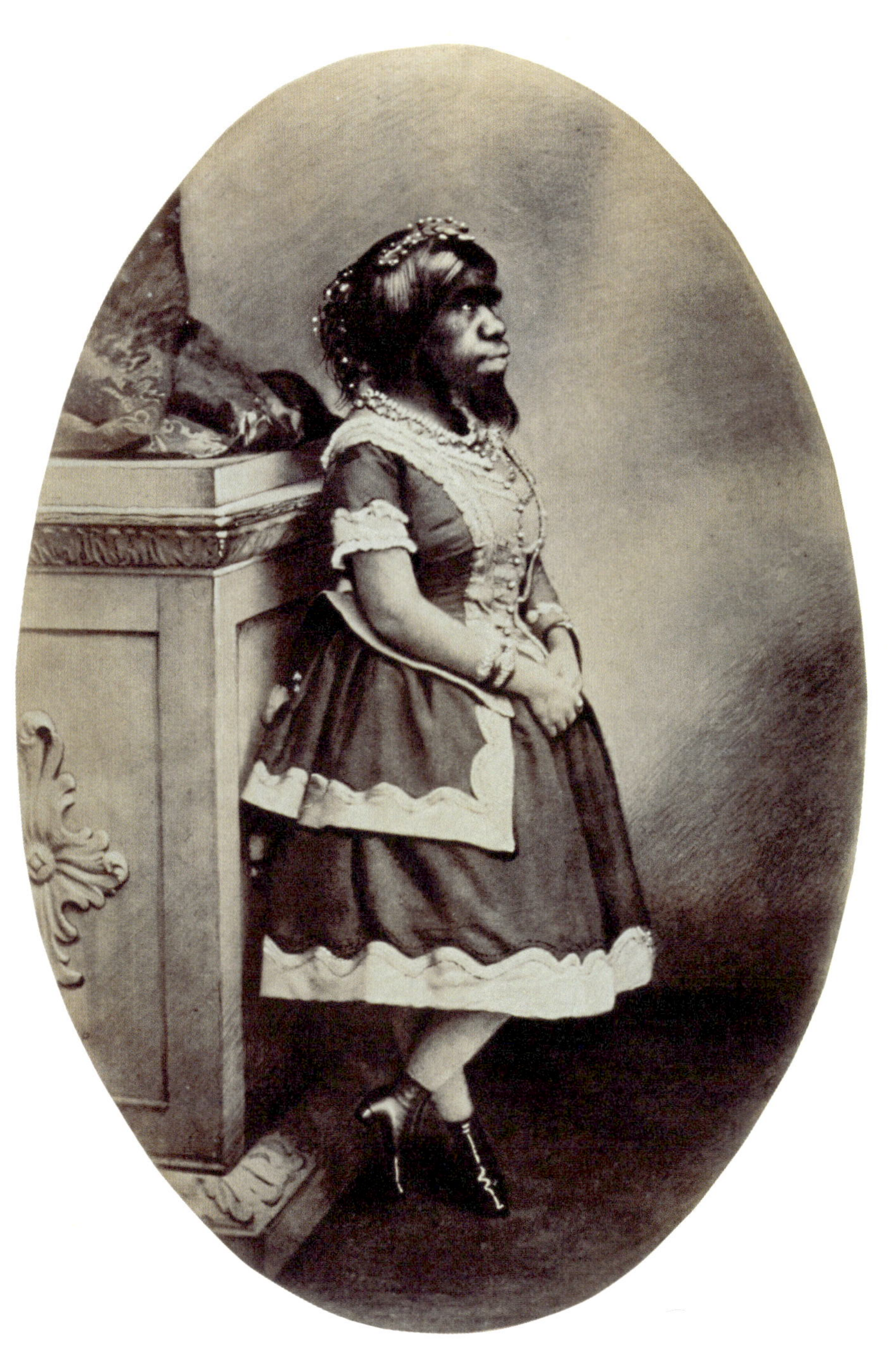

The Eye of the Beholder

JULIA PASTRANA'S LONG JOURNEY HOME

---

with essays by

LAURA ANDERSON BARBATA

JAN BONDESON

ROSEMARIE GARLAND-THOMSON

GRANT H. KESTER

BESS LOVEJOY

NICHOLAS MÁRQUEZ-GRANT

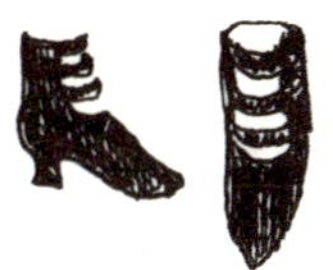

EDITED BY

LAURA ANDERSON BARBATA AND DONNA WINGATE

LUCIA | MARQUAND

SEATTLE

JAN BONDESON

ROSEMARIE GARLAND-THOMSON

JAN BONDESON

GRANT H. KESTER

NICHOLAS MÁRQUEZ-GRANT

LAURA ANDERSON BARBATA

BESS LOVEJOY

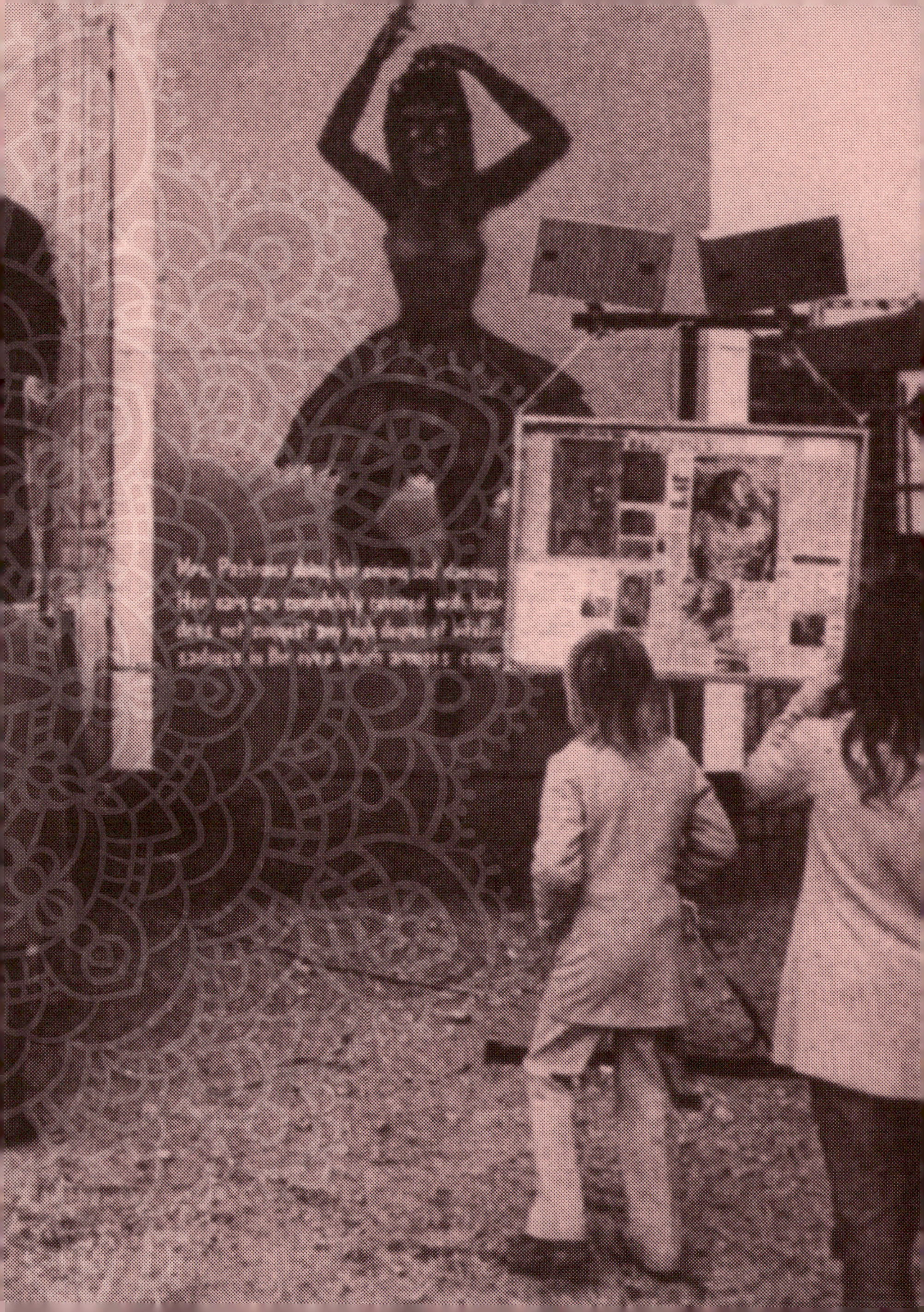

The Strange Story of Julia Pastrana

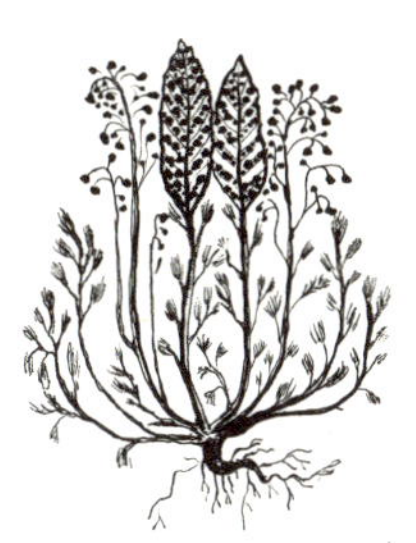

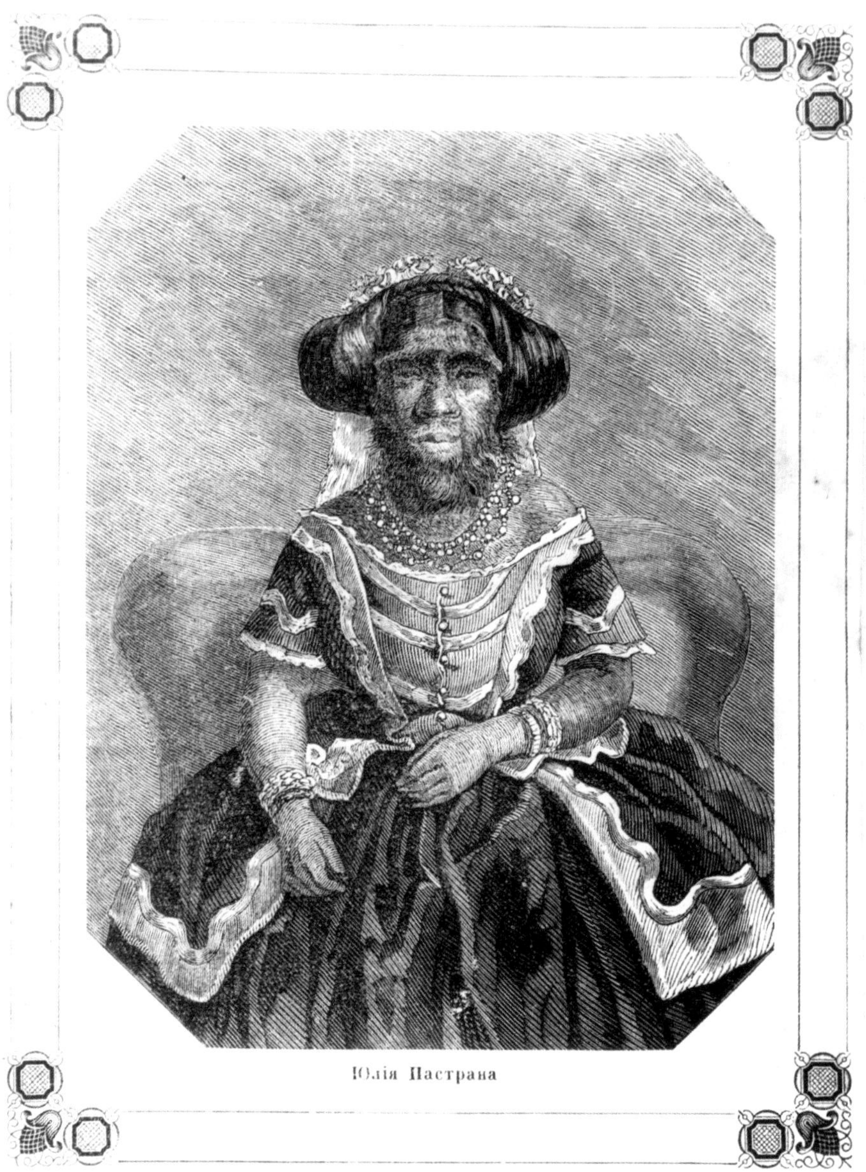

Юлія Пастрана

Drawing of Julia Pastrana, Russia, 1860

The Strange Story of
Julia Pastrana

JAN BONDESON

This essay provides a summary of the life of the Victorian "Ape-woman" or "Nondescript," Julia Pastrana (1834–1860), who has gained immortality as one of the most extreme cases of congenital excessive hairiness on record.[1] When she performed for paying viewers in the United States and Europe from 1854 until 1860, people thronged to see her, and she was many times described in the medical press of the time. Julia Pastrana remains unique in the annals of human exploitation, in that after her death during childbirth her body and that of her little son were mummified, and the corpses were exhibited for another 113 years.

The Early History of Julia Pastrana

The early life of Julia Pastrana is veiled in mystery. She appears to have been born in 1834, and is said to have belonged to a tribe of Indians who inhabited the Sierra Madre mountains in Mexico. According to contemporary exhibition pamphlets, she might have been the daughter of an Indian woman named Espinosa, who had become separated from her tribe in 1830.[2] Some years later, when Pastrana's supposed mother died, the child was sent to the nearest town. It is

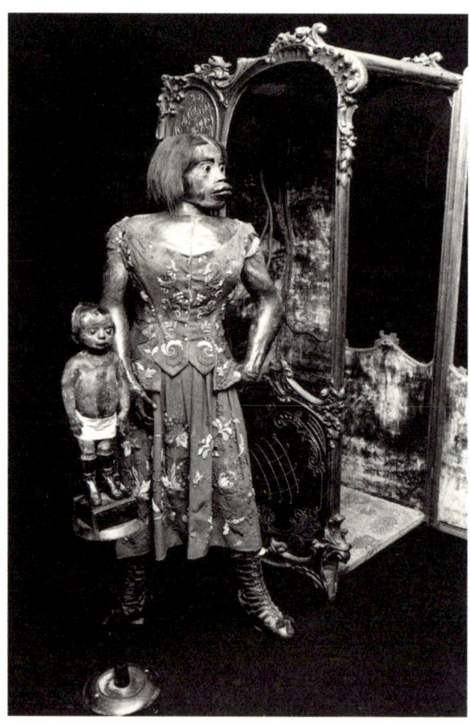

Julia Pastrana and her son, embalmed,
beside exhibition case

not stated whether her body was already covered by hair, but this is likely to have been the case, because she was taken into the family of Pedro Sanchez, governor of the state of Sinaloa at the foot of the Sierra Madre, who might well have wanted to study her as a curiosity. She was brought up to be a serving girl, and stayed in the governor's house until April 1854, when she decided to return to her tribe after being poorly treated. While she was on the way there, her extraordinary appearance was observed by an American named M. Rates, and she was persuaded to accompany him to the United States, where he would exhibit her for money.

In December 1854 Rates and Pastrana came to New York by way of New Orleans. The "Marvelous Hybrid, or Bear Woman," as she was first called, was exhibited at the Gothic Hall, 316 Broadway. As a contemporary newspaper account put it, "The eyes of this *lusus natura* [*sic*] beam with intelligence, while its jaws, jagged fangs and ears are terrifically hideous. . . . Nearly its whole frame is coated with long glossy hair. Its voice is harmonious, for this semi-human being is perfectly docile, and speaks the Spanish language." In New York, Pastrana attracted a good deal of attention, both from the public and from men of science. She was first examined by Alexander B. Mott, a medical doctor, who declared her to be a hybrid between human and orangutan, and therefore "one of the most extraordinary beings of the present day." With a new showman, J. W. Beach, Pastrana went on to New Orleans and many other American cities. In Cleveland she was seen by Professor S. Brainerd, another doctor, who examined her hair under the microscope and found that she had "no trace of Negro blood." Instead, the professor claimed that her hairy skin and protruding jaws "entitle her, I think, to the rank of a DISTINCT SPECIES."

Mott's and Brainerd's certificates were added to the exhibition pamphlet, in which it was stated that all the Indians of Pastrana's tribe were as hairy as her, and that their features had "a close resemblance to those of a bear or Orang Outang."[3] When the exhibition went on to Boston, she was shown at the Horticultural Hall during a fair. In the three-page exhibition pamphlet, a crude drawing of her is reproduced. Julia Pastrana was also shown before the Boston Natural History Society, and Samuel Kneeland Jr., the ex-curator of comparative anatomy for the society, declared in an affidavit that she was entirely human and "a perfect woman, performing all the functions of her sex." When she arrived in Baltimore in November 1855, Pastrana married Theodore Lent, who then became her manager.[4] While in Baltimore, Pastrana was invited to a military ball, where everyone present was introduced to her and shook her hand; some of the more daring military gentlemen even danced the waltz and schottische with her. Lent and Pastrana kept touring the United States well into August 1856, when "The Bear Woman—Half Human, Half Beast," as she was now called, came to Oswego.[5]

London newspapers advertised in July 1857 that "a Grand and Novel Attraction" had come to the metropolis: "Miss JULIA PASTRANA, the NONDESCRIPT, from the United States and Canada, where she has held her levees in all the principal cities, and created the greatest possible excitement, being pronounced by the most eminent Naturalists and Physicians the Wonder of the World." Theodore Lent put advertisements into many daily newspapers, in which no superlatives were spared in describing her various attractions. Lent feared that the well-informed English public would not believe the story that all the Indians of Pastrana's tribe were as hairy and apelike as her. Therefore, it was instead stated that she was "a hybrid, wherein the nature of woman predominates over the ourang-outangs," Julia's mother having strayed into a mountain region devoid of human beings but full of apes, baboons, and bears.[6] This ignores, of course, the fact that apes and baboons are not to be found in the Americas.

According to the exhibition pamphlet, Julia stood four feet six inches tall and weighed 120 pounds. She was good-natured and sociable, could speak English, French, and Spanish, as well as her native tongue, and had learned to sew, cook, wash, and iron during her sojourn in the household of Governor Sanchez. She delighted in travel, and her health was excellent. It was remarked that she learned things and retained knowledge as avidly as an eight-year-old child. She was kindly and affable during the shows, and willing to submit to any examination in order to demonstrate that her extraordinary appearance was not an imposture. In the pamphlet she was said to be always cheerful and perfectly contented with her situation in life. Lent, who might well have written or at least supplied material for the pamphlet, seems to have considered her a model freak, a house-trained monster that behaved well in front of audiences. It was stated without irony that she did not see the necessity of making money, but "there are hopes that she will acquire in time the money-getting faculty, equal to that of the rest of the family of man." Lent himself did not lack this faculty: the Nondescript attracted a good deal of publicity in the newspapers, and the exhibition soon became one of the most popular in town. During the shows, Julia entertained audiences by singing romances in English and Spanish, and dancing the Highland fling, the schottische, and other "fancy dances." Most of the accounts of Julia agree that she was a good dancer and sang well in a mezzo-soprano voice. After the entertainment, those who wished could get to know her better: "Miss Julia is pleased when the Ladies and Gentlemen ask her Questions, and examine her pretty Whiskers, of which she is very proud."[7]

The London reviews of Pastrana's performances provide interesting reading. The journalists, who had expected some dull, repulsive freak, were amazed to find her intelligent and happy. She sang well, spoke English with ease, and danced with spirit and grace. Although short and quite stout, she had a comely figure, and her hands and feet were slender and pretty. But even the jolly London journalists, who had been invited to an elegant lunch by the affable Lent, could not help feeling sorrow when they contrasted Julia's apparent happiness with her hideous face, long beard, and hairy skin. When she sang "The Last Rose of Summer" and another song called "Who Will Have Me?," they were touched by the pathos with which she appealed to the audience.[8] The exhibition of the Nondescript naturally attracted much attention also from men of science. A certain Dr. J. Z. Laurence described her as thickset and well-proportioned in body, as well as "intelligent and quick." Her body was hairy except for the palms of the hands and the soles of the feet, "especially on those parts that are ordinarily covered with hairs in the male sex." The hair was very thick and jet black, and had no disposition to curl, not even in the long beard and whiskers. He added that her breasts were remarkably well developed, and that "she menstruates regularly."[9] The naturalist Frank Buckland, who also saw and spoke to Pastrana, stated that "her features were simply hideous on account of the profusion of hair growing on her forehead, and her black beard; but her figure was exceedingly good and graceful, and her tiny foot and well-turned ankle, *bien chaussé*, perfection itself."[10]

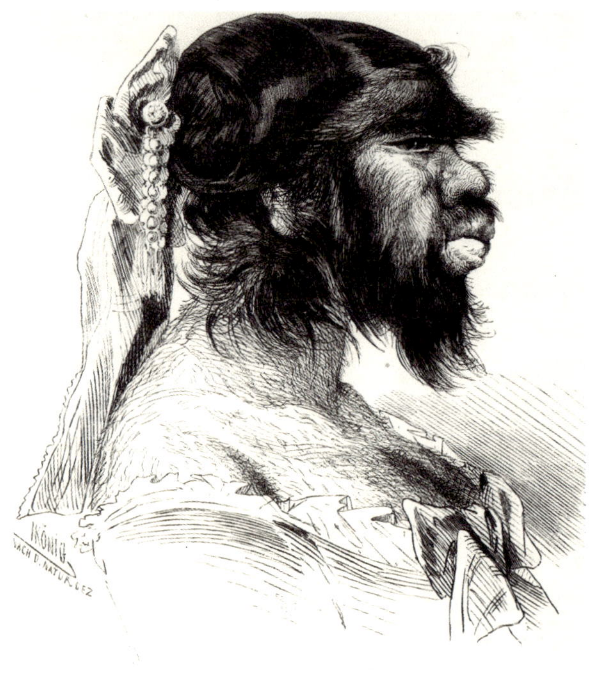

Drawing of Julia Pastrana by German artist
Herbert König, 1857

Travels on the Continent

Pastrana and Lent remained in London until September 1857, when they went on a tour of Liverpool and Newcastle, before leaving England in late 1857 and going to Berlin, where she again attracted much publicity. The German authorities discouraged degrading monster shows, but Lent managed to secure permission to exhibit her by emphasizing that she only performed as a singer and dancer. When they reached Leipzig, a play called *Der curierte Meyer* was written especially for her participation and performed at the Kroll theater. The plot of the play was that a stupid German dairyman fell in love with a woman who always wore a veil; when he was not on stage, Pastrana lifted the veil to the great amusement of the audience. This burlesque fun continued for several acts, before she showed her face to the dairyman, who was instantly cured of his infatuation. However, the German police had spies present on opening night, and the theater was closed after only two performances, on the grounds that the play was immoral and obscene. Furthermore, some German obstetricians objected strongly to the public exhibition of Pastrana, suggesting that pregnant ladies might miscarry at the sight of her, or even have children exactly like her through a "maternal impression."[11] Thus Lent had to make do with having Julia dancing Spanish *pepita* dances and singing English popular songs. Soon after the scandal surrounding the play, a magazine published an interview with Pastrana, illustrated with a drawing of her by the artist Herbert König. Her face and ears were hairy, and she had impressive whiskers, mustache, and beard. Her nose was very broad and flat, and the ears uncommonly large. Her lips were exceedingly thick, and the tongue large and shapeless. The newspaperman was impressed by her fluent conversation: she spoke of her triumphs on the stage during her tour of America and England. She said that she had had more than twenty offers of marriage during the American tour, but she had turned them down, since the suitors were not rich enough; the interviewer suspected that Lent had told her to say this in order to attract wealthy admirers.[12]

Early in 1858, Lent took Pastrana to Vienna. The exhibition was as popular as ever, and was visited by several medical men. Professor Sigmund, a Viennese anthropologist, published a short report declaring that he had never seen anything remotely like her and considered her type of hairiness to be unique. Pastrana was unwilling to submit to the professor's examination of her body, but she was persuaded by Lent, to whom she was touchingly devoted. Sigmund also had the opportunity to speak to her in private. He found that she was no semihuman monster trained to perform a few tricks, but instead was intelligent, happy, and pleased with her position in life. In view of her supposed illiteracy, he was impressed by the range of her knowledge on various subjects.[13] Pastrana never left her apartment during daytime; her manager thought that her drawing power would be diminished if she was seen by nonpaying spectators, but in the evenings

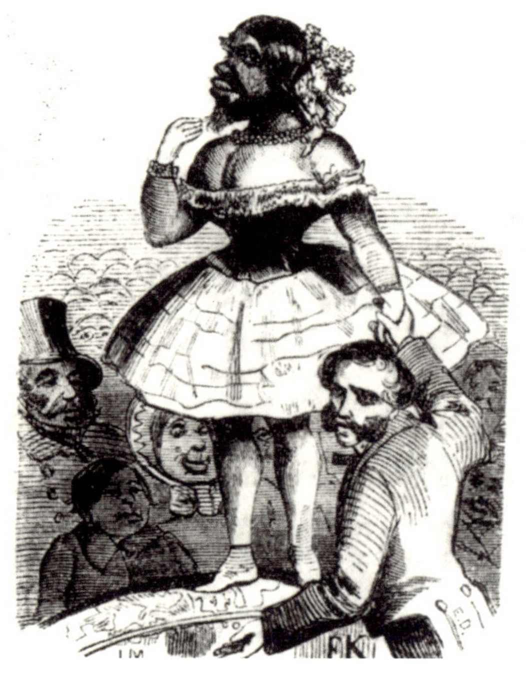

Julia Pastrana and Theodore Lent in a
Polish advertisement, 1858

she and Lent often went to the circus after she had put on a heavy veil. The German circus owner Hermann Otto agreed that Julia was clever and eager to learn, and that she was good-hearted and a skilled judge of people. Her abnormal appearance gave her much pain, and she felt ashamed to be shown as a freak of nature. When her impresario instructed her to carry a flower in her hand during the shows, and to wear an elaborate headdress, it was only to further emphasize the difference between her and the rest of her sex. According to Otto, Julia was an avid reader, and knew the world through books only. A popular Austrian singer and actress named Friederike Gossmann

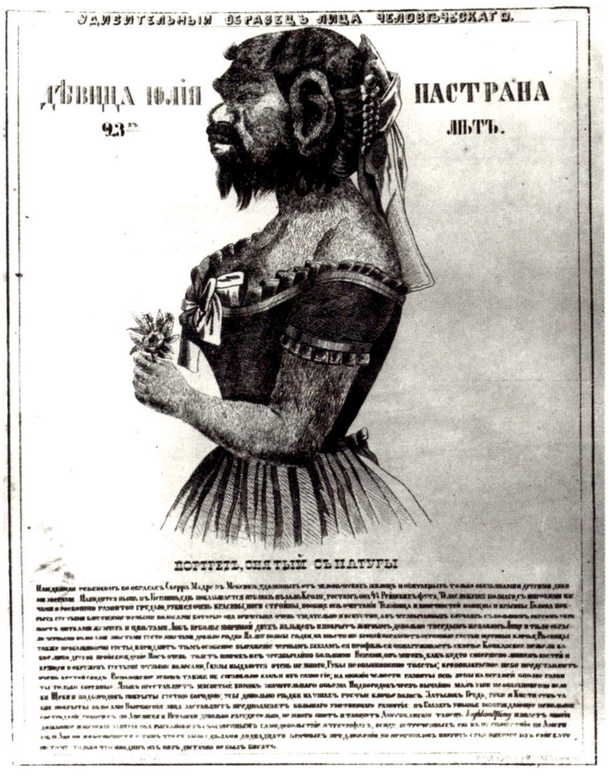

Julia Pastrana in a Russian broadside, 1860

knew Pastrana well and visited her many times, being deeply touched by her tragic fate.[14] In late 1858 she visited Poland, and seems to have caused quite a sensation in Warsaw.

Julia Pastrana's Death

In late 1859, Lent and Pastrana went to Moscow. As always, the show was a success, and they made more money than ever. After some months, Julia noticed that she was pregnant. The doctors feared a difficult childbirth due to her narrow pelvis, and she was attended by

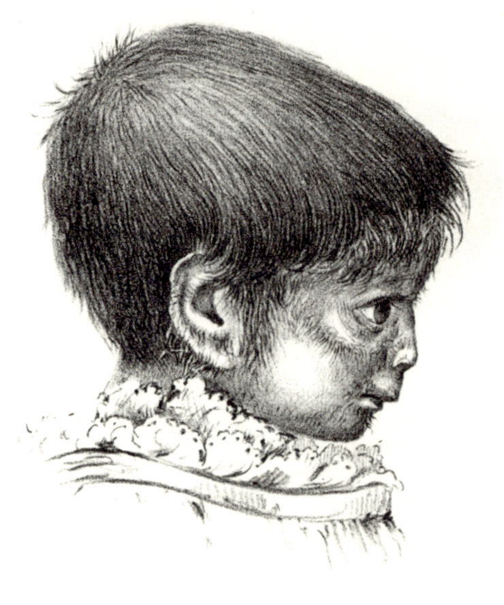

Drawing of Julia Pastrana's son, c. 1860

several obstetricians from the Moscow Accoucheur-Institut. Due to the size of the infant, obstetrical forceps were resorted to, and some lacerations could not be avoided. Julia Pastrana gave birth to a boy on March 20. She had hoped that the baby would be like his father, but his body was also hairy. The infant soon fell into a state of asphyxia but was resuscitated by the medical attendants; finally, the child died after only thirty-five hours. The distraught mother herself died on the fifth day after the delivery. According to romantic interpretations this was from a broken heart, but the pathologist ascribed it to "metro-peritonitis puerperalis." As usual, Lent was highly aware of the situation's commercial possibilities; it even seems that a crowd of titled spectators visited Pastrana on her deathbed and heard her purported last words: "I die happy; I know I have been loved for myself."

The macabre Theodore Lent was of course highly put out, having lost his prime source of income, but he managed to retrieve some capital by selling the corpses of his wife and child to a Professor Sokolov of Moscow University. Sokolov took the bodies to his Anatomical Institute in order to embalm them, using a new method of his own devising. Before the embalming, he made a thorough examination of the corpses. Pastrana's body was four feet six inches tall and weighed 112 pounds; the head was rather large in proportion to the body, and united to it by a short, stocky neck. The neck, arms, and legs were covered with hair, but the hairy growth terminated on the back in an angle, the apex of which pointed downward. The corpse's head was "unprecedented in the history of the development of the human body." All parts of it except the eyes were covered with black, bristly hairs. The beard was quite full, with whiskers hanging down on both sides like two plaits. The broad, flat nose had wide apertures, and the lips were very thick and tightly drawn. The gums were excessively thick, with a number of excrescences. The body of the infant was also examined: it was 19¼ inches long and weighed about eight pounds. The formation of the head very much resembled that of the mother. The infant's forehead was covered with dense hairs down to the eyebrows, and the neck, shoulders, and back were also totally covered with hair.[15]

Sokolov embalmed the bodies by injecting a decay-arresting mixture with a secret composition; they were photographed during this process.[16] The child's body was quite fresh, and there was no difficulty in embalming it. The mother's body was a more difficult matter, since it had decomposed a good deal. It had to be injected several times, and it took a long time before it was free from smell. All in all the embalming process took six months. The parts of the mummy that had started to decompose were gray, but the rest of the skin retained its dusky yellow hue. The breasts were somewhat wrinkled, but the face was little changed during the process of mummification, except that the eyes became somewhat sunken, the lips slightly thinner than in life, and the gums shrank. According to Frank Buckland, there was "great rascality connected with the whole business" of the embalming, but he was "not at liberty to mention the particulars."[17] It is certain that a contract between Lent and the professor was drawn up, and it is possible that the corpses were shown to visitors or otherwise indelicately treated.

The Embalmed Female Nondescript

Sokolov placed the embalmed bodies of Julia Pastrana and her child in the anatomical museum of the University of Moscow, where they became quite an attraction. However, when Lent saw how extremely lifelike the mummies had become, he tried to get them back. Since a certificate of his marriage to Julia, attested by the American consul, had to be presented for Lent to establish his claim, it seems likely that legal procedures had to be used to persuade Sokolov to give them up. According to another version, Lent had to pay Sokolov the equivalent of £800 for the mummies, having previously sold the corpses to him for £500. In February 1862 the world's most famous bearded lady again appeared before many admirers in London. The price of entrance was a shilling, which was considerably lower than during Pastrana's lifetime, but Lent could keep the exhibition open for longer hours. Furthermore, the mummy of the child was set up next to its mother on a small pedestal. Julia's mummy was dressed in an elaborate Russian dancer's costume, while the child was attired in a sailor's suit.

The remarkable exhibition of "The Embalmed Female Nondescript" was much noted in the popular press, and in the medical journal *The Lancet* it was stated that "all interested in the methods of preserving the dead will do well to examine the result of this curious and completely successful system."[18] When Frank Buckland saw the mummy, he exclaimed "Julia Pastrana!" Lent assured him that it really was the famous Nondescript, and he let Buckland examine the mummies closely. The senior taxidermist of the British Museum, Abraham Bartlett, who accompanied Buckland, had never seen mummies as well made as these. Frank Buckland described Julia Pastrana's mummy with these words: "The figure was dressed in the ordinary exhibition costume used in life, and placed erect on the table. The limbs were by no means shrunken or contracted, the arms, chest, etc., retaining their former roundness and well-formed appearance. The face was marvellous; exactly like an exceedingly good portrait in wax, but it was *not* formed in wax. The closest examination convinced me that it was the true skin, prepared in some wonderful way; the huge deformed lips and the squat nose remaining exactly as in life; and the beard and luxuriant growth of soft black hair on and about the face were in no respect changed from their former appearance."[19]

When the novelty of the Embalmed Female Nondescript had begun to fade, the mummies were lent to an English traveling museum of curiosities. In 1864 they were taken on a tour through Sweden together with a German anatomical museum.[20] Theodore Lent was now searching for another "artist" to exploit, and when he passed through Karlsbad he heard that a young lady in this town had a considerable beard. Although she was kept locked in the garden of her family's town house, Lent managed to get acquainted with her, and some weeks later he asked her parents for her hand in marriage. After some time, her father permitted the marriage, but only on the grounds that Lent promise never to exhibit his wife for money. The cunning showman agreed to these demands, but soon after the wedding he took away his wife's shaving tools and made plans for a grand tour through Europe. He announced his new bearded wife under the name Miss Zenora Pastrana, in order to exploit her predecessor's notoriety (see p. 22). In the exhibition handbills, it was stated that she was Julia's sister. Again, the talented Lent succeeded beyond all reasonable expectations: for more than ten years, they signed lucrative contracts with Europe's finest circuses and gave private performances for several royal families. Initially, the mummies were also on tour with them, but not for long; perhaps Zenora did not want to see her predecessor's ghastly, stiff grin and feel the cold stare from the black glass eyes. At any rate, the mummies were lent to the Präuscher Volksmuseum at the Prater in Vienna; the mother of the proprietor agreed to pay Lent a yearly rent of 320 talers.

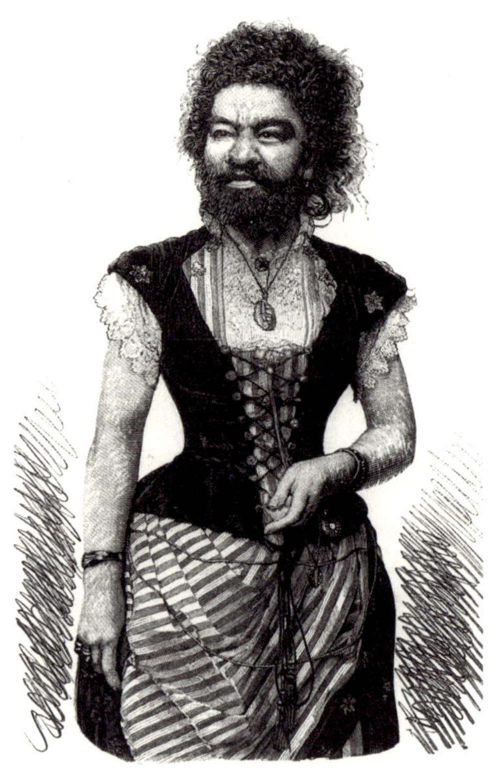

Portrait of Marie Barthel, later known as
Zenora Pastrana, c. 1864–80

In the early 1880s, Lent and Zenora retired from show business and went to St. Petersburg, where they purchased a small waxworks museum. After the lucrative tours with his two bearded wives, Lent was a wealthy man, and he allowed the Präuscher Museum to keep the mummies for a considerable annual payment. In 1884, however, he was struck by "acute weakening of the brain," and danced about in the streets, tearing up the banknotes and stock certificates that he had earned in such a peculiar way, and throwing them into the river Neva. He was taken to a Russian insane asylum, and it is unlikely that he survived long within its walls.[21] In 1888 Zenora Pastrana left Russia for Munich, fetching the two mummies on the way, which like the rest of Lent's estate were now her property. In November of that year she presented herself and Julia Pastrana's mummy before the Anthropological Society of Munich. The reason for this was probably to dispel the rumors that she and the mummified celebrity were in fact the same person, as Lent had tried to make people believe.

In 1889 Zenora gave the mummies to a Munich impresario named J. B. Gassner. She had by then settled in Dresden and married a man twenty years her junior. Gassner exhibited the mummies at various German fairs, and in 1895 he took them to a large circus convention in Vienna, where he sold them. In 1921 they were bought by the Norwegian fairground owner Håkon Jaeger Lund, who was building up a "chamber of horrors" at his large amusement park near Oslo. The mummies of Julia Pastrana and her son were part of this chamber of horrors for many years, being exhibited alongside many other bizarre preparations, such as half a man's corpse in a glass box, a human skin including the scalp, and numerous monsters in glass bottles, as well as a large collection of wax molds illustrating various diseases. During these years, the mummies disappeared as far as the scientific world was concerned. In 1926 the German circus historian Alfred Lehmann gave a radio talk on Julia and Zenora Pastrana, and he ended it by inquiring for the present whereabouts of the mummies of Julia and her son.[22] Although numerous people replied to his inquiries, and described seeing the two bearded celebrities at some stage of their careers, nobody knew where Julia Pastrana's mummy was kept.

NOTES

1   The major scholarly articles on Julia Pastrana are those by A. E. W. Miles, *Proceedings of the Royal Society of Medicine* 67 (1974), 160–64, and J. Bondeson and A. E. W. Miles, *American Journal of Medical Genetics* 47 (1993), 198–212; some additions have been made by J. Bondeson in *Cabinet of Medical Curiosities* (Ithaca, NY: Cornell University Press, 1997), 216–44, and *The Pig-Faced Lady of Manchester Square* (Stroud, UK: The History Press, 2004), 23–68.

2   The story is that when Espinosa was found in a cave six years later by some cowboys, she told them that she had been captured by a party of hostile Indians, who had imprisoned her in the cave, but no human beings could be found near these parts. The place where she was found was said to be "a region of country abounding in monkeys, baboons, and bears."

The woman was carrying a two-year-old girl, and she "professed to love this child dearly, though she disclaimed being its parent." With her husband, Espinosa took care of the child, and had her christened Julia Pastrana.

3 There are at least three original exhibition pamphlets kept in various repositories. The University of Virginia Library has *Opate Indian! The Misnomered Bear Woman Julia Pastrana*, published in Worcester in August 1855; the New York Public Library and the Yale University Library have *Hybrid Indian! The Misnomered Bear Woman Julia Pastrana*, published when she was in Boston in September 1855. Longer and more informative is *Account of Miss Pastrana the Nondescript, and the Double-Bodied Boy*, published in London in 1857; copies are kept by the British Library and by the Houghton Library of Harvard University.

4 *Buffalo Daily Courier*, November 16, 1855.

5 *Oswego Daily Times*, August 16, 1856.

6 *Account of Miss Pastrana the Nondescript, and the Double-Bodied Boy* (London, 1857).

7 Ibid.

8 *Morning Chronicle*, July 2 and August 10, 1857; *Morning Post*, August 10, 1857; *Era*, July 19, 1857; *Lloyd's Weekly Newspaper*, July 19, 1857.

9 J. Z. Laurence, *Lancet* 2 (1857): 48.

10 F. T. Buckland, *Curiosities of Natural History*, vol. 2 (London, 1865), 44–51.

11 On this obscure phenomenon, see J. Bondeson, *Cabinet of Medical Curiosities* (Ithaca, NY: Cornell University Press, 1997), 144–69.

12 *Die Gartenlaube* 48 (1857): 657–59.

13 *Wiener Medizinische Wochenschrift* 8 (1858): 108–10.

14 H. W. Otto, *Fahrend Volk* (Leipzig, 1895), 123–26.

15 J. Sokolov, *Lancet* 1 (1862): 467–69.

16 These photographs were reproduced by A. E. W. Miles in *Proceedings of the Royal Society of Medicine* 67 (1974): 160–64, from an obscure Russian article.

17 F. T. Buckland, *Curiosities of Natural History*, vol. 2.

18 *Penny Illustrated Paper*, March 1, 1862; *Freeman's Journal*, March 13, 1862; *Lancet* 1 (1862): 294.

19 F. T. Buckland, *Curiosities of Natural History*, vol. 2.

20 *Svenske Arbetaren*, April 7, 1864.

21 F. Drimmer, *Very Special People* (New York: Amjon, 1976), 311–19.

22 A. Lehmann, *Zwischen Schaubuden und Karusells* (Frankfurt, 1952), 93–95.

»zwarte haar op en om het gelaat zijn in alle opzichten gebleven als
»vroeger. Er is geen onaangename lucht, noch iets anders bij het
»lichaam, maar men kan zich moeielijk voorstellen dat dit eene mummie
»van een menschelijk wezen en geen kunstmatig gevormd model zou
»zijn. De uitstekende taxidermist, mr. BARTLETT, een man van lang-
»durige ondervinding, die de meeste gorilla's en andere groote dieren
»voor het Britsch Museum, Crystal Palace, enz. heeft opgezet, ver-
»gezelde mij en gaf mij ook te kennen dat dit het verwonderlijkste

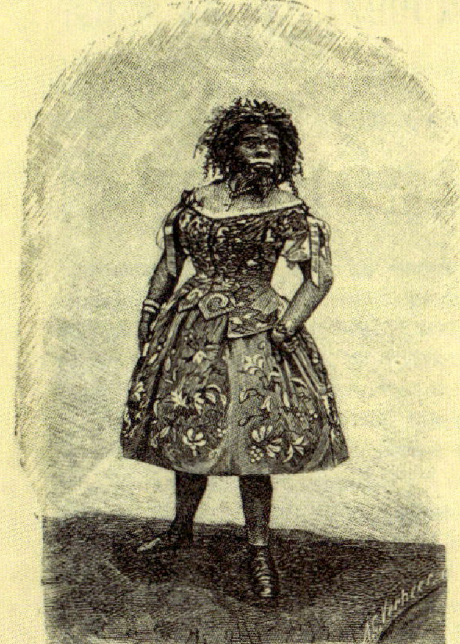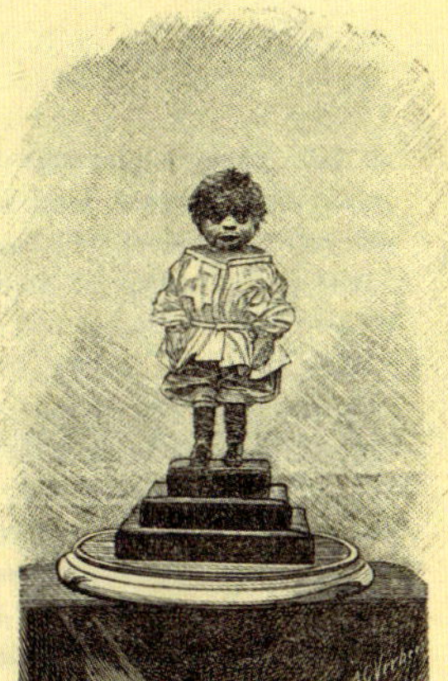

JULIA PASTRANA en haar kind.

»soort van balsemen was, dat ooit aan het publiek werd aangeboden,
»en noch hij, noch ik konde begrijpen, welke middelen daarvoor
»waren gebruikt."

Indien wij derhalve alles nagaan, wat over dit zonderlinge wezen
is in het midden gebracht, dan meen ik dat wij tot het besluit mogen
komen, dat de moeder van JULIA PASTRANA met vrij groote zekerheid

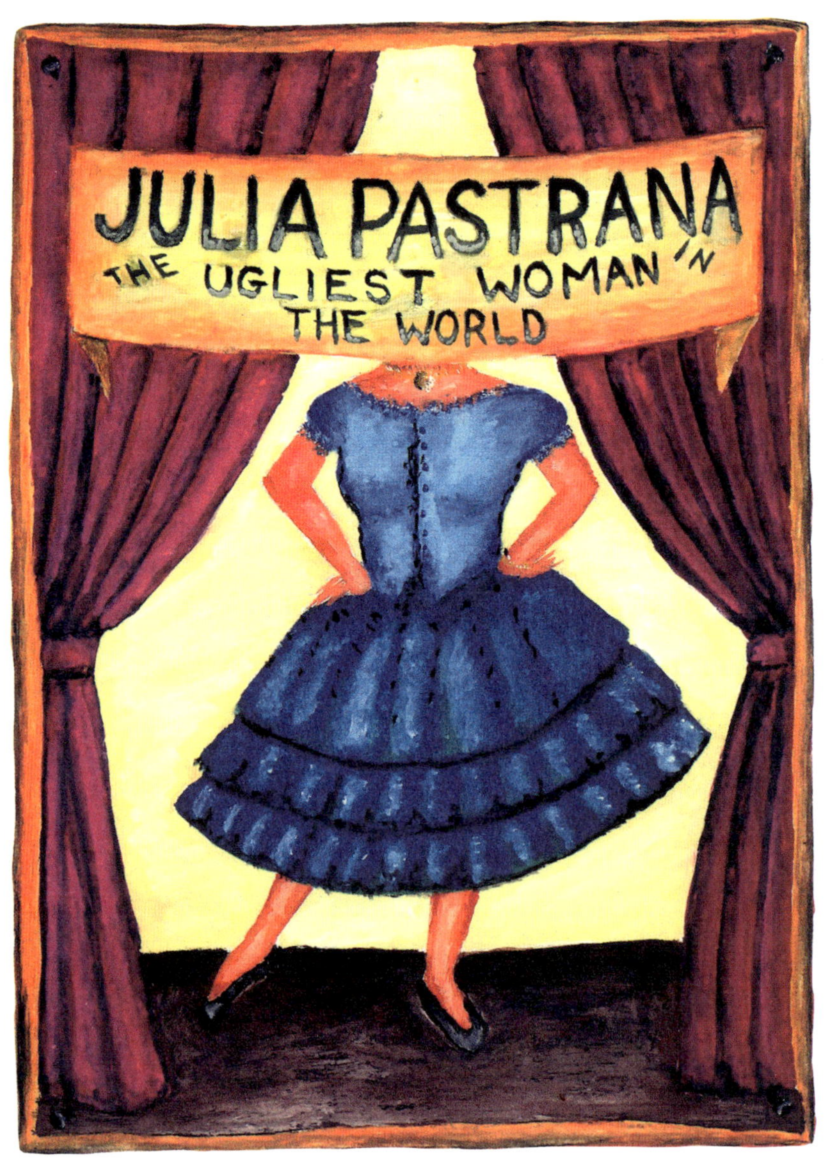

Poster by Kathleen Culebro for the play *The True History of the Tragic Life and Triumphant Death of Julia Pastrana, the Ugliest Woman in the World*, 2003

Laura Anderson Barbata and Erik Tlaseca, page from *La Extraordinaria Historia de Julia Pastrana*, zine no. 1, 2015; risograph

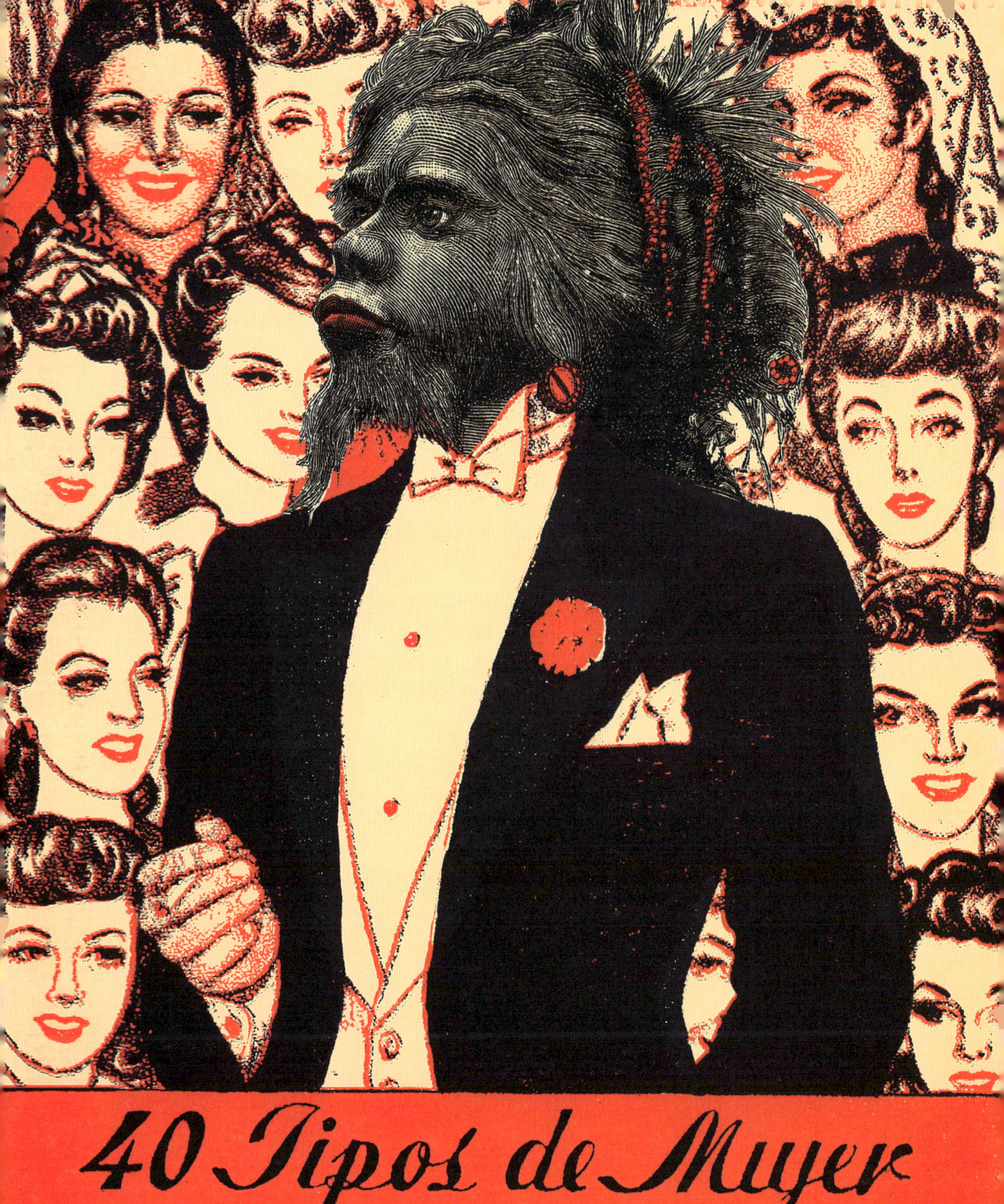
40 Tipos de Mujer
y Normas para Actuar en la
Vida Social y Mundana

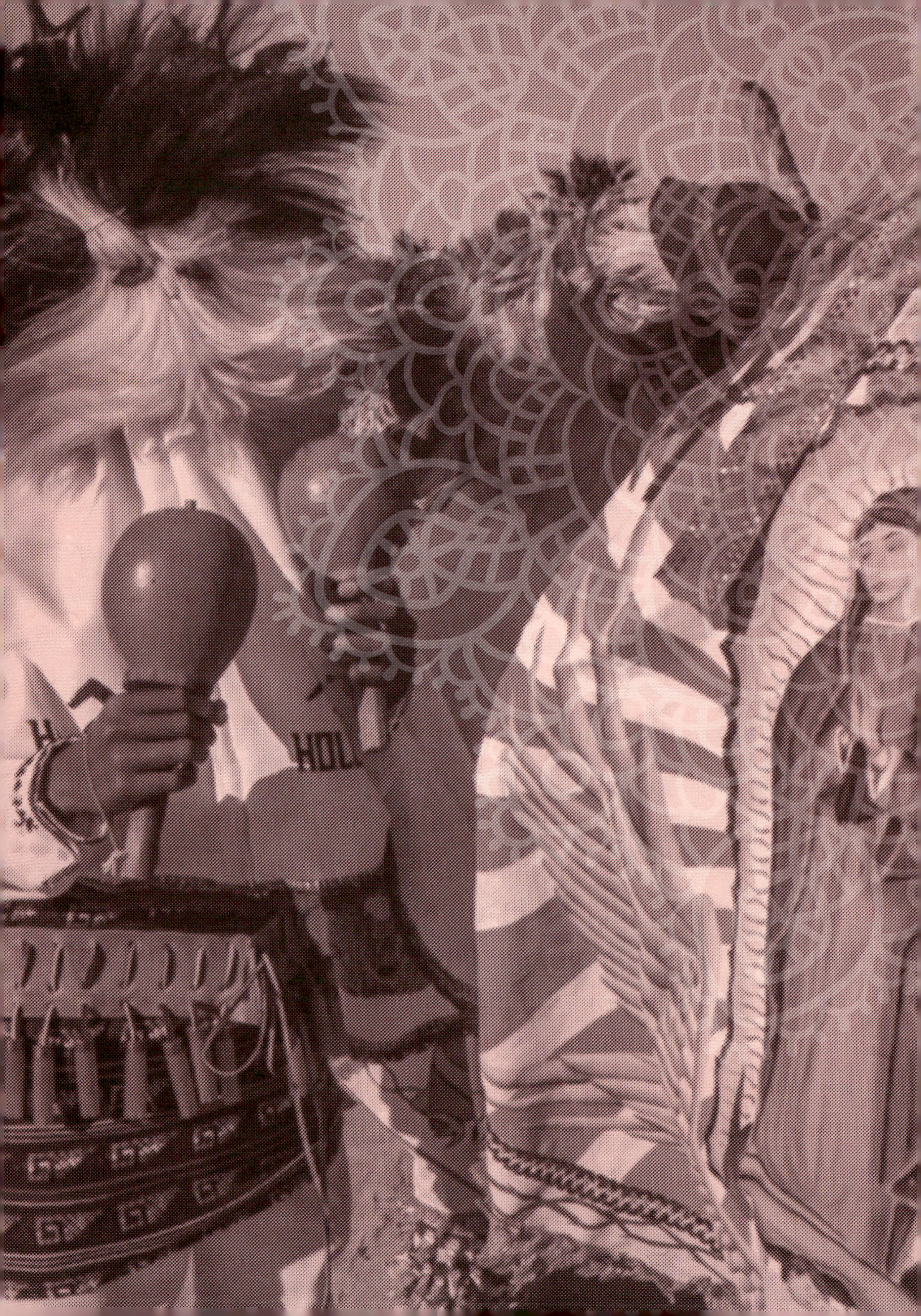
HOL

Julia Pastrana, the "Extraordinary Lady"

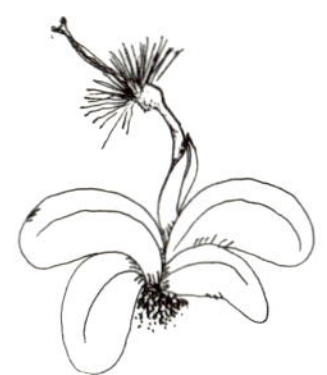

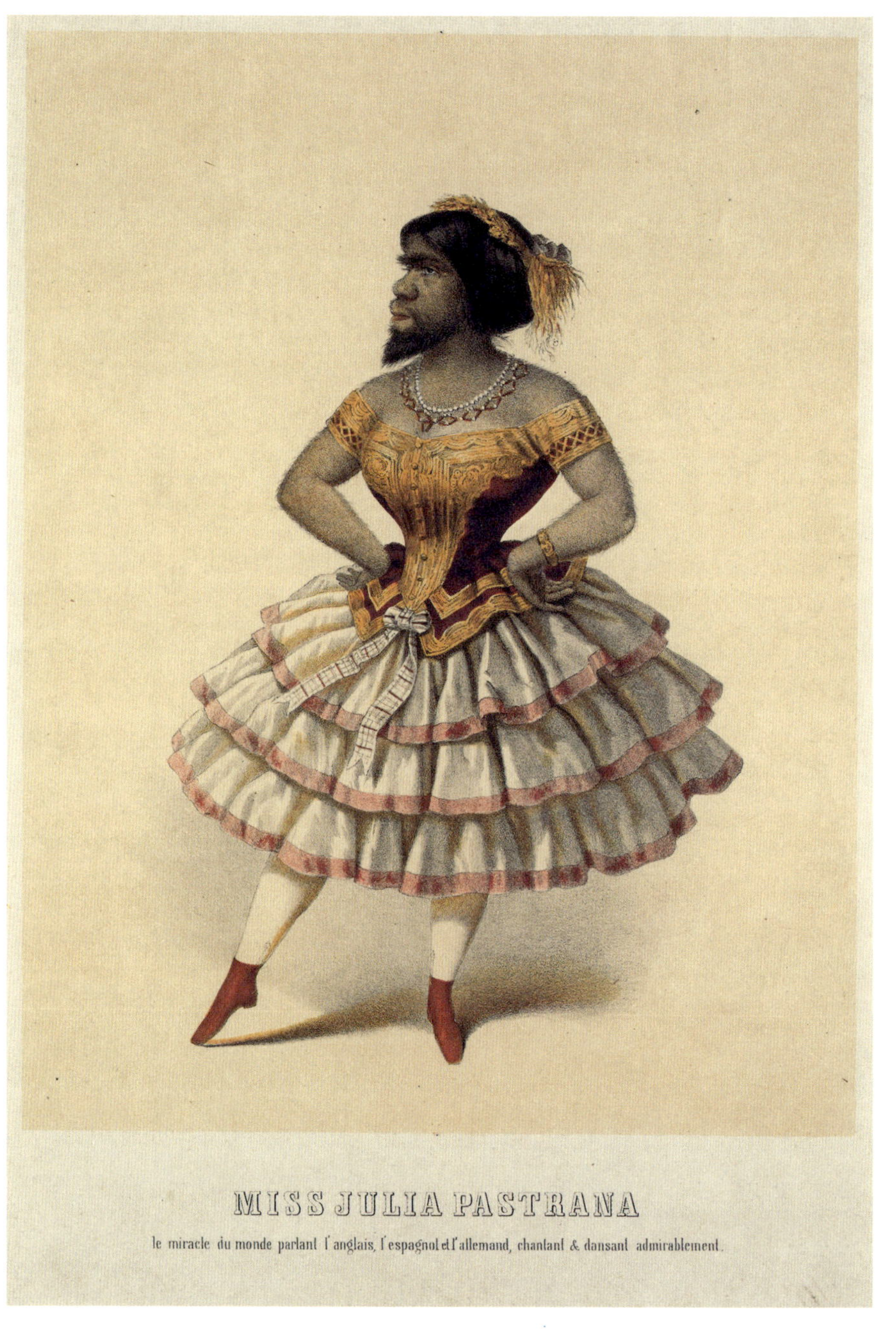

Portrait of Julia Pastrana in dance attire, c. 1857–58

Julia Pastrana, the "Extraordinary Lady"

ROSEMARIE GARLAND-THOMSON

My interest in Julia Pastrana as an important figure in the cultural history of disability stretches back across the course of my work, and I see the repatriation of her remains as part of the ongoing processes of building a world where the human variations we call disability are respected and accommodated rather than targeted for exploitation or elimination. My argument here, which I have developed over a number of years, is that seemingly unremarkable social practices, such as staring, reveal a great deal of complexity when closely analyzed.[1] Julia Pastrana's display for profit and entertainment was a prototype of the popular nineteenth-century American freak shows. This essay explores the matrix of spatial, visual, and textual rhetorics that comprise the narratives of the body that staring produces. Because displays such as Pastrana's were intensely mediated, conventionalized, and exaggerated forms of staring, they serve as especially vivid instances from which to read the complex and often contradictory narratives of bodily difference that staring generates. My aim here is twofold: first, to excavate the ways that Pastrana's display at once enforces and challenges the line between the self and the other, the human and the nonhuman, the ordinary and the extraordinary, that such spectacles rely upon; and, second, to suggest how discursive systems such as race, gender, humanness, and normativity intertwine in the social practices that constitute them. What such an examination ultimately reveals is that practices such as staring that are designed to create otherness always complicate, and often supersede, the identities and oppositions upon which they are founded.

Freak Shows in Victorian America

Julia Pastrana's exhibition was an early manifestation of the many freak shows that in the second half of the nineteenth and the early twentieth centuries capitalized upon and institutionalized the ancient practice of displaying "monsters" and prodigies as forms of religious augury. Prodigious bodies—whether the fanciful hybrids of myth, such as centaurs, satyrs, and minotaurs, or the congenitally deformed newborns who were imagined as signs from the gods—have obsessed humankind since antiquity. As the narrative of the natural world shifted from one of divine determination to secular explanation, early science viewed exceptional bodies as clues to the order of things as well as examples upon which to hone medical expertise. Irregular bodies continued to be interpreted as exegeses of the divine and natural orders by figures as respected as Cotton Mather and John Winthrop well into the seventeenth century. At the same time, these extraordinary bodies were commercialized at public fairs and on streets by showmen who charged for viewings, and also were narrativized in "monster" ballads, which offered morals drawn from the wondrous bodies.[2]

In Victorian America, a number of now-discrete disciplines and specialized practices, such as ethnography, anthropology, museum culture, anatomy, embryology, taxidermy, circuses, musical reviews, and beauty pageants, were interwoven into a discourse of the freak show. These disciplines can be sorted into two broad, competing cultural discourses that controlled the extraordinary body: entertainment—a popular, commercialized discourse—and science—the more elite, authoritative narrative of such bodies. Entertainment trafficked mainly in the rhetoric of the marvelous and wondrous, while science enlisted the logic of rationality, mastery, authority, and pathology.

By 1841, P. T. Barnum's early entertainment industry had institutionalized the once-itinerant practice of showing monsters in inns and on streets in his American Museum, which aspired to middle-class status, with temperance tracts, appeals to education, entrepreneurship, and other gestures toward bourgeois respectability.[3] Science had meanwhile institutionalized its preoccupation with monsters in the discipline of teratology, which developed elaborate taxonomies of physical deviation. The meanings imposed upon the unsettling bodies of "freaks" were articulated through many of the emerging discourses fundamental to nineteenth-century culture: not only science and entertainment, but pathology, sentimentality, anthropology, gender, and beauty. The showman, the entrepreneur, the curator, the professor of science, the impresario, the writer, the teratologist, Queen Victoria, and the most ordinary of citizens responded with wonder and delight in the communal articulation of embodied identity that was the freak show.

The immensely popular displays of figures such as Julia Pastrana were an aspect of a larger culture of exhibition that developed as a part of nineteenth-century America's concern with appearances. The secularizing, mobile, rapidly changing social order dominated increasingly by market economics, individualism, and a developing mass culture engendered both a trust in and an anxiety about how things looked. With the stable indices of a fixed social hierarchy eradicated by democracy, the shifting social and economic ranking promised by an egalitarian order needed to be displayed in an ever more subtle and inconstant system of signs. Consequently, reading everchanging meaning, status, and truth in external appearances became a challenge and an obsession for Americans enthralled with looking: museums, circuses, grand expositions, photographs, freak shows, parades, theater, and department store displays flourished as early glimmerings of what political theorist Guy Debord would later call "the society of the spectacle."

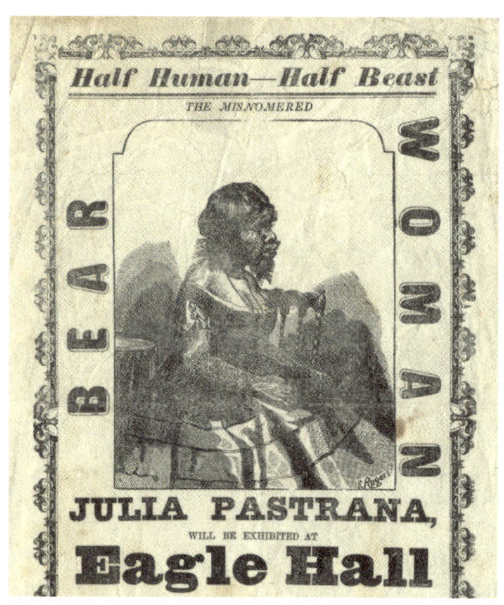

Announcement for performance at Eagle
Hall in Ogdensburgh, NY, August 16, 1856;
broadside

Since traditional structures such as kinship, titles, geography, guilds, official costuming, and other markers no longer clearly communicated one's position in society, the body was a prime indicator of social identity. Fashion, manners, and appearances became the variable registers of position and identity as the newly decontextualized body took on the burden of communication left by the demise of a formally and rigidly classed society. This context fueled the nineteenth century's fascination with the exhibition of freaks—identifying the self in and against displays of bodies whose physical particularities were embellished through hyperbolic, sensationalized performance.

The Dynamics of Staring

Pastrana's exhibition imposed upon her body the cultural meanings her historical moment required. America's preoccupation with appearances and anxieties about identity in the unstable system that was modernity in part fueled the public interest in displays of extraordinary bodies. This ritualized form of staring explored the somatic boundaries of what counted as human and ordinary at a time when new rights, demands, and privileges were assigned based on imagined human categories. Just as Pastrana was being displayed, the terms of citizenship for newly democratized nations were taking shape and being contested. The franchise and the rights it represented had been expanded in Jacksonian America, even as slavery forced a consideration of what constituted the human, and the woman's suffrage movement began pressing for a more universal conception of the citizen. In this historical context, the stakes of who was included and who was excluded in the category of "human" were high and under debate. Displays such as Pastrana's were both a manifestation of and an occasion for this debate. The spectacle of Julia Pastrana challenged her audiences by enacting a complex iconography of self and other that at once installed and destabilized the borders of human identity.

Staring is a highly structured genre of social relations that produces the narrative of human bodily variation we now call "physical disability," although the vocabulary used to describe these physical variations changes over time. The cultural work of staring is frequently to normalize the viewer by spectacularizing the body on view, fixing it in a position of difference. Yet even as staring attempts to enforce difference, an analysis of its dynamics suggests how seemingly firm identity categories inflect and intrude upon one another. Indeed, what sustains staring are the very entanglements and contradictions of the identities it works at creating. Staring is, ultimately, an intense visual exchange that makes meaning.[4]

Staring enacts a cultural choreography between a disembodied spectator and an embodied spectacle that attempts to verify norms and establish differences. Staring is a mediation between viewer and viewed that exaggerates particularity by turning the visible body into a series of theatrical props, gestures, or poses imbued with hyperbolic significance. For instance, the conventions of staring literally

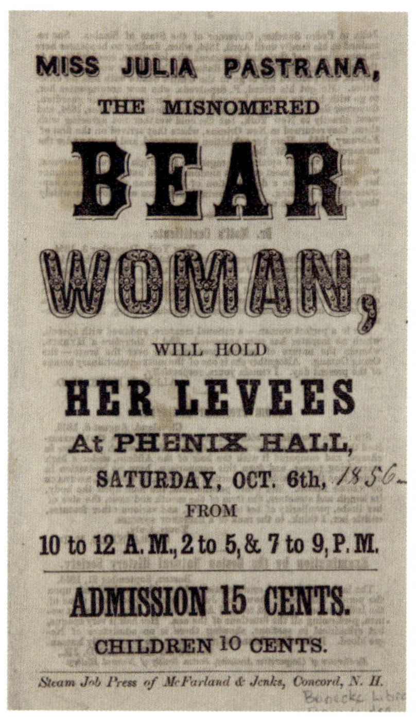

Announcement for the appearance of
"The Misnomered Bear Woman," 1856

spotlighted differences and incongruities, such as Pastrana's "jagged fangs," the "hideous" yet "intelligent" face, the "long glossy hair" covering the body, and the "harmonious" voice.[5] Moreover, the display was always sensationalized and exaggerated by jarring contrasts and perplexing contradictions: Pastrana's hirsute face was set off with feminizing hair ribbons; her singing emphasized the distorted dentition; this apparent lady was covered with thick, black hair.

Staring thus produces narratives of the body such as the deviant, the delightful, the marvelous, the primitive, the exotic, the alarming, and the pathetic. As a kind of cultural didacticism where an array of scripts, roles, and positions can be writ large, staring struggles to establish a border between the canonical body of the citizen and the iconoclastic body of the freak as stable signifiers of identity and cultural legitimacy. Staring at Pastrana offered viewers an arena of self-contemplation for the price of a ticket.

Although Pastrana's presentation magnified contradictions and confused categories, the choreography of staring that structured the relation between Pastrana and her viewers was rigidly prescribed and monitored. For example, the mediating "printed history" that accompanied Pastrana's exhibition explicitly instructed her viewers as to their appropriate roles, entitlements, and expectations. The spatial conventions that controlled the visual dynamic between spectator and object of speculation created the nonreciprocal relationship of the stare. The entirely visual nature of the stare, mediated by the conventional show language, enforces distance, precluding the more intimate exchange of touch or dialogue. Pastrana was on a stage or in some other highly controlled setting whenever audiences saw her.[6] Staring in this context grants all perspective and agency to the starer, who sees, moves, defines, judges, names, responds, thrills, and delights. The pamphlet accompanying Pastrana's exhibition sets up a rhetorical "we" that fuses showman, audience, and prospective viewers into a single, staring, normative perspective that looks, advances, experiences, and testifies:

> *Language fails us, when we attempt to depict the mingled sensations that filled our minds, at* even a first sight *of Miss Julia Pastrana. A* closer inspection *struck us with awe; a* lengthened interview *created astonishment unbounded; and a* minute examination, *compared with the printed history of her in our hands, which we purchased there, including an intense attention to her various entertaining performances (referred to in the above advertisement), so inspired us with amazement and delight, that,* "Strangely-formed Being!"— "Singular-looking Creature!"—"Wonderful Curiosity of Nature!" *and other ejaculations manifesting the excitement we were under, involuntarily escaped from our lips, and which were no sooner overheard by the spectators nearest*

*to us, but they were caught up and responded to in a similar
strain by every lady and gentleman present; so extraordinary
and fearfully wonderfully they deemed the "Nondescript,"
that their eyes feasted upon.*[7]

In this narrative Pastrana is the passive object upon whom the
viewer advances from "first sight," to a "closer inspection," to a
"lengthened interview," and finally to a "minute examination." With
each move closer, the starer responds with increasing intensity, from
"sensation," to "astonishment," to "amazement," "delight," and "excitement." Here is the rhetoric of wonder, designed to evoke what literary theorist Stephen Greenblatt has called "exalted attention."[8] While
this trajectory is one of arousal and fulfillment, designed primarily
to get viewers' money, it is also one of license, in which the viewer
is not only satisfied but empowered as an epistemological authority.
The exhibition is an occasion for the onlooker to "feast" upon privileged knowledge. Thus the hyperbolic show language enlists a profitable synesthesia in which the eye that looks becomes the mouth that
"feast[s]." The spectacle of Pastrana, the "nondescript," becomes
here a visual form of cannibalism in which the ordinary spectator
consumes the ancient, wondrous power of the extraordinary body
and transforms it into the authority of a knowing, nonparticular-
ized subject of modernity who, by contrast to Pastrana, is comfort-
ingly normal.

Pastrana's body functioned as a text that unsettled the onlookers'
world view, even as they tried to find a reassuring coherence about
the order of things, their place in that order, and about what human
identity might be. Grasping the truths embedded in appearances was
the compelling challenge that such displays offered onlookers, driv-
ing them in huge numbers to the exhibitions.[9] By describing Pastrana
as a "nondescript," a species neither previously nor easily classi-
fied in natural history, and a "misnomered," the promotional material suggested that she was a category dilemma.[10] Applied to many
other anomalies as well, the term "nondescript" lifted her out of the

coherent empiricist scheme that catalogued and ranked living things and flung her into a tantalizing realm of ambiguity, where onlookers either anxiously or sanguinely hone their personal authority as interpreters of the material world. The scientific taxonomies she eluded depended upon empirical observation and predictable reoccurrence that the staring dynamic replicated and parodied, investing the authority of the observer in the spectator. Indeed, the fundamental dynamic of Pastrana's display was to expose her body as the object of observation and interpretation while eclipsing the observer, who has the power to define. By framing her as "nondescript" and "misnomered" within some natural order, her publicists invited viewers to define her in relation to themselves and to verify their imagined arrangement of the world and their place within it.

The ultimate aim of this nineteenth-century obsession with classification was to justify a political, economic, and moral hierarchy that posited the figure of a certain type of Anglo male as superior to all living things and the legitimate heir to power and privilege. This ontological blueprint of status depended upon establishing discrete categories authenticated by the material differences we call species, race, and gender. Pastrana's body and presentation troubled several oppositions fundamental to the accepted social order, challenging its coherence, refuting its logic, sparking debate, firing anxiety—all the while making Pastrana's handlers rich and making her famous. The conventions of the stare recruited Pastrana's body in order to question five foundational cultural oppositions that structured the nineteenth-century social order: human/animal, civilized/primitive, normal/pathological, male/female, and self/other.

The Human/Animal Opposition

Narratives from Genesis, to the divine order posited by the Great Chain of Being, to the evolutionary ideas of Charles Darwin had long sought to establish a natural order that elevated "man" above animals and differentiated them absolutely. The dominion Genesis promised to man over the world required a distinct and hierarchical relation between man and beast. The idea of natural rights that animated American democracy hinged upon who might be included in the definition of a citizen. The democratic suggestion that simple humanity might be the criterion for citizenship threatened social hierarchies by implying power sharing among all humans. Consequently, much nineteenth-century science devoted itself to policing the category of the human by questioning the full humanity of women and people of color in order to justify the exclusionary practices of slavery and limited enfranchisement.[11]

Pastrana's exhibition capitalized on this anxiously contested notion of the human by presenting her as a creature part human and part beast. Such show sobriquets as "Bear Woman," "Baboon Lady," and "Ape Woman" enlist her hirsute body in a fantasy of species fusion that harkens back to early interpretations of prodigious bodies.[12] The unsettling appearance of bodies like Pastrana's in a prescientific era was explained as the result of unnatural unions between animals and humans. For instance, some of what are now known to be dermatological disorders produced narratives of "fish people"; the occasional extremely hirsute person such as Pastrana was taken as the offspring of a furry beast and a human; unusually formed newborns were imagined as the progeny of pigs (a frequent disguise of the devil). Indeed, man's sense of being above animals in the natural order was apparently so fragile, and a strict boundary so essential to man's sense of a privileged identity, that bestiality—thought to produce hybrids— became a capital offense in England in 1534.[13]

The sensationalized entertainment conventions that directed Pastrana's exhibition appealed to this earlier, vanished era of superstition and the fabulous by exploiting the once popular suspicion that animals and humans could interbreed, kindling both the anxiety of identity and the wonder of the miraculous. A souvenir book of her "curious history" announces, for example, "Her Remarkable Formation, and Mysterious Parentage, and how she was discovered in a cave, suckled by her Indian Mother, DWELLING ONLY WITH BABOONS,

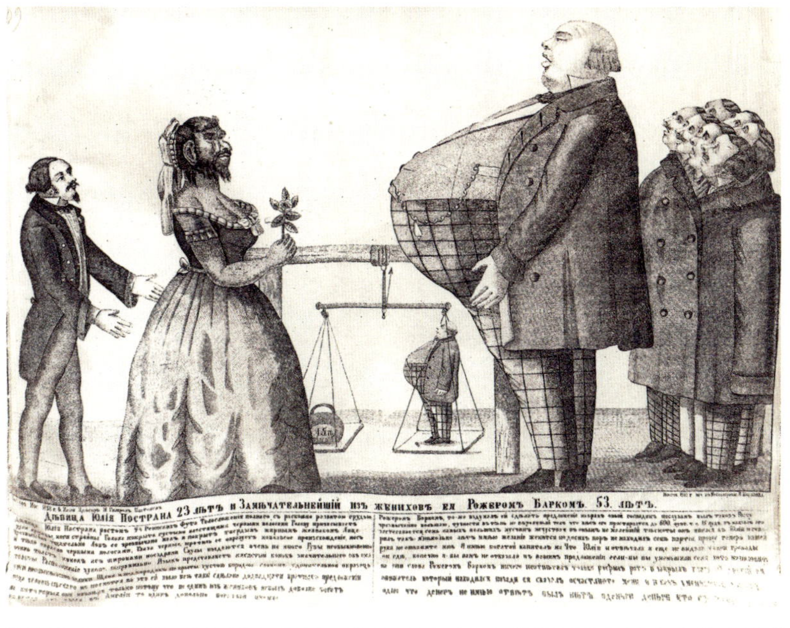

Theodore Lent and Julia Pastrana in Russia, 1858; lithograph

BEARS, AND MONKEYS." This titillating narrative suggests bestiality between the Indian mother and the animals at the same time that it recruits the excitement and awe of the enigmatic. With this strategy, exhibitors could seduce viewers by simultaneously assuaging potential anxieties about identity that hybridity might evoke and appealing to the viewers' authority to solve the mystery of her classification for themselves.[14]

Pastrana's exhibition appealed simultaneously to the ancient traditions of the wondrous and to the newest narratives of science. In addition to summoning the image of the hybrid marvel, her black, coarse hair and her extremely pronounced dentition were used to invoke the emerging scientific discourse of evolution by seeming to validate the troubling cousinship between humans and apes. One doctor who supposedly examined her testified that "from her uncouth gait, it may be conjectured that the mysterious animal moves as if an elongation of the spinal column should have taken place, producing a tail, which in consequence of humanity predominating, has been denied."[15] Hybridity in this account has produced a monster who is abnormal rather than marvelous, one who is arrested in evolutionary progress between beast and human.

Although no advertising I could find actually uses the term in reference to her, Pastrana is an early prototype of the "missing link," a figure from popularizations of Darwinian thought that flourished in exhibits throughout the century.[16] Thus, under the banner of popular entertainment, the rhetoric of the marvelous, and the authority of the evolutionary the question of who was human enough to be granted the natural rights promised by democracy could be posed. And the answer was implicit in the presentation: entertaining and captivating as Pastrana might be, her "hybrid" and "semi-human" figure confirmed by contrast the viewers' status as fully human, legitimate citizens.

The Civilized/Primitive Opposition

Pastrana's body also provides an opportunity to analyze the distinction between the civilized and the primitive, an element of racial discourse inflected by science that underpins the then-emergent narrative of self and other we now call anthropology. Because the display of monsters and freaks offended the sensibilities of an increasingly rigid and influential bourgeois respectability, the shows sought legitimacy under the guise of education by invoking the increasingly elite discourses of science and medicine.[17] The narrative pamphlets assure prospective audiences that "she has appeared in all the principal cities and towns, exciting the greatest curiosity, especially among the medical faculty and naturalists."[18] Yet in the nineteenth century, ethnography and monster displays had not fully separated into the realms of high and low culture as they have today.[19] Medical men and naturalists participated in her exhibition and wrote about her in their publications and memoirs. The souvenir pamphlets accompanying Pastrana's exhibition recruited scientific figures to authenticate her and mobilized the language of ethnology to lend authority to the often fraudulent biographies they offered to explain her unusual embodiment.

The pamphlets offered a racist, proto-Darwinian ethnography of her "semi-human" tribe, the so-called Root Digger Indians, that cast them as primitives whose practices were in opposition to those marking a civilized society. In the authoritative, ostensibly objective language used by nineteenth-century ethnographers, the pamphlets describe this "race" or "tribe" by detailing a supposed diet of "grasshoppers, snails, and wasps." Besides subsisting on gathered foods repugnant to the Western imagination, the "male digger never hunts, but usually depends on the exertions of his squaw" to provide food. Such a practice suggests unmanliness and ineptitude according to bourgeois conceptions of male family roles. A final testimony to these Indians' uncivilized state is their violation of the middle-class disciplinary codes of work, thrift, and cleanliness, practices that constitute virtue in the Western self: "They get their food daily, and never lay up anything. They have no cause to labor," readers are assured, and "of all the Aborigines . . . the Digger Indians are certainly the most filthy and abominable."[20] Such ethnographic descriptions simultaneously validated the civility of even the most humble or socially insecure viewer by offering an authoritative, contrasting fantasy of unequivocal primitiveness.

In opposition to but alongside ethnographic discourse was the embellished language of wonder as well, perhaps intended to draw in those readers whose repugnance had overcome their curiosity. Maintaining a balance between intriguing and disgusting the bourgeois sensibility was any freak show's rhetorical challenge. If the show were to make its audiences more civilized, it had to be careful not to allow viewers to develop a crude interest in the barbaric. An appeal to myth, wonder, and—most important—progress mitigated the coarseness of the primitive. The crude conditions of the Diggers provided a scenic background for the emergence of Julia Pastrana herself, the figure audiences paid to see. Pastrana is billed as a marvelous anomaly differentiated from the routine pack of primitives: she is "the Extraordinary Lady just imported from the regions of wonder."[21]

This narrative of the prodigious Pastrana affirms the march toward evolutionary advancement that Westerners were imagined to lead. She appears as the wondrous exemplar of civilization's sway over the primitive. In a doubled confusion of boundaries, the pamphlets claim that Pastrana is herself a hybrid between a semibrute Digger and a civilized woman. Having shown herself "capable of being cultivated and improved," Pastrana differs from her tribesmen because of her exposure to civilization.[22] After a detailed description of her simian body, a pamphlet asserts that she is "good natured, sociable, and accommodating," in contrast to her tribesmen, who are "very spiteful and hard to govern."[23] She "can speak the English and Spanish languages—dance, sing, sew, cook, wash, iron—these latter accomplishments being acquired, of course, since her introduction into civilized life."[24] She now "eats the same food as any other person, and speaks the English language."[25] It is her ultraprimitive hirsuteness and dentition juxtaposed with her civilized demeanor that make her singular and wondrous. In this narrative of progress, Pastrana's exploitation becomes a salvation, her colonization becomes a conversion, and her display becomes a testimony.

The Normal/Pathological Opposition

The authoritative discourse of medicine, an increasingly elite cousin of science, also framed Pastrana's body as a taxonomical enigma. The rhetoric of entertainment sometimes recruits the authority of medicine, dovetailing with a hint of the marvelous, as in Dr. Alex B. Mott's 1854 certificate of Pastrana's examination: "She is therefore a Hybrid," Mott concludes, "wherein the nature of woman predominates over the brute. . . . Altogether she is the most extraordinary being of the day" (see p. 46).[26] While exhibition language tends to blend wonder and science, the medical discourse purges all vestiges of awe.

Detailed observations expressed in dispassionate, elite, specialized jargon characterize Pastrana as abnormal. The esteemed British medical journal *The Lancet,* for example, trades the marvelous for the "peculiar" in its delineation of her: "Her face is peculiar: the alae of the nose are remarkably flattened and expanded, and so soft as to seem to be destitute of cartilages; the mouth is large and the lips everted—by an extraordinary thickening of the alveolar border of the upper jaw in front—below, by a warty hard growth arising from the gum."[27] Similarly, the widely published *Anomalies and Curiosities of Medicine,* compiled by the distinguished doctors George M. Gould and Walter L. Pyle, presents Pastrana as having "defective dentition" and "pronounced prognathism."[28] Gould and Pyle's book has the format and style of an encyclopedia or textbook, even though a majority of the information and illustrations come, unacknowledged, from freak shows. Thus, the entertainment discourse parades its collaboration with medicine, whereas the medical discourse suppresses the fact that doctors were actually attending the shows to examine Pastrana. What we see here, then, is the incipient demise of the freak show as the legitimate articulator of the extraordinary body and its replacement by medical discourse of pathology.

Pathology transforms hybridity into abnormality. It converts the oddity into the specimen. Whereas the spectacle of the freak exhibit tries to expand the possibilities of interpretation through sensationalism and exaggeration, the spectacle of the specimen attempts to contain those possibilities through classification and mastery. The remarkable exhibition of Pastrana's body from 1860 through 1972 illustrated this discursive shift from prodigy to pathology more strikingly than did most other cases. After her death in 1860, her embalmed body circulated for more than one hundred years as either a medical specimen or a side show, depending upon the context of its presentation. Although the pathological construction of Pastrana eventually predominated as freak shows became increasingly unacceptable to middle-class sensibilities, the narrative of Pastrana as wonder has not been easily subdued.

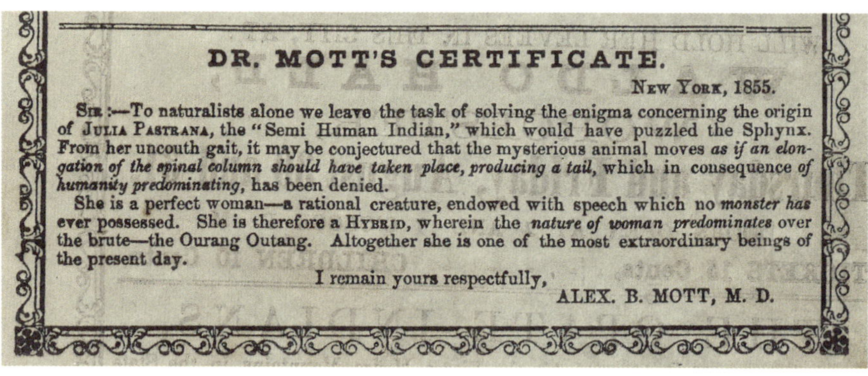

Inspection certificate of Alex B. Mott, M.D.; from *Opate Indian! The Misnomered Bear Woman,* 1855; broadside

The most intense pathologizing of Pastrana's body, both discursively and materially, occurred with her actual embalming, along with that of her child, in 1860 by Dr. J. Sokolov of Moscow University and his accompanying detailed account of that procedure in an article published in an 1862 issue of *The Lancet*. The article contains, by far, the most comprehensive description of Pastrana's body, including precise measurements and weights of every part of her anatomy, from her little finger to her "pelvicular diameter."[29] In graphic detail, Sokolov narrates the complete process of embalming both mother and child, exhaustively noting the colors, smells, textures, and extent of the decomposition against which he raced. In addition, he provides the particulars of Pastrana's difficult childbirth and the subsequent deaths of both mother and child, including diagnoses, dates, times, and names of the accoucheurs in attendance. The report includes as well an indignant explanation of how the American consul and Pastrana's husband/manager procured the bodies, which "well deserved a place among the rarities of the [Anatomical Institute's] museum," affirming that "wherever they may be they have a claim upon the scientific world."[30] Sokolov's account is essentially an autopsy report, which does not invoke a single trace of Pastrana's or her son's humanity. Both become absolute specimens in this narrative. The only subjectivity that emerges is Sokolov's pride of craftsmanship in restoring the semblance of life to dead flesh.

After being embalmed, Pastrana—in a Russian dancer's dress and with her tiny hirsute son on an elevated platform beside her—became a spectacle once again in tawdry side shows, exhibition halls, traveling circuses, and museums as prestigious as the Prater in Vienna. The famous British naturalist Francis T. Buckland, who saw her body exhibited at 191 Piccadilly, discursively reinvokes a vestige of awe by describing her in a section on human mummies in his 1888 *Curiosities of Natural History*: "The face," he notes admiringly, "was marvelous." At the same time, his recollection "of seeing and speaking to this poor Julia Pastrana when in life" restores her semihumanity, her position midway between the human and the other.[31]

The Male/Female Opposition

As if to confound the anxious nineteenth-century preoccupation about distinctions between men and women that underpinned the ideology of separate spheres, both the entertainment and the scientific discourses highlight gender transgression in their framing of Pastrana's body. For example, a characteristic medical report in *The Lancet* depends upon gendered traits as a map with which to make sense of her body. She is described as

> *a female whose main peculiarity consists in her possessing*
> *hairs nearly all over the body, and more especially on those*
> *parts which are ordinarily clothed with hairs in the male*
> *sex. . . . She has a large tuft of hair depending from the chin—*
> *a* beard, *continuous with smaller growths on the upper lip*
> *and cheeks—moustache and whiskers. . . . Indeed, the whole*
> *of the body, excepting the palms of the hands and the soles*
> *of the feet, is more or less clothed with hairs. In this respect*
> *she agrees, in an exaggerated degree, with what is not very*
> *uncommonly observed in the male sex.*[32]

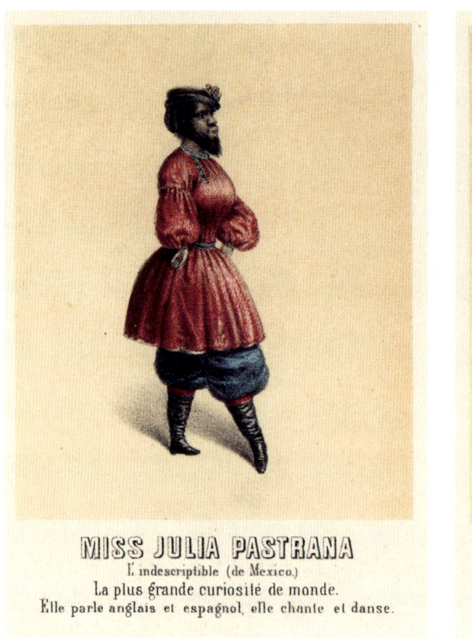

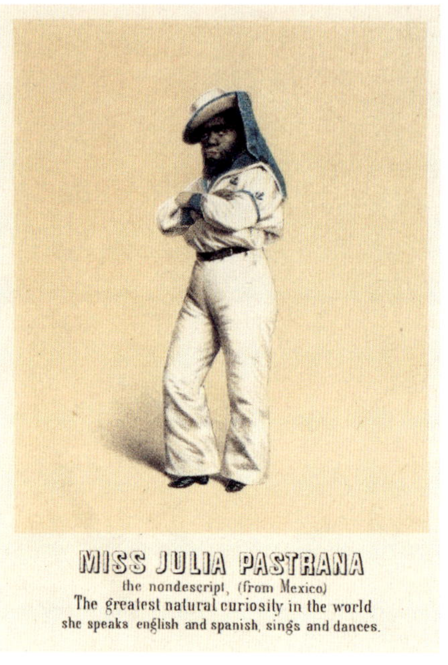

Portraits of Julia Pastrana in dance attire, c. 1850s

Pastrana's hirsuteness becomes here not the mark of an ape but the mark of a man. The journal then goes on to juxtapose these signs of the masculine with "other respects" in which Pastrana "agrees with the female. Her breasts are remarkably full and well-developed. She menstruates regularly. . . . The voice is that of a female."[33] The same body that merged the human and animal now confuses the male and female. This gendered reading of her body creates her as a hermaphrodite, an imagined ontological category that populated late-nineteenth and early-twentieth-century freak shows.[34] Indeed, both the medical and show rhetorics conflate Pastrana's multiple bodily abnormalities into a single transgression of gender: she is "a bearded woman."[35] Gender expectations become the template which render her extraordinary by placing her outside the system.

In the onstage part of her exhibition (the offstage portion being medical examinations), she performed the theatrics of femininity

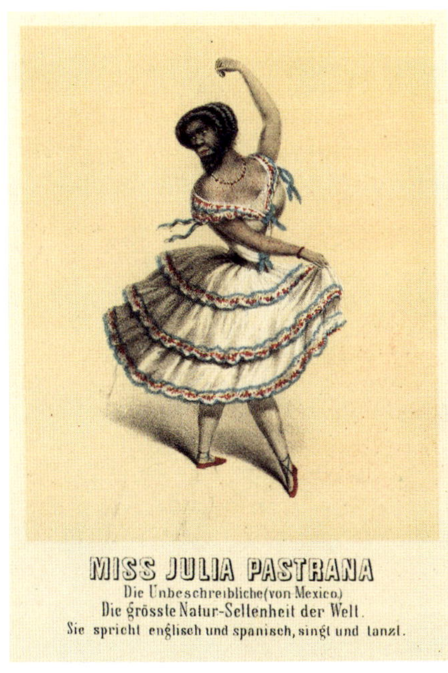

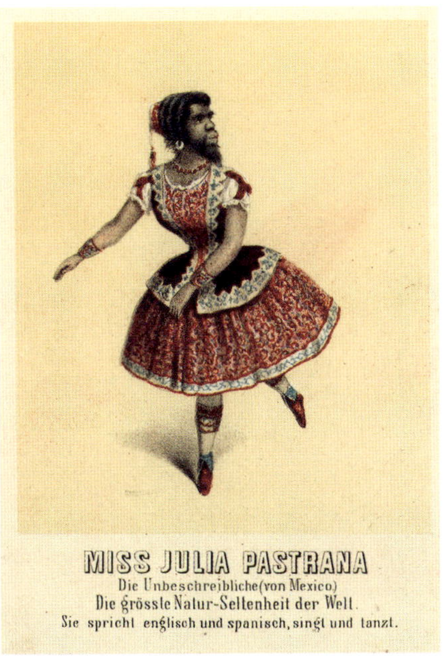

Portraits of Julia Pastrana in dance attire, c. 1850s

by dancing the popular *pepita*, doing Highland flings, and singing "Mexican songs in a quiet, sad voice like the Creoles."[36] Her costuming included roses, ribbons, elaborate headdresses, and the Russian dancer's dress she wore after being embalmed. Such hyperbolically feminine attire contrasted with her supposedly masculine face to create the disconcerting, illusory visual fusion of male and female.

The naturalist Francis T. Buckland, who examined her in life and in death, summons the language of gender to interpret Pastrana as a hybrid of the beautiful, elite lady and the bearded monster:

Her eyes were deep black, and somewhat prominent, and their lids had long, thick eyelashes: her features were simply hideous on account of the profusion of hair growing on her forehead, and her black beard; but her figure was exceedingly good and graceful, and her tiny foot and well-turned ankle,

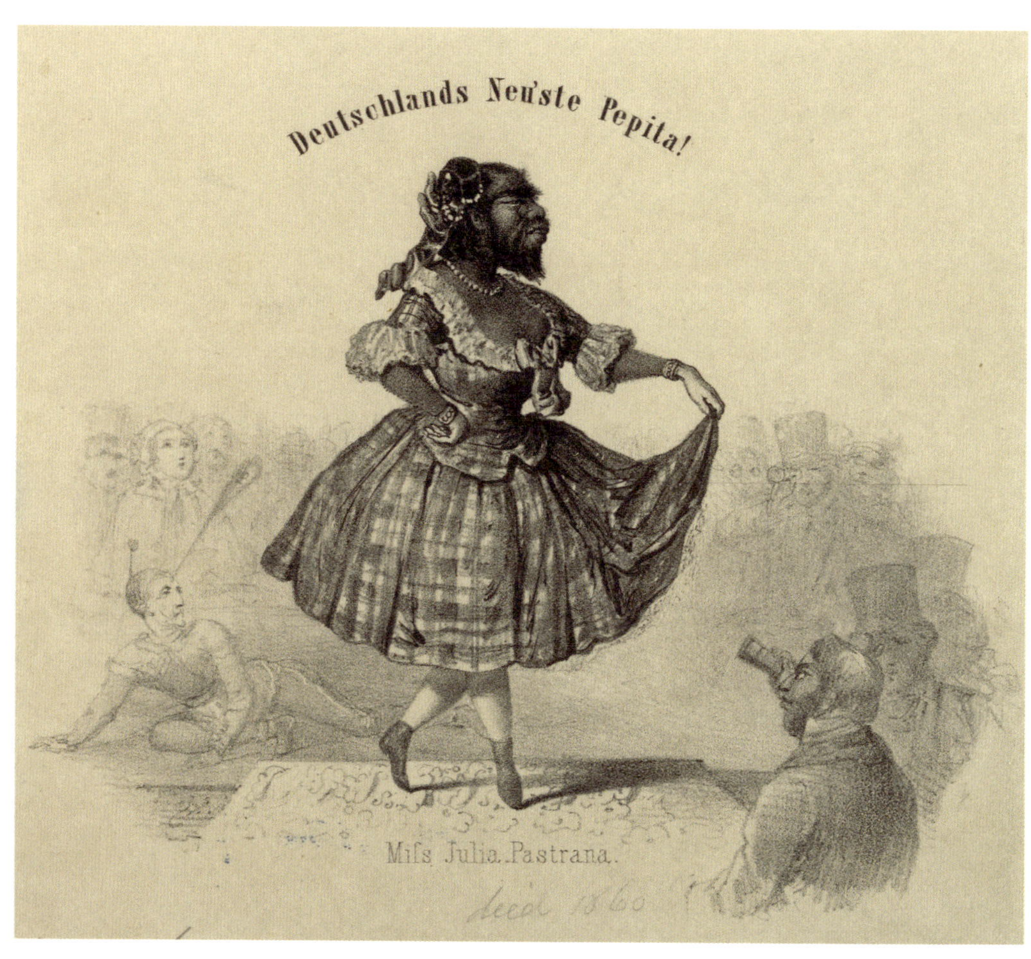

Duetschlands Neu'ste Pepita! Miss Julia Pastrana, c. 1850s

*. . . perfection itself. She had a sweet voice, great taste in
music and dancing, and could speak three languages. She
was charitable and gave largely to local institutions from
her earnings.*[37]

Here Buckland is at once attracted to and repulsed by Pastrana's
seeming fusion of the "hideous" and "perfection itself." Using the
gender system as a template to interpret her physical traits, he reads
her body as a merger of the male and female that enhances rather
than dilutes each identity. The show narratives capitalized upon this
response, heightening the anxious fascination with gender confusion
in order to draw in customers.

But if Pastrana's exhibition provoked discomfort, it also assuaged
the uneasiness viewers felt about themselves and their places in
the world. One account, for example, of Pastrana attending a ball
in Baltimore provides "a very genteel young man in citizen's dress"
an opportunity to demonstrate a kind of heroic civility despite the
discomfort that her gender trespass arouses. The highly embellished—
and probably fictional—story presents an ultrafeminized, Cinderella-
like Pastrana costumed in "a blue dress, trimmed with silver lace,
white kid gloves, black satin slippers, bracelets, watch, and splendid
set of Jewellery, including a diamond ring, which had just been made
a present to her." The reader—and prospective audience member—is
assured that "had [Pastrana's] face been screened from observation"
her femininity would have made her "the cynosure of all eyes" at the
ball. Like a proper bourgeois lady, Pastrana waltzes gracefully and
adeptly "by some *natural* intuition," inspiring a "handsome gallant
[to run up] to Miss Julia with considerable eagerness." But when
the couples face one another to dance, "the young gentleman" is
overcome momentarily by "fright or some other undefined emotion"
and exhibits "a degree of embarrassment strangely at variance with
his character." Nevertheless, he recovers in a "creditable manner"
and the ball proceeds gaily with him as its hero.[38]

The story leaves the source of his discomfort unnarrated, stressing only the severity of his response to Pastrana's transgressive face and his "genteel" recovery. This vignette assures the readers that they can maintain bourgeois decorum and self-control in the face of this shocking violation of what they imagined as a world discretely ordered into male and female. Pastrana's exhibition becomes a kind of test of the (male) spectator's capacity to absorb the instability of categories that structure self and world, "an enchanting occasion" for him to master his insecurity despite the "fright" and discomfort such ambiguity kindles.[39] This narrative of spectatorship thus instructs the viewer about how to respond to the assault on his world view that Pastrana presents.

The Self/Other Opposition

The affirmation of the viewer produced by Pastrana's exhibition is nowhere clearer than in the sentimental discourse of self and other that characterized her display. In this relational choreography, the response she elicits from her onlookers defines them, ultimately placing them in the order of things that she seemingly so upsets. Coached by the promotional material, spectators could expect a thrilling, even delightful, excursion through a disintegration and reintegration of their sense of self within the social order of Victorian America. This is perhaps what the audience was paying for. As I have already suggested, Pastrana's presentation as semihuman legitimated the status of her onlookers as fully human and thus potential citizens in a democratic order. But it was the sentimental discourse of self and other deployed in Pastrana's display that established precisely what kind of citizen her viewers might be.

Sentimentality was one element in the nineteenth-century discourse that increasingly differentiated the bourgeoisie from the working classes. The sentimental was part of a rhetoric of upward social mobility registering the refined sensibility, genteel manners, and sense of stewardship that characterized emergent middle-class respectability.[40]

In terms of bourgeois taste, such exhibitions moved from the crude to the refined and back again to the vulgar on exactly the same historical trajectory as the prevalence of sentimental discourse. By the 1860s P. T. Barnum was courting Queen Victoria and charming the world with Tom Thumb, but by 1923 one writer condemned him for the "complete indifference to the semi-humanity or sub-humanity of the horrible creatures that he often exhibited," insisting that "a nature with a shred of sensitiveness would have recoiled from the public display of these monstrosities and the sickening morbid curiosity they fostered."[41] What made spectacles such as Pastrana's exhibition acceptable and profitable was their suitability to sentimental discourse, the exercise of which was a major marker of bourgeois status in Victorian America.

Sentimentality was the production and demonstration of a certain affect that structured a social relation between the person who could show fine feeling and the one who could induce it. Pity, the primary sentimental affect, is the genteel response that often characterized relations between the bourgeoisie and the poor, the disabled, and the primitive. Pity is repugnance refined: the other becomes sympathetic rather than brutish in the service of cultivating a bourgeois self. The sentimental relationship is nonreciprocal, as it elevates the self to a position of stewardship over the other.[42] Pity thus defines its object even as it depends upon that object for its enactment. In other words, pity needs an incitement to which it must respond. Julia Pastrana's immense popularity may be explained by her function as an anchor for the respectable sentiment of pity that the newly solidifying middle class needed to display and that its aspirants needed to perfect.

Such an appeal to the ennobling emotion of pity is rather shamelessly exploited in the promotional material for Pastrana's exhibition. One account of her display insists that "there is nothing in her appearance in the least calculated to offend the sensibilities of the most

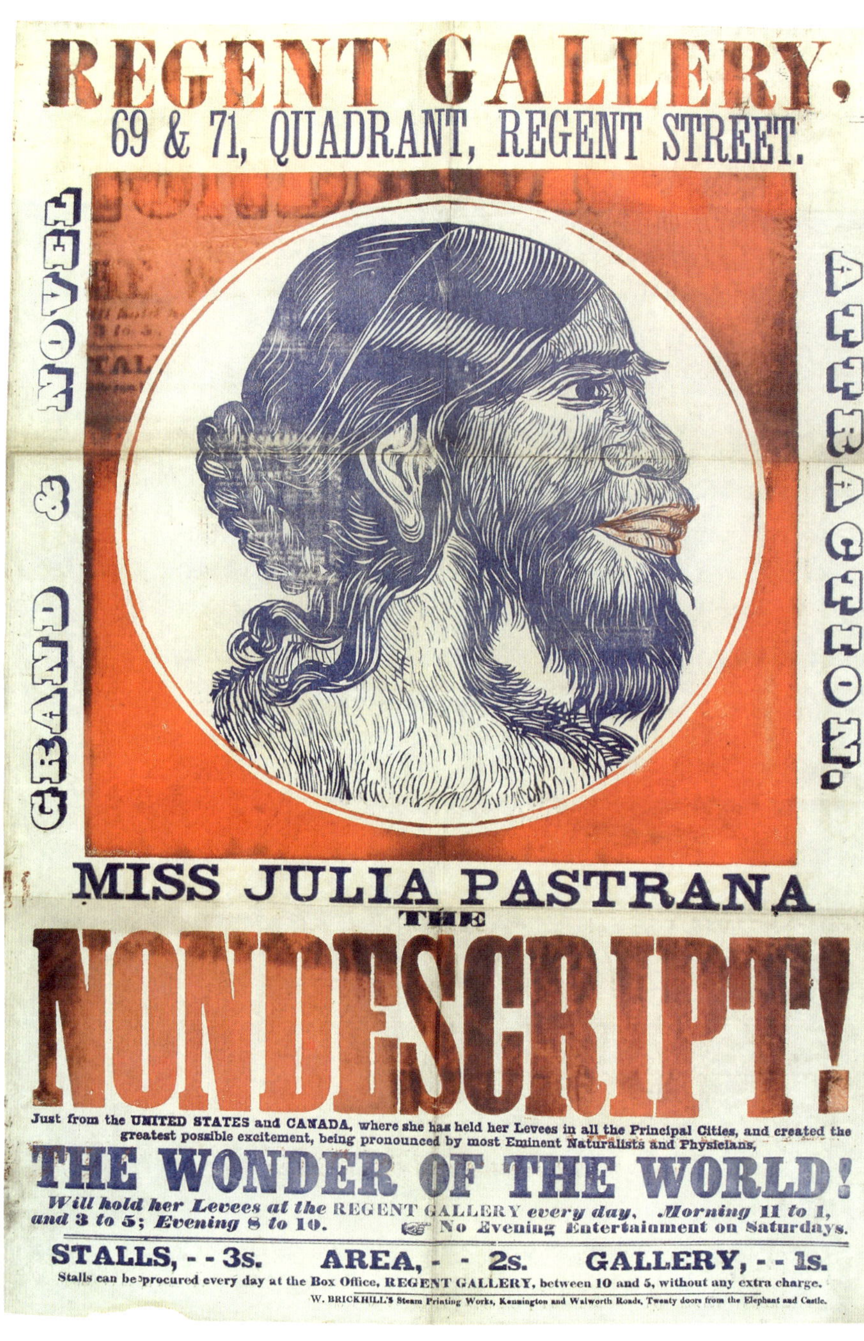

Advertisement for exhibition at Regent Gallery, London, 1857; woodcut

fastidious, whether viewed socially, morally, or physically. A feeling of pity, rather than of repugnance or antipathy is generally experienced in the bosom of all who pay her a visit."[43] Here pity keeps the onlookers "fastidious," delivering them from an interest in the lurid and from the "morbid curiosity" that such shows were often later accused of pandering to.

Similarly, Hermann Otto, who saw Pastrana's embalmed corpse on display in Vienna after ostensibly interviewing her in life, avows in his memoir, "I felt tremendous pity for this thing who could no longer see or hear, feel joy or pain, or my sorrow. I remembered her smiling face saying [of her manager/husband] 'He loves me for my own sake.'"[44] The ground for Otto's pity is what he imagines as Pastrana's capacity for the same human emotions he feels. Even though he recognizes that "poor Pastrana was known for her ugliness," Otto's interest in her transcends any fascination with the disturbing differentness of her body or with its violation of the gender order. Indeed, Otto differentiates his stare from both the medical gaze, which he says "was fascinated with Julia," and the vulgar stare:

> *To the world, she was nothing more than an aberration,*
> *something grotesque that was paraded before others for*
> *money and trained to do tricks like circus animals. For those*
> *few who knew her better, she was a warm, thoughtful, capable*
> *being with a big heart. They knew her sorrow at being on the*
> *fringe of society, not part of it, of not knowing the normal*
> *joys of family, home, love.*[45]

Otto uses sentimental rhetoric to suggest here that the state of total otherness Pastrana's "grotesque" bodily "aberration" creates for "the world" could be inflected and thus redeemed by affective properties imagined as "normal," such as "a big heart" and being "warm" and "thoughtful." Thus, he envisions her as pitiful rather than repulsive because she is like him emotionally, if not physically. By projecting the self onto the other in this manner, Otto finds verification of his own humanizing sentiments in Pastrana. His ability to pity her makes him more sensitive and cultivated, more bourgeois, than the other base spectators who comprise "the world."

Sentimentality thus hybridizes the self and the other by positing an exchange of feeling so that the other inspires elevating and humanizing sensibilities in the self which then projects those sentiments back onto the other. This sentimental economy merges identification through pity with differentiation through otherness to produce Pastrana as the hybrid of the "sensitive monster," whose role it is to instruct, edify, and thus construct the middle-class self. Through viewing Pastrana the starers become better people, citizens higher on the ladder of bourgeois respectability.

Sentimental discourse leashes spectator and spectacle together in a performance of identity that compels, delights, troubles, and affirms by confusing categories and blurring boundaries. Yet the ritual and highly stylized quality of that performance seals it off from ordinary experience, and the commercial nature of the encounter demands that it serve the viewer. In the end, for all the ambiguity staring introduces, it gestures in a conciliatory, almost nostalgic way toward affirming the boundaries that organize the order of things: "Go and see Julia Pastrana, the 'Nondescript,'" a souvenir narrative instructs, "and learn wisdom, subdued by becoming humility. Go and endeavor to realize where man's bestial attributes terminate and where those that are *Divine* begin!"[46] It was perhaps this at once sentimental and titillating suggestion that one might be able to determine a line between the "bestial" and the "divine" self that drew viewers to Pastrana. Yet her startling body invariably exceeded the discourses that audiences were invited to try to impose upon it. This exhibition was, as such, not about her, but rather about who her spectators imagined they were.

My purpose in probing the spatial and textual discourses that made up Julia Pastrana's exhibition is to show how actual social practices manipulated and complicated the often contradictory cultural categories in which they trafficked. In the case of Pastrana, the staring

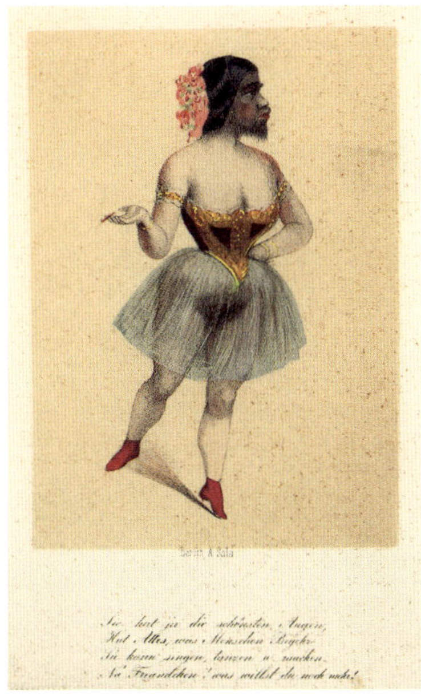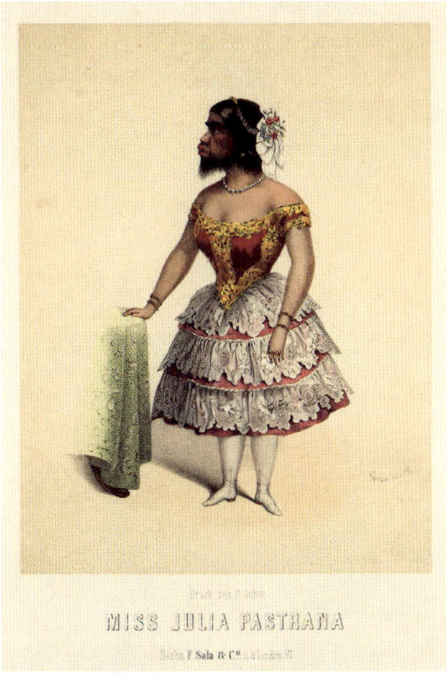

Portraits of Julia Pastrana in dance attire, c. 1850s

orchestrated by her handlers provocatively challenged the fundamental categories upon which the social order relied, so as to intensify anxieties in the viewers. By destabilizing comforting categories of identity such as human/animal, civilized/primitive, normal/pathological, male/female, and self/other, staring at Julia Pastrana mobilized viewers' fears and concerns to create the obsessed fascination that drove profits. So while the freak show seemingly depended upon an absolute distinction between the freak and the patron, the looked-upon and the looker, it in fact relentlessly contested those boundaries in order to perpetuate itself and to make money. But, of course, while it made money, the freak show also made meaning: in an age of mechanical reproduction, social instability, and economic transformation, it disseminated narratives of human bodily variation that spoke to the sociopolitical concerns of the historical moment.

NOTES

An earlier version of this essay was published as "Narratives of Deviance and Delight: Staring at Julia Pastrana, 'The Extraordinary Lady,'" in *Beyond the Binary*, ed. T. Powell (Rutgers University Press, 1998) and reprinted as "Making Freaks: Visual Rhetorics and the Making of Julia Pastrana" in *Thinking the Limits of the Body*, ed. Jeffrey Jerome Cohen and Gail Weiss (Albany: State University of New York Press, 2003). The essay in its current form updates my analysis of staring and the exhibition of Julia Pastrana presented in that earlier piece, taking into consideration her recent repatriation and the resurgence in media interest that accompanied it. I would like to gratefully acknowledge the assistance of C. Melissa Anderson in preparing this essay.

1   See Rosemarie Garland-Thomson, *Staring: How We Look* (New York: Oxford University Press, 2009).

2   For a history of the displays of monsters and freaks, sometimes referred to now as "freak studies," see Richard D. Altick, *The Shows of London* (Cambridge: Harvard University Press, 1978); Leslie A. Fiedler, *Freaks: Myths and Images of the Secret Self* (New York: Simon and Schuster, 1978); John Block Friedman, *The Monstrous Races in Medieval Art and Thought* (Cambridge: Harvard University Press, 1981); Frederick Drimmer, *Very Special People* (New York: Amjon Press, 1983); Robert Bogdan, *Freak Show: Presenting Human Oddities for Amusement and Profit* (Chicago: University of Chicago Press, 1988); Dudley Wilson, *Signs and Portents: Monstrous Births from the Middle Ages to the Enlightenment* (London: Routledge, 1993); Michael P. Winship, "Prodigies, Puritanism, and the Perils of Natural Philosophy: The Example of Cotton Mather," *William and Mary Quarterly*, 3rd series, no. 1 (January 1994): 92–105; Rosemarie Garland-Thomson, ed., *Freakery: Cultural Spectacles of the Extraordinary Body* (New York: New York University Press, 1996), especially chapters 1 and 10; Lorraine J. Daston and Katherine Park, *Wonders and the Order of Nature, 1150–1750* (New York: Zone Books, 1998); Rachel Adams, *Sideshow U.S.A.: Freaks and the American Cultural Imagination* (Chicago: University of Chicago Press, 2001); Ben Reiss, *The Showman and the Slave: Race, Death and Memory in Barnum's America* (Cambridge: Harvard University Press, 2001); Lillian Craton, *The Victorian Freak Show: The Significance of Disability and Physical Differences in 19th-Century Fiction* (Amherst, NY: Cambria Press, 2009); and Garland-Thomson, *Staring*.

3   For more on Barnum's influence in American popular culture, see Neil Harris, *Humbug: The Art of P. T. Barnum* (Boston: Little Brown, 1973); A. H. Saxon, *P. T. Barnum: The Legend and the Man* (New York University Press, 1989); Bluford Adams, *E Pluribus Barnum: The Great Showman and the Making of U.S. Popular Culture* (Minneapolis: University of Minnesota Press, 1997); and Reiss, *The Showman and the Slave*.

4   Garland-Thomson, *Staring*.

5   George C. D. Odell, *Annals of the New York Stage*, vol. 6, 1850–1857, reprint (New York: AMS Press, 1970), 413.

6   Because glimpsing a freak could be charged for, managers did not allow freaks to go freely about or to have nonpaying relationships.

7   "Curious History of the Baboon Lady, Miss Julia Pastrana," pamphlet, Harvard Theater Collection, 5.

8   Stephen Greenblatt, "Resonance and Wonder," in *Exhibiting Cultures: The Politics and Poetics of Museum Display*, eds. Ivan Karp and Steven D. Lavine (Washington, D.C.: Smithsonian Institution Press, 1991), 82.

9   Neil Harris, in *Humbug*, argues that the attraction of freak shows was that they challenged audiences to recognize fakes, or "humbugs."

10 *Miss Julia Pastrana, the Misnomered Bear Woman*, pamphlet, 1855, New York City Public Library.

11 Stephen Jay Gould, *The Mismeasure of Man* (New York: Norton, 1981).

12 "Curious History;" *Miss Julia Pastrana.*

13 Keith Thomas, *Man and the Natural World* (New York: Pantheon, 1983), 135.

14 "Curious History," 2.

15 *Miss Julia Pastrana.* Because so many of the accounts of Pastrana and other freaks are found in ephemeral promotional material, it is impossible to know whether the statements in them supposedly made by doctors and other authorities are authentic. Nevertheless, it is the cultural concepts that frame the freaks' bodies for public view rather than the authenticity of them that is useful for this analysis.

16 For a discussion of "missing link" figures, see James W. Cook Jr., "Of Men, Missing Links, and Nondescripts: The Strange Career of P. T. Barnum's 'What Is It?' Exhibition," in *Freakery*, ed. Garland-Thomson, 139–57.

17 Bruce A. McConachie, "Museum Theater and the Problem of Respectability for Mid-Century Urban Americans," in *The American Stage: Social and Economic Issues from the Colonial Period to the Present*, eds. Ron Engle and Tice L. Miller, 65–80 (New York: Cambridge University Press, 1993). On science and medicine in the freak show, see also Andrea Stulman Dennett, *Weird and Wonderful: The Dime Museum in American History* (New York: New York University Press, 1997); David T. Mitchell and Sharon L. Snyder, eds. *The Body and Physical Difference: Discourses of Disability* (Ann Arbor: Michigan University Press, 1997), especially the introduction; Lillian Craton, *The Victorian Freak Show: The Significance of Disability and Physical Differences in 19th-Century Fiction* (Amherst, NY: Cambria Press, 2009); Nadja Durbach, *Spectacles of Deformity: Freak Shows and Modern British Culture* (Berkeley: University of California Press, 2010).

18 "Curious History," 8.

19 For examples of the conflation of ethnography and show business, see Phillips Verner Bradford and Harvey Blume, *Ota Benga: The Pygmy in the Zoo* (New York: St. Martin's Press, 1992); Christopher A. Vaughan, "Ogling Igorots: The Politics and Commerce of Exhibiting Cultural Otherness, 1898–1913," in *Freakery*, ed. Rosemarie Garland Thomson, 219–33; and Adams, *Sideshow U.S.A.* For a discussion of high and low culture, see Lawrence W. Levine, *Highbrow/Lowbrow: The Emergence of Cultural Hierarchy in America* (Cambridge: Harvard University Press, 1988).

20 "Curious History," 6–7.

21 "Curious History," 5.

22 *Miss Julia Pastrana.*

23 "Curious History," 7.

24 Ibid.

25 *Miss Julia Pastrana.*

26 "Curious History," 8; *Miss Julia Pastrana.*

27 J. Z. Laurence, "A Short Account of the Bearded and Hairy Female," *The Lancet* 2 (July 11, 1857), 48.

28 George M. Gould and Walter L. Pyle, *Anomalies and Curiosities of Medicine* (Philadelphia: W. B. Saunders, 1897), 229.

29 J. Sokolov, "Julia Pastrana and Her Child," *The Lancet* 1 (May 3, 1862), quotation at 468.

30 Ibid., 468. Also see Francis T. Buckland, *Curiosities of Natural History*, vol. 4 (London: Richard Bentley and Son, 1888), 41.

31 Buckland, ibid.

32 Laurence, "A Short Account," 48.

33 Ibid.

34 See also Alice Domurat Dreger, *Hermaphrodites and the Medical Invention of Sex* (Cambridge: Harvard University Press, 1998). Medical accounts of Pastrana's body in the late twentieth century do not invoke gender to produce pathology. Rather, they focus on the terminology of her abnormality. For example, a 1993 article argues that Pastrana was an example of "congenital, generalized hypertrichosis terminalis with gingival hyperplasia," rather than one of "hypertrichosis lanuginosa"; see Jan Bondeson and A. E. W. Miles, "Julia Pastrana, the Nondescript: An Example of Congenital, Generalized Hypertrichosis Terminalis with Gingival Hyperplasia," *American Journal of Medical Genetics* 47 (1993): 198–212.

35 Gould and Pyle, *Anomalies and Curiosities*, 229.

36 Hermann W. Otto, *Fahrend Volk* (Leipzig: J. J. Weber, 1895), 123. My translation.

37 Buckland, *Curiosities*, 42.

38 "Curious History," 9.

39 Ibid., 9–10.

40 Karen Halttunen, *Confidence Men and Painted Women: A Study of Middle-Class Culture in America, 1830–1870* (New Haven: Yale University Press, 1982); Yi-Fu Tuan, *Dominance and Affection: The Making of Pets* (New Haven: Yale University Press, 1984); Lori Merish, *Sentimental Materialism: Gender, Commodity Culture, and Nineteenth-Century American Literature* (Durham, NC: Duke University Press, 2000).

41 Gamaliel Bradford, *Damaged Souls* (Port Washington, NY: Kennikat Press, 1923), 216.

42 See Julie Ellison, *Cato's Tears and the Making of Anglo-American Emotion* (Chicago: University of Chicago Press, 1999); Susan Sontag, *Regarding the Pain of Others* (New York: Penguin Books, 2003); and Merish, *Sentimental Materialism*.

43 "Curious History," 12.

44 Otto, *Fahrend Volk*, 125.

45 Ibid., 123–24.

46 "Curious History," 12.

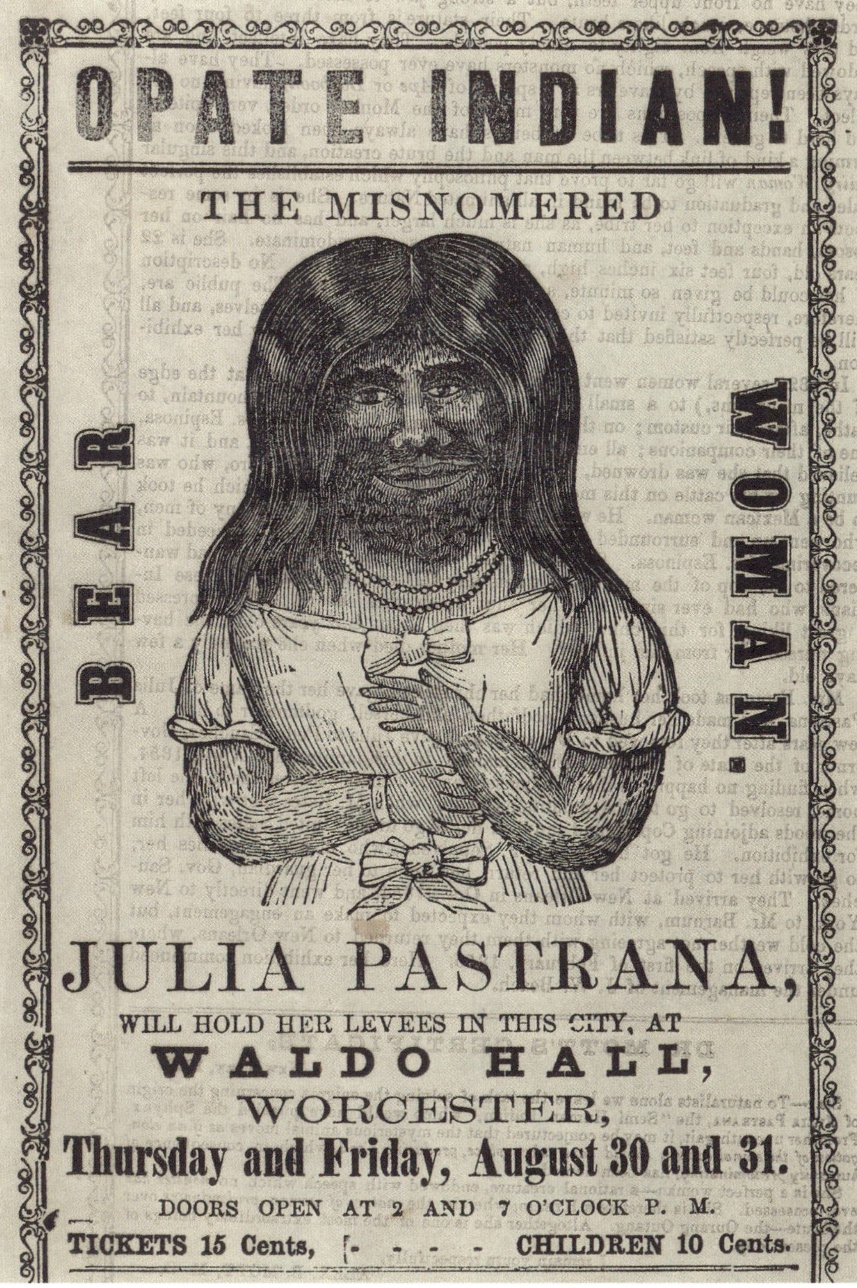

Announcement for exhibition at Waldo Hall, Worcester, 1855; broadside

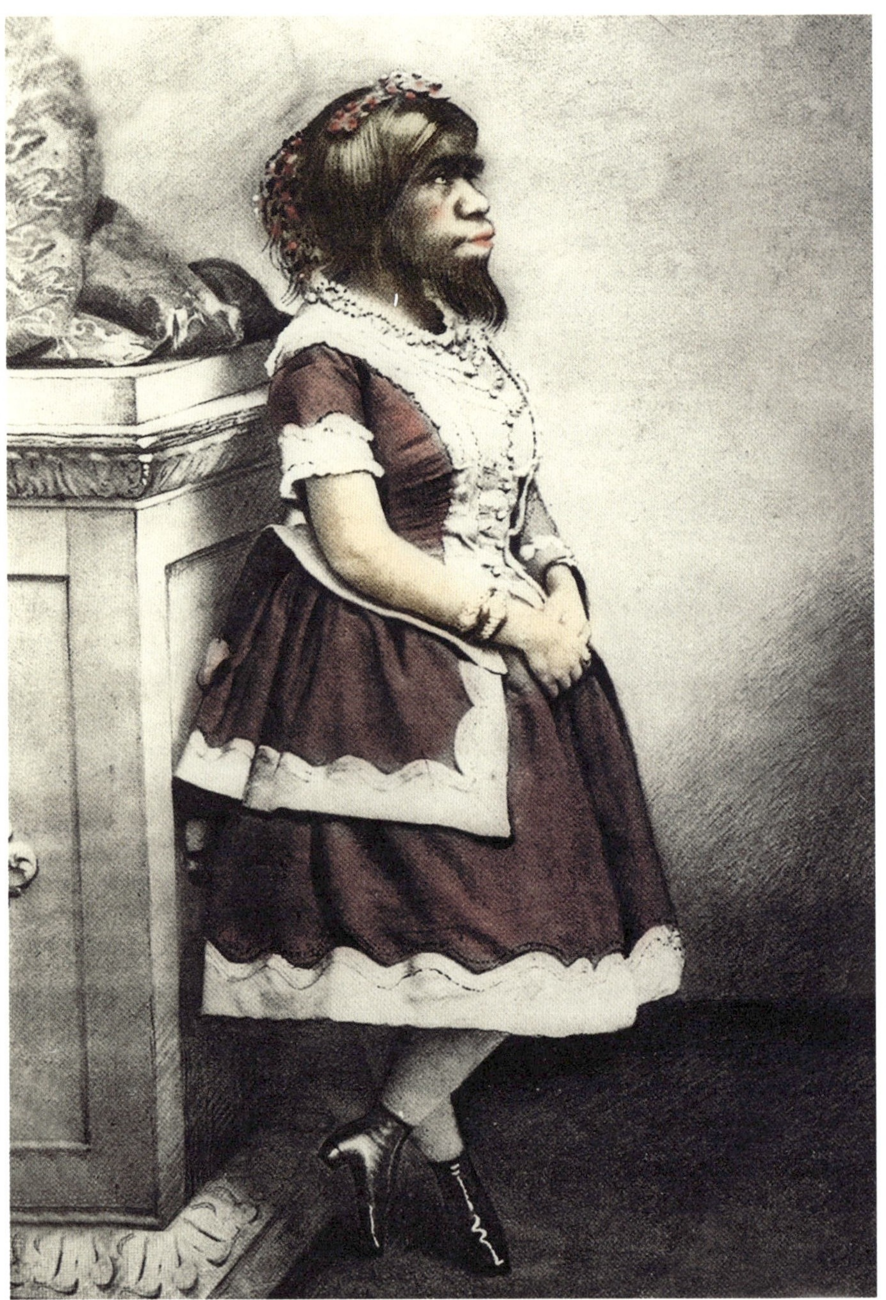

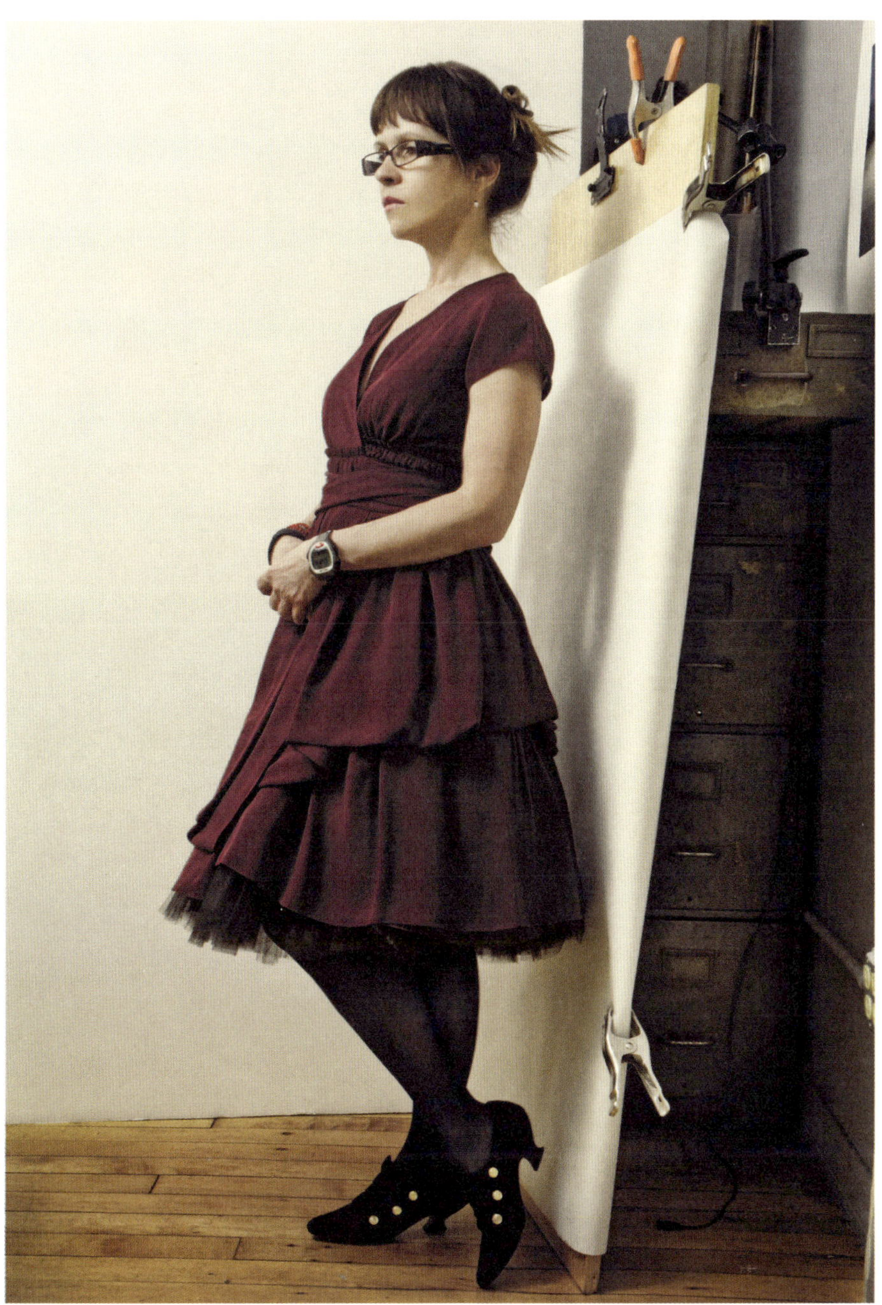

Laura Anderson Barbata, *Julia y Laura,* 2013; photographs on fiber paper; ed. 5

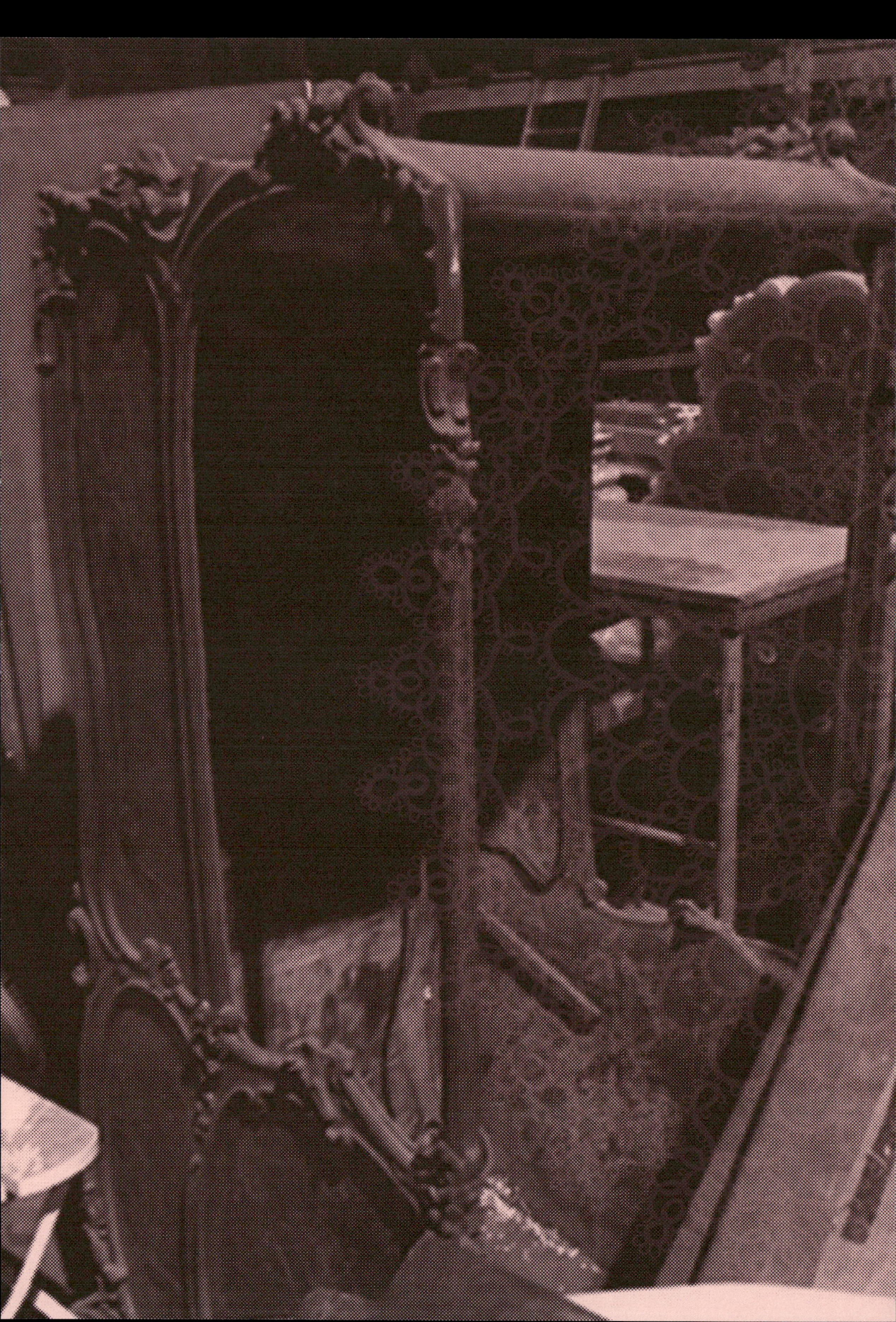

My Quest for Julia Pastrana's Mummy

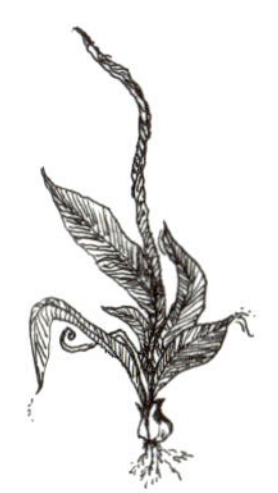

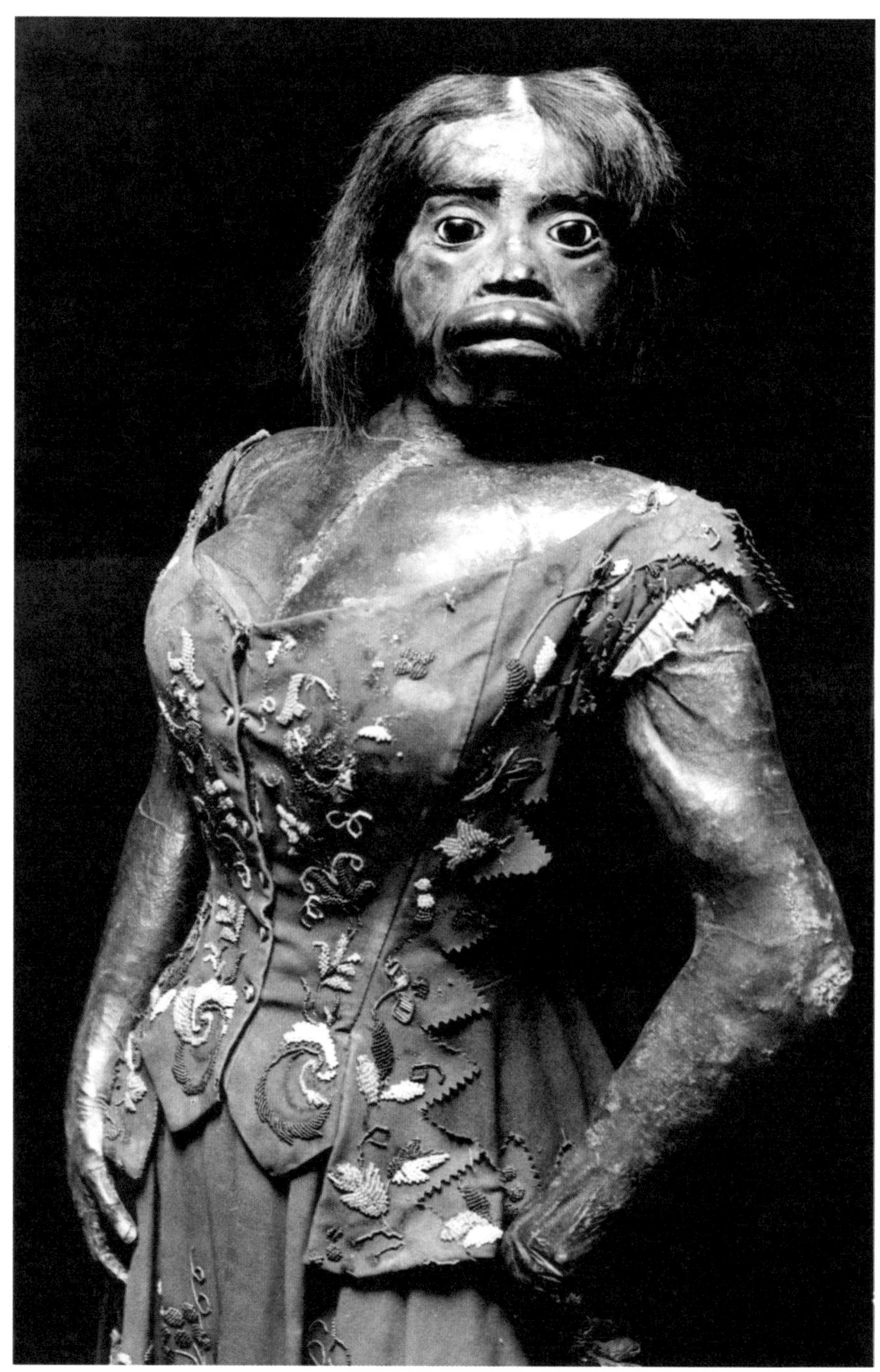

Julia Pastrana embalmed, 1971

My Quest for Julia Pastrana's Mummy

JAN BONDESON

In 1988, when I was a young doctor, I became fascinated with the strange tale of Julia Pastrana. Not only was her life story singularly tragic, eclipsing those of the Sicilian Fairy and the Elephant Man, but the sordid exploitation of her mummified remains, for many decades, was without precedent in the annals of the freak show. Since the more trustworthy sources agree that Julia Pastrana was an intelligent woman of affectionate and gentle disposition, the true tragedy of her fate can scarcely be imagined. Having an interest in clinical genetics, I decided to try to find the mummies of Pastrana and her son, and to establish Pastrana's correct diagnosis.

This quest turned out to be far from an easy undertaking, since in 1988 no one knew the whereabouts of their remains. It was possible, however, to trace the later movements of the mummies in some detail. In early 1943 the medical director of the German forces in Oslo ordered that the wax molds and other exhibits in the Lund amusement park's chamber of horrors be confiscated, so the wax could be used for war production. But the fairground owner managed to save the preparations, suggesting that they be taken on an extended tour to Sweden, and that the profits from the exhibitions would benefit the treasury of the Third Reich.[1] He loaded three railway trucks full of displays, including the mummy of Julia Pastrana, and toured Sweden, exhibiting the objects at various fairs and markets.

In 1953 the chamber of horrors was permanently stored in a warehouse in Linköping, Sweden. It was soon rumored that the warehouse was haunted by monstrous apelike creatures, and some daring youths broke into it to investigate. They were struck with horror when they saw Julia Pastrana's mummy staring at them from its dusty, cobwebbed sedan chair, and they fled the building in panic. The most intrepid of them later returned to take a photograph of the mummy, the first for more than eighty years. The ravages of time are clearly visible: the mummy's jewelry is missing and its elaborate coiffure is destroyed; furthermore, the extraordinary chin beard and whiskers are gone. The mummy of Pastrana's son had also lost a good deal of its hair, as well as being deprived of its elaborate costume. In 1959 the chamber of horrors was exhibited at a large agricultural fair in Oslo. The weather was very hot, and the sight of the hideous wax figures and the "stuffed apewoman" was too strong a sensation for many a Norwegian countryman; ambulances had to pay several daily calls to pick up visitors who had fainted. By the early 1960s the market for the chamber of horrors had become less lucrative, and it was permanently stored in a warehouse outside Oslo.

The Mummies Are Again Exploited

In September 1969 the name Julia Pastrana entered the headlines again after more than one hundred years. Judge Hofheinz, a wealthy American collector of curiosities, was eager to purchase the two mummies, but their owner, Hans Jaeger Lund, considered the offer of $10,000 to be insufficient. He threatened to take the mummies on tour again, after cleaning them up with a vacuum. These bizarre proceedings attracted much curiosity from the Swedish and Norwegian press, and there were several articles about the valuable mummies. In one of them, Lund indicated the existence of an old Russian document (now lost), dated 1860 and containing an affidavit that the corpses of Julia

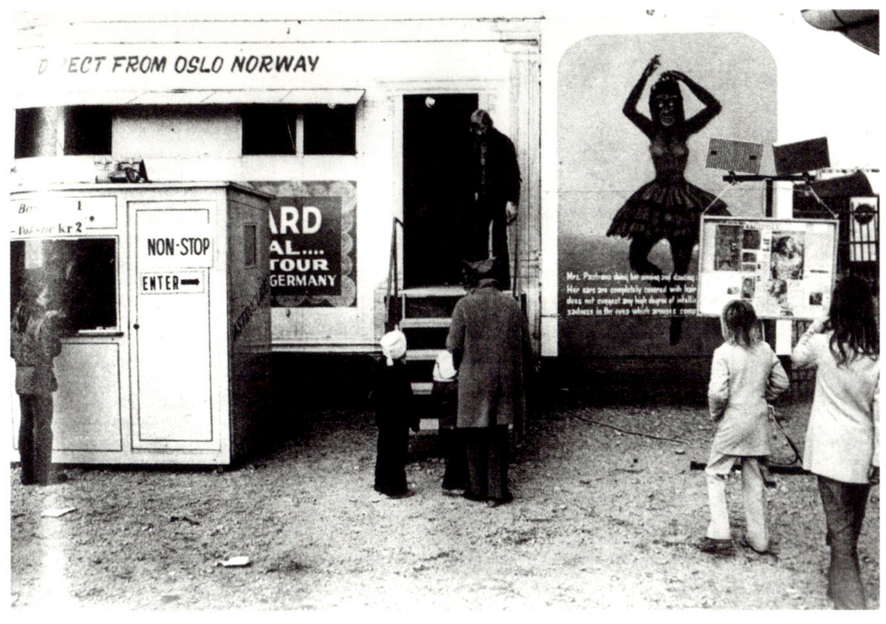

Julia Pastrana exhibition in the United States, c. 1971–72

Pastrana and her son had been made into genuine mummies. Although the American collector increased his offer several times, Lund still declined to sell the mummies, instead exhibiting them in both Sweden and Norway during 1970. They were quite a public attraction, due to newspaper publicity and the objections to such a degrading show from various religious organizations. In the end Hofheinz suffered a stroke. Lund, instead of receiving $500,000, which had been Hofheinz's final offer, now had no prospective buyer.[2]

In 1971 the mummies were exhibited in Norway and Denmark, and the following year they were rented by an American traveling amusement park called the Million Dollar Midways, which took them on tour throughout the United States. They were placed in a cage made of unbreakable glass to prevent them being stolen; this contraption was carried on an enormous circus caravan. Although several American venues closed the exhibition after a few days, since it was considered immoral and degrading, the enterprise was a monetary success. In 1973 Lund again planned to exhibit Julia Pastrana in Norway, but there was a public outcry against this, and the church objected to the use of a dead body in such a sordid commercial way. The Bishop of Oslo demanded that the mummies be confiscated and buried by the Norwegian church. The witty Lund replied that if the Norwegian clergy wanted to bury mummies, they could start in Egypt! When his plans were thwarted, he instead rented the mummies to a Swedish traveling fair.

During this tour, Pastrana became a public attraction equal to the most popular entertainers, and when she was exhibited in various small towns, people thronged to see the mummies in the Russian sedan chair, which was exhibited in the large caravan with its glass cage. The mummy of the little son was standing beside that of the mother, with his feet in black boots, nailed to a pedestal. Just as when Julia Pastrana had been shown in London in 1857, the exhibition hand-bills declared her to be a hybrid of human and ape.

In Hudiksvall, a small town in central Sweden, the local board of health closed the exhibition, and a petition was sent to the Swedish Home Office requesting that exhibition of dead bodies be prohibited by law. Julia Pastrana and her son had made their final tour, and the caravan was stored at the fairground's winter quarters near Oslo. In August 1976 the fairground was broken into, and the burglars forced the lock of the mummies' caravan. Julia Pastrana's dress was torn open. The child mummy's arms and lower jaw were knocked off; it was also removed from its pedestal and thrown in a ditch outside. The damaged child's mummy was later eaten by mice, and Julia now stood alone in her glass cage. During the summer of 1979, the fairground was again broken into, and Julia Pastrana's mummy was among the objects missing. It was presumed that it had been stolen by vandals and later destroyed.

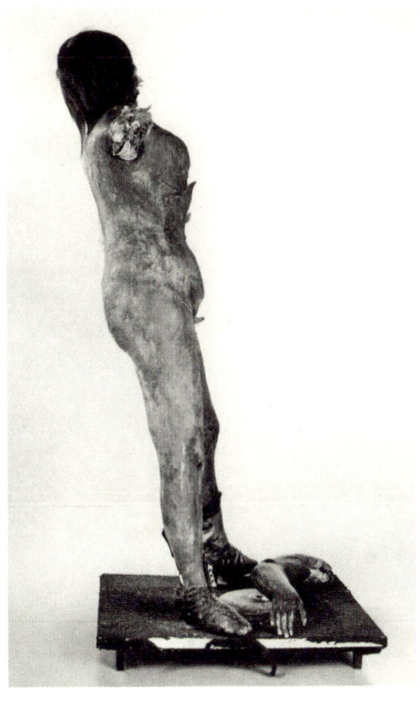

Julia Pastrana's body as it was
found by the author in 1990

The Mummy Is Rediscovered

In February 1990, a Norwegian detective magazine revealed that the restless mummy of the "apewoman" was still in existence. It turned out that in 1979 the Oslo police had been notified that some children had found a mummified human arm at a dump in an Oslo suburb. The rest of Julia Pastrana's mummy was found in an abandoned caravan nearby. Strangely enough, the owner was not notified by the police, and the mummy was instead put in storage at the Institute of Forensic Medicine at a hospital in Oslo.

It did not take long for me to get on a plane to Oslo, as the correspondent of a Swedish medical magazine, having first obtained permission to see the mummy from the director of the Institute of Forensic Medicine.[3] An elderly assistant took me down into the basement, where it was kept in a cupboard with vacuum cleaners and other utensils. It was a sad and pitiful sight, standing on a small wooden board covered with fabric. The right arm had been torn off and was lying in front of the mummy; furthermore, the right side of the face had been torn open, and one glass eye was missing. The Russian dancer's costume had been ripped off by the thieves, and the mummy was completely unclothed, apart from the remains of the original boots. The abnormal hairiness of the forehead was still evident, and parts of the whiskers were also preserved. The preparation of the corpse had been performed in a very skillful fashion, using minimal sutures, although it was obvious that stuffing had been employed to prevent the effects of shrinking.

Julia Pastrana's Diagnosis

For many years, the majority of anthropologists and dermatologists considered Julia Pastrana to be a case of congenital hypertrichosis lanuginosa (inherited increased hairiness with lanugo, a fine, downy hair), a genetic disorder with autosomal dominant inheritance. (An autosome is a non-sex-linked gene, and dominance means that inheritance from only one parent is possible.)[4] Due to persistence of the lanugo, the bodies of the individuals with congenital hypertrichosis lanuginosa are covered with long, soft, wavy hair. A remarkable early case was Petrus Gonzales, who had such hair all over his body. He was taken to the court of King Henry II of France as a curiosity, married there, and had three children, who all inherited the same form of hairiness. At least one of them transmitted the condition into a third generation. A severely diminished number of teeth has often been observed in conjunction with congenital hypertrichosis lanuginosa. An example of this is Shwe-Maong, a man from Burma who was enveloped from head to foot in a mass of wavy hair. Both he and his descendants had only four or five teeth in each jaw, and where there were no teeth, the alveolar processes (the ridges of bone containing the tooth sockets) were missing also.[5]

Some older writers divided individuals with congenital hypertrichosis lanuginosa into "dog-faced" and "monkey-faced" groups.[6] The majority of cases fell into the former group, including Petrus Gonzales and his offspring, the hairy Burmese, and the Russian peasant Andrian and his son Fedor, who had been exhibited in London in 1874. The latter group included Julia Pastrana and her son, as well as Krao, a hairy young girl from Bangkok who was widely exhibited during the 1890s. Studying Petrus Gonzales, Shwe-Maong, and other established cases of congenital hypertrichosis lanuginosa on one hand, and Pastrana and Krao on the other, several discrepancies can be noted. While the entire faces of the former group are covered with long hair, the latter group has more of a male pattern, with long whiskers and beard but shorter hair on the rest of the face. Furthermore, Pastrana and Krao had short, hard, jet-black hair covering the body, while the others had very long (up to ten centimeters), thick, and soft lanugo hair.

Upon a thorough examination of Pastrana's remaining hair, the impression was that it resembled normal terminal hair rather than lanugo. In order to verify this, a microscopic examination of head and beard hair samples obtained from Pastrana's mummy was performed; all features observed were consistent with human terminal facial hair. Replacement of lanugo with terminal hair never occurs in congenital hypertrichosis lanuginosa, proving that Julia Pastrana did not have this disorder. But what, then, was the cause of her condition? An important clue is given by the appearance of her teeth and jaws, which had fascinated many of those who saw her during life. A curious rumor started by the exhibition pamphlets said that Pastrana had double gums and two sets of teeth. Plaster casts of her upper and lower dentition, kept in the Odontological Museum of the Royal College of Surgeons in London, show greatly thickened alveolar processes, and it is difficult on the casts to distinguish probable cusps of teeth from nodules of overgrown gum.[7] Even in life such nodules could be whitish and thus easily confused with teeth, which would explain the ill-informed rumor. The plaster casts and the accounts of Pastrana during life agree that she suffered from severe gingival hyperplasia (overdevelopment of the gum). Whether this was present at birth is not known, but it was evident as early as 1855, when she was

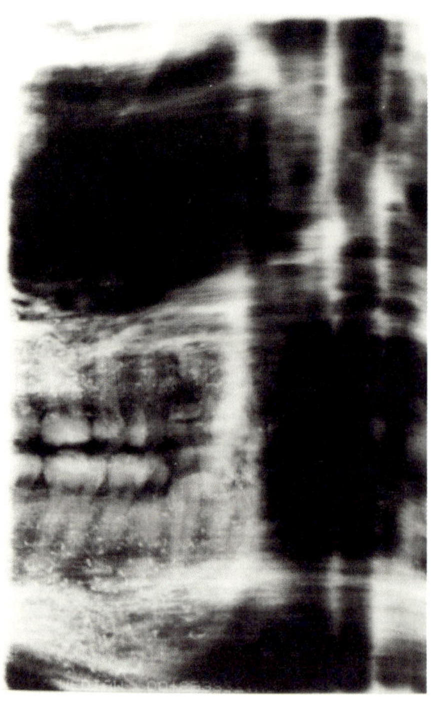

Radiograph of Julia Pastrana's head

twenty-one years of age. It seems highly probable that this condition was progressive, and gradually buried such teeth as had erupted. No observer during her lifetime would have been able to ascertain what was beneath the overgrown gum. Since the jaw region of the mummy is relatively undamaged, it has been possible to do this today. A skull radiograph and panoramic radiographs of her jaws demonstrate that she had complete permanent (secondary) dentition, with the possible exception of the upper left lateral incisor. With these findings in mind, it was possible to diagnose Pastrana as an extreme case of congenital hypertrichosis (with terminal hair) and gingival hyperplasia, an established, autosomally dominant syndrome.[8] It seems very likely that Krao had the same condition. The previous classification into "monkey-faced" and "dog-faced" subgroups is thus not only uncouth but also completely erroneous: the patients belong to two completely

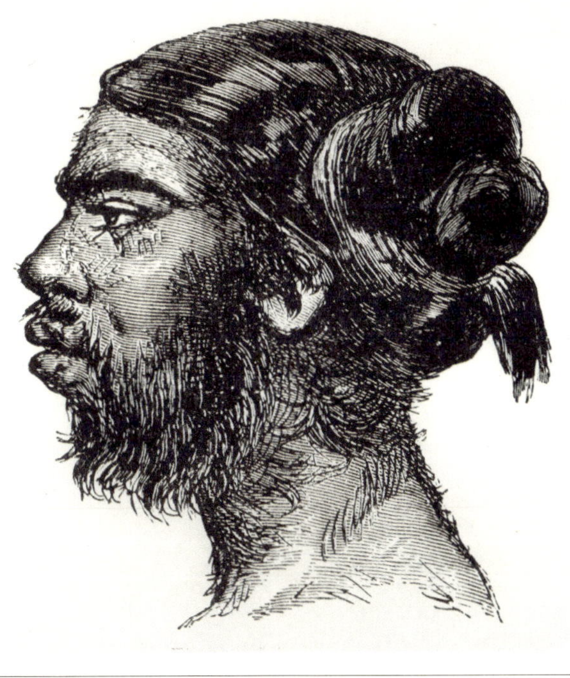

Drawing of Julia Pastrana for exhibition in Paris, c. 1857–58

different genetic syndromes, with excessive hairiness as the only common denominator.

Modern medical science recognizes three major subgroups of inherited excessive hairiness.[9] First, there is traditional congenital hypertrichosis lanuginosa, which affected many of the historical cases, like Barbara Urslerin (one of the earliest documented examples), the Gonzales family, the hairy Burmese, and Andrian and Fedor. Although most cases are sporadic, and the result of spontaneous mutations, there is one example of a three-generation pedigree (the Gonzales family) and one example of a four-generation pedigree (the hairy Burmese). Second, there is the syndrome of excessive hairiness with terminal hair and overgrowth of the gums, which affected Pastrana and Krao. This syndrome is also autosomally dominant, and clearly has variable expression. Some individuals have only mild gingival hyperplasia, others more severe overgrowth of the gums, and also excessive hairiness. The extremes, like Pastrana and Krao, are the only ones to have an extent of hairiness resembling the historical cases of hypertrichosis. Third, a syndrome of X-linked hypertrichosis, often associated with deafness as well as dental and palatal anomalies, has been described in Mexico in recent years.[10] This syndrome is unlikely to have been involved in any of the historical cases.

The question whether excessive hairiness is an atavism is still debated today. An atavism is defined as the reappearance of a lost characteristic, either of morphology or behavior, which is typical of remote ancestors, and not seen in the parents or recent ancestors of the individual in question. Examples of such an ancestral phenotype are hind limbs in whales and three-toed (polydactylous) horses; in humans, supernumerary nipples, the presence of a vestigial tail, and a heart deformity leading to a coronary circulation similar to that of reptiles have been presented as examples of atavisms.[11] The model used to explain them is that the genetic and developmental information originally utilized in the production of these characteristics has not been lost during evolution, but lies dormant within the genome and can still be "turned on" by a mutation.

Although most earlier writers accepted the concept of congenital hypertrichosis as an atavism, it seems reasonable to raise a few objections. The fact that there are (at least) three separate genetic defects causing congenital hypertrichosis, one of them X-linked, the two others autosomal (with mutations in two different chromosomes), would weaken the case for this condition being the result of the reactivation of an ancestral pattern of development. The associated defects—toothlessness and overgrowth of the gums—cannot be considered as ancestral qualities. Some of the historical cases have had an extremely hairy nose, something untypical of primates. Nor is there any evidence of any primitive or animal-like characteristics in individuals with congenital hypertrichosis. The alleged apelike characteristics of Julia Pastrana are still widely believed by credulous and careless authors. But for any person who has examined a chimpanzee, it is apparent that the shape of its face is due to the protuberance of the jaws and not to any abnormality of the gums. The radiographs of the head of Pastrana's mummy show that her jaws were of a normal shape, and the casts of her jaws indicate that her prognathic appearance was entirely due to overgrowth of the gums. It is impossible to prove that congenital hypertrichosis is not an atavism, since the concept of atavism is in itself an arbitrary one, but the arguments mentioned here are against it. The sinister interpretation of the word "atavism," implying that the affected individuals, like a hairy child or a baby with a tail, are "primitive" or "apelike," thus opening the door to racist and bigoted interpretations, is of course entirely unfounded.

NOTES

1 Mr. Bjørn Lund, private communication; Swedish newspapers, 1969–70.
2 Julia Pastrana's Russian sedan chair was still kept at Lund's Tivoli as recently as 1990, together with an archive of newspaper clippings, exhibition posters, and other material concerning her. I possess copies of much of this material, as well as a wealth of other Scandinavian newspaper coverage of Julia's postmortem career in Scandinavia.
3 *Draco pro Medico* 30, no. 8 (1990): 17–24; and 32, no. 4 (1992): 23–26.
4 W.-R. Felgenhauer, *Journal de Genetique Humaine* 17 (1969): 1–44; P. Beighton, *Archives of Dermatology* 101 (1970): 669–72.
5 J. Bondeson and A. E. W. Miles, *Journal of the Royal Society of Medicine* 89 (1996): 403–8.
6 M. Bartels, *Zeitschrift für Ethnologie* 16 (1884): 106–13; A. Brandt, *Biologisches Centralblatt* 17 (1897): 161–79.
7 As figured by A. E. W. Miles, *Proceedings of the Royal Society of Medicine* 67 (1974): 160–64.
8 G. R. Winter and M. J. Simpkiss, *Archives of Diseases in Childhood* 49 (1974): 394–99; F. Vontobel, *Helvetica Paediatrica Acta* 28 (1973): 401–11.
9 As outlined by J. Bondeson in *The Pig-Faced Lady of Manchester Square* (Stroud, UK: Tempus Publishing, 2004), 23–68.
10 M. Tapin-Strapps et al., *Clinical Genetics* 63 (2003): 418–22.
11 R. Tyson et al., *Veterinary Radiology and Ultrasound* 45 (2004): 315–17; I. Walia et al., *Texas Heart Institute Journal* 37 (2010): 687–90.

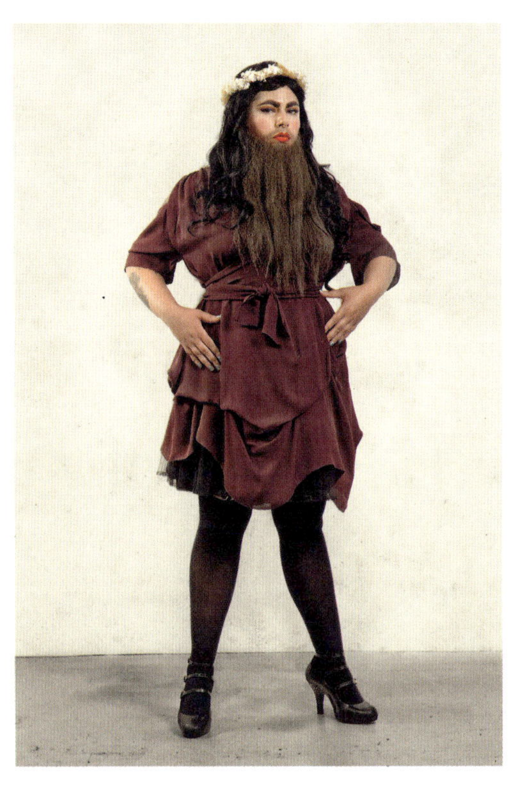 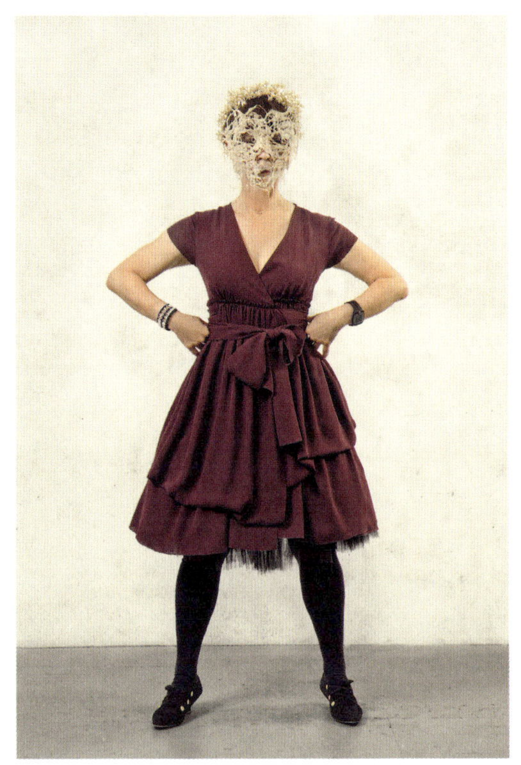

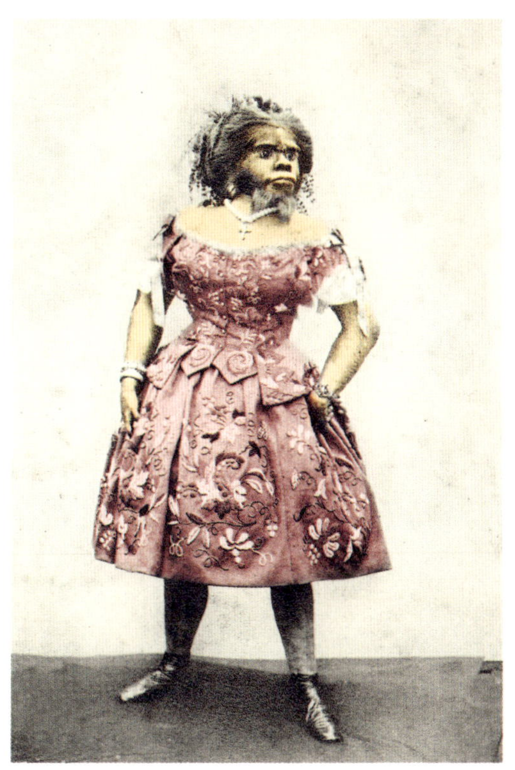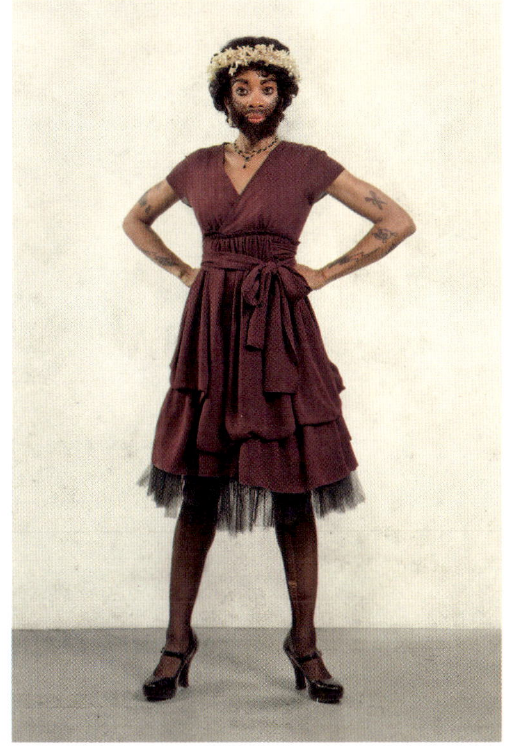

4 Julias (Divina Gran Sparkle, Laura Anderson Barbata, Julia Pastrana, and Fem Appeal), 2016; photographs on cotton fiber paper

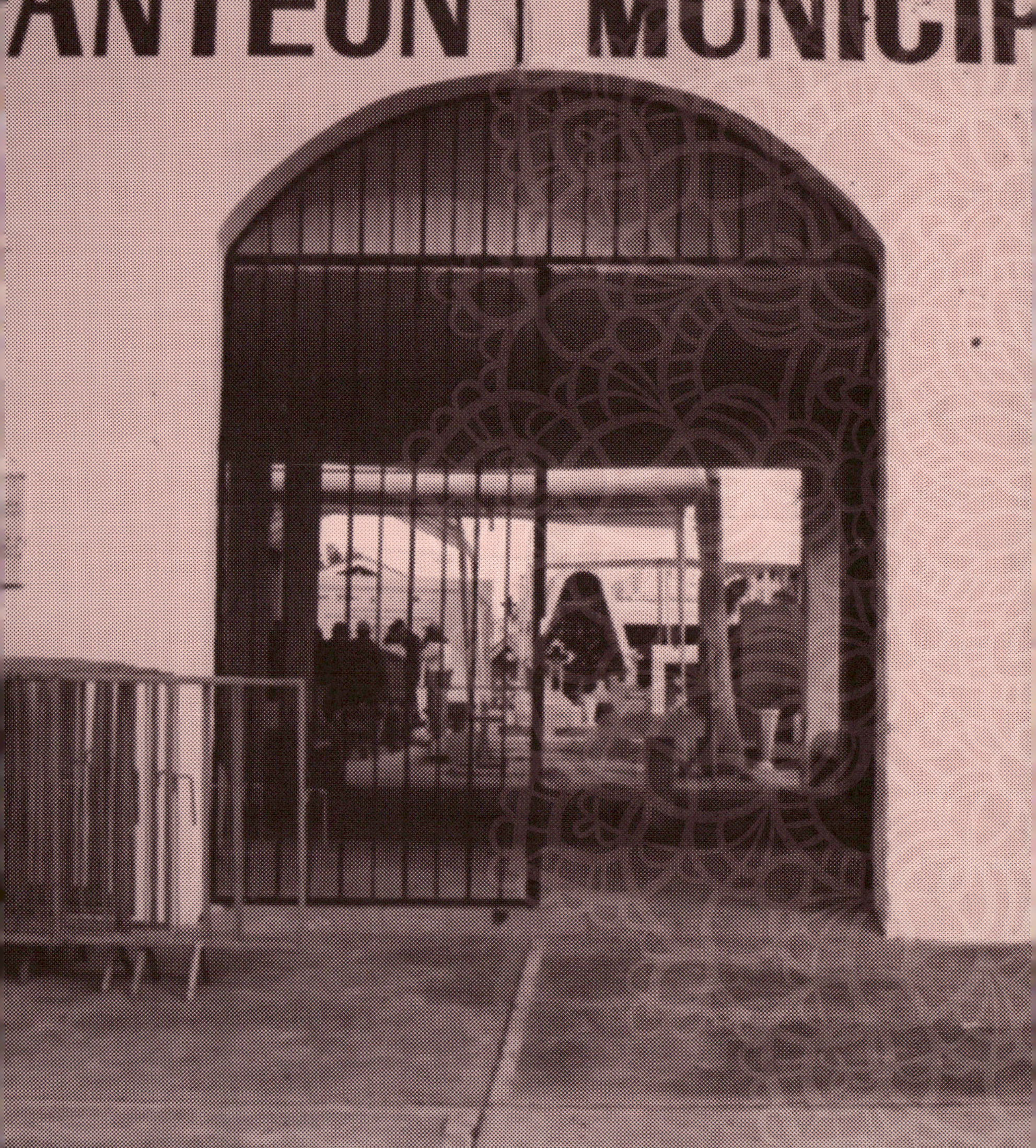
PANTEON
MUNICIP

Julia Pastrana and the Art of Restitution

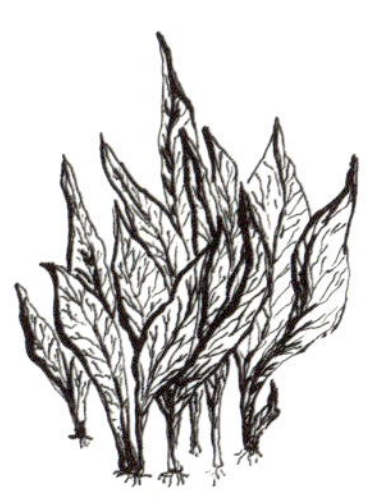

JULIA PASTRANA.

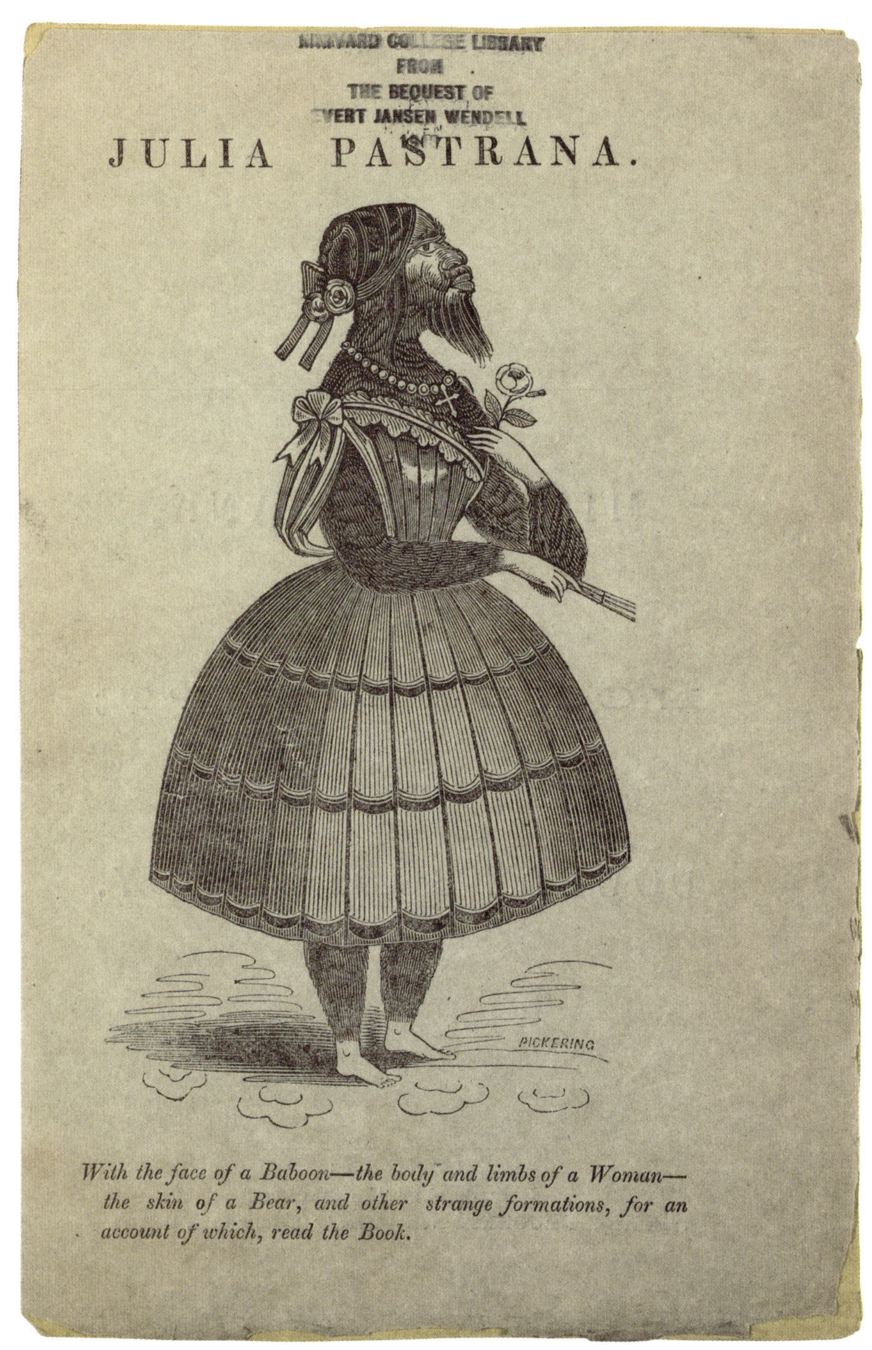

*With the face of a Baboon—the body and limbs of a Woman—
the skin of a Bear, and other strange formations, for an
account of which, read the Book.*

Front cover of *Account of Miss Pastrana, the Nondescript;
and the Double-Bodied Boy,* 1856; pamphlet

Julia Pastrana and the
Art of Restitution

GRANT H. KESTER

> *Primitive man could not have been happy,*
> *nor often long-lived, nor ever beautiful.*
>
> — "Some Human Monsters: The Lessons Taught by Wild Men
> and Hairy Men," *New York Times*, March 21, 1886[1]

The Perils of the Nondescript

The discipline of art history begins with an act of theft. While Europe's colonial expansion resulted in the movement of vast amounts of wealth into the economies of the West, it also involved the transportation of another kind of loot: archaeological and cultural artifacts, ranging from the Parthenon frieze to Congolese nail fetishes. During the late eighteenth and early nineteenth centuries museums and ethnographic collections in London, Paris, and Berlin began to fill with objects that confronted modern Europeans with evidence of vital, non-Christian cultures, both historical and contemporary, whose values, language, and rituals were either archaeologically inaccessible or profoundly different from their own. These objects, each carrying its own secret history, forced their way into the consciousness of European thinkers. The result was an extended inquiry into the nature of civilization and the meaning of art. The modern discipline of art history emerged in response to this encounter with cultural difference, which presented itself as both a threat and an opportunity. It was, of course, Winckelmann's encounter with the objects discovered as part of the eighteenth-century excavations at Pompeii and Herculaneum that laid the foundations for the field.

The reaction to this flood of often perplexing cultural artifacts took two main forms. On the one hand they provided a salutary reminder that there are many other cultures, and many ways of being civilized, each with its own value. However, this perspective was largely superseded by a second view, which would exercise a decisive influence on the evolution of art history and our subsequent understanding of the significance of art. It is a view that conjures up historical context only in order to dissolve it, retaining the dried husk of the cultural artifact as a vessel for a transhistorical aesthetic drive that may be present in all civilizations and cultures, but that only reaches its apotheosis in European art of the present day. We can gain some sense of this perspective from Karl Schnaase's *Niederländische Brief* [Letters from the Netherlands], published in Stuttgart in 1834. In these letters Schnaase, who would go on to become one of the most influential art historians of the nineteenth century, asks how a contemporary European might comprehend artworks that are rooted in cultures outside his own. "If artistic form depends upon religion," Schnaase writes, "how can we Christians . . . accept ancient pagan [artistic] forms?"[2] In other words, how can we have a conversation with a culture if we can't understand it? Or if its beliefs are alien or foreign to our own?

For Schnaase the solution to this impasse involved the analysis of a historical dynamic by which art and religion evolve in constant dialogue with each other: "Both combine to create the essence of humanity, and they complement each other; each needs the other to help it progress into the future." In mankind's "raw state," art and religion are blurred or mingled together. However, as civilization evolves, each asserts its own separate identity through an ongoing dialectical exchange. "They complement each other," Schnaase notes, "but if they are in opposition, if there is too much of one, the other suffers." This quasi-autonomy, however, is eventually superseded. With the emergence of a fully mature society, art and religion achieve a final harmonious reconciliation ("only when they are united at the highest level of production is the highest life reached").[3] History, then, traces an ever-upward spiral, out of the inchoate disorder of humanity in its raw state to the quasi-divine resolution of both spiritual and creative impulses, as monotheistic Christianity replaces the primitive beliefs of pagan or heathen cultures. The Hegelian teleological overtones are unmistakable (Schnaase attended Hegel's lectures in Heidelberg and Berlin).

Schnaase's insight is emblematic of a deeper tendency in early art historical research, which involved the postulation of a transcendent, form-giving intelligence that operates beyond the merely contingent influence of specific cultural or historical contexts. Thus, our ignorance of an object's performative function within a given culture can become an advantage, rather than a liability, as it allows us to more easily grasp its underlying, transhistorical, formal significance. Here we encounter the incipient expression of a tendency to define aesthetic experience in terms of a necessary uncoupling from any referential or representational integration with the world, which would become more fully developed in the dialogue concerning abstraction during the twentieth century. From this perspective art history as a discipline has an oddly paradoxical relationship to history. On the one hand it remains deeply invested in reconstructing the specific conditions of an object's original creation, but on the other hand it requires us to remove that object from its original receptive context in order to allow its transcendent features to become more visible. Each work of art contains an embryonic kernel of this immanent aesthetic quality.

As Schnaase's work suggests, there was an opening at this time for a hermeneutic framework that would allow the mysterious and inexplicable objects then being imported to the West to be made semantically accessible and conceptually productive for contemporary European viewers. The concept of a formal intelligence, manifested in widely

THE HYBRID, OR SEMI-HUMAN INDIAN, FROM MEXICO.—Stuyvesant Institute, No. 659 Broadway.—Christmas Holidays cannot be more agreeably passed than in attending the Levees of JULIA PASTRANA, whose dulcet voice enchants the ladies. Julietta Grisi is not more popular. Dr. Mott's impressive epistle concerning the duality of "La Muger Osa," astounds the public. The Troglodyte of ancient days is recognized—"four feet in height, with eyes like the owl, and gifted with speech—the link between mankind and the ourang-outang." Admission 25 cents.

Julia Pastrana featured in the *New York Times* entertainment section ("Amusements"), December 27, 1854

disparate works and driven by a force that existed independently of specific cultural or historical conditions, provided a fortuitous framework for accomplishing precisely this task. We might say, then, that art history begins as a form of negative ethnography. It constitutes a kind of organized forgetting that seeks to deny the specificity of non-European cultural forms and practices and the "dangerous memories" they carry with them. It also involves a displacement from the experiences of those viewers who are most connected to the lifeworld out of which the object was initially produced. Instead it privileges the synoptic perspective of the critic or historian, who is able to situate the individual work of art within the larger tapestry of an ever-evolving *Kunstwollen*.[4]

Dangerous Memories

In 1834, the same year that Schnaase published his *Niederländische Brief* in Stuttgart, Julia Pastrana was born in a small town in Sinaloa, Mexico. Her story is elsewhere presented in this publication. I will only note here the most pertinent details. She was born with a genetic condition known as generalized hypertrichosis terminalis (extra hair covering her face and body), and also had gingival hyperplasia, which enlarged her gums and lips. She bore a child with Theodore Lent, her opportunistic husband and promoter, and spent most of her

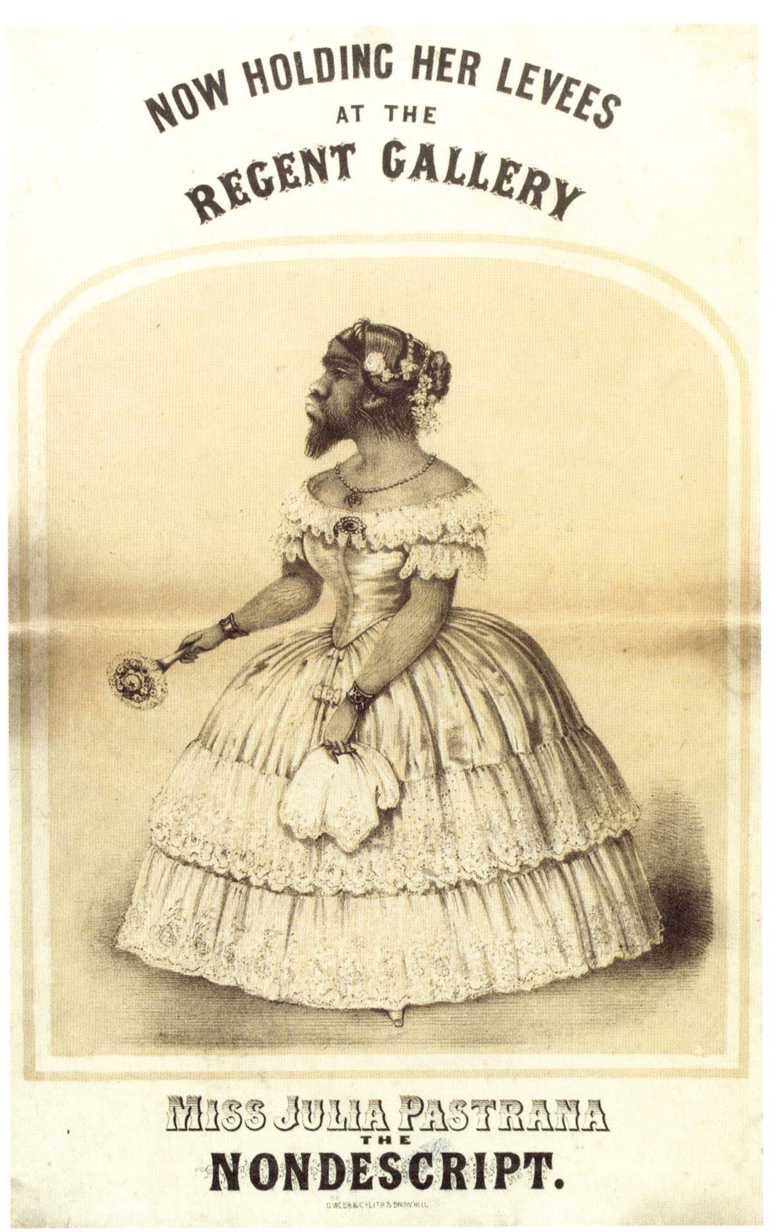

Announcement for Julia Pastrana's performance at Regent Gallery, London, 1857; broadside

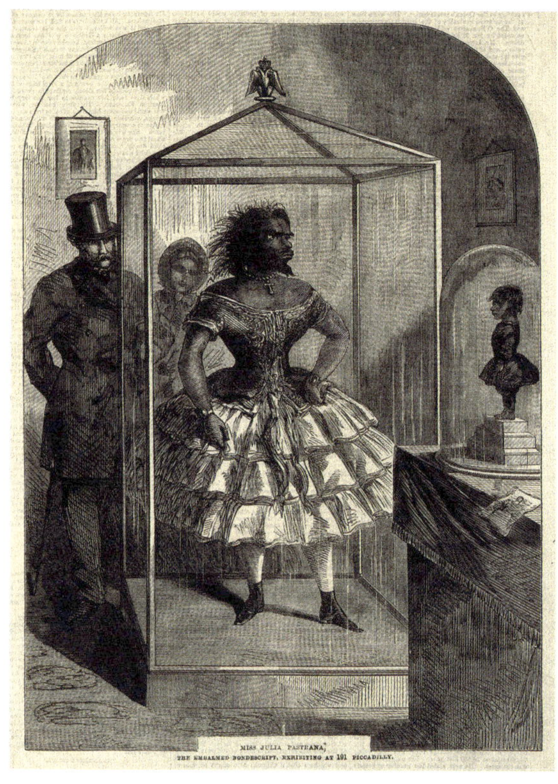

Julia Pastrana and her son embalmed in separate
glass display cases, *The Penny Illustrated Paper*,
London, 1862

all-too-brief adult life traveling through Europe and North America,
where she was displayed before paying audiences. Typically these
exhibitions would feature performances in which Pastrana would
dance or sing. She even appeared in the lead role of a play (with a
plot written around her unusual physical appearance) while touring
Germany. Her appeal was based on the perceived disjunction
between her obvious cultural refinement and her animal-like physical
appearance. Public exhibitions of her body, organized by her husband,
consistently focused on her atavistic or primitive quality. She was
advertised variously as "The Marvelous Hybrid or Bear Woman," "The

Ape Woman," and, according to the *New York Times,* as the missing link "between mankind and the ourang-outang") (see p. 86). During a tour of London, Lent began presenting her as "The Nondescript" (literally, that which can't be described or explained) (see p. 87). Pastrana died following childbirth in 1860 along with her son, after which her husband sold both bodies to the University of Moscow for dissection and preservation (he would buy them back a short time later after realizing he could make further profit by exhibiting her as "The Embalmed Nondescript").

In the final sad chapter of her life story, Pastrana's body and that of her child were consigned to a carnival chamber of horrors for the edification of bored Norwegians, only to end up in a storage facility in Oslo, where they were desecrated by teenagers as a prank. Beneath all of this lies the infinite sadness of a human life and a human spirit reduced to a kind of object, not by her appearance but by the cultural prejudices of ostensibly civilized peoples. Pastrana was the primitive artifact in living form, carrying within herself a kernel of civilized humanity that, once removed from its point of origin, and uncoupled from her beastlike exterior, could be allowed to shine forth. She reassured her European viewers of the eventual triumph of the civilized over the primitive, of aesthetic transcendence over the semantic resistance of the "nondescript." In her long travels through Europe and the United States Pastrana was forced to act out the familiar drama of the primitive and the indigenous, which can only gain acceptance within the spaces of modernity by renouncing their origins and taking on the role of the unrefined specimen that promises the eventual emergence of something far more resplendent.

In returning Pastrana to the place of her birth, Laura Anderson Barbata reverses this journey, finally putting an end to Pastrana's restless wandering. This process, while logistically quite complex, exhibits a philosophical clarity.[5] Pastrana's body was no longer to be warehoused like a resource, traded like an asset, or exhibited like a product, but finally honored and returned to the earth. Barbata made a special effort to frame and ritualize Pastrana's homecoming. This

In memoriam

Julia Pastrana

*1834 Mexico †1860 Russia.

A mass for Julia Pastrana
will be held on Monday
12 September 2005,
6 pm at St. Joseph Chapel,
Akersveien 6, 0177 Oslo.

Obituary announcement, *Aftenposten*,
Oslo, Norway, 2005

included the publication of a formal obituary in Oslo and the staging
of a Catholic Mass for Pastrana in Norway, as well as the final burial
of her body in Sinaloa, in accordance with the Catholic faith. A key
feature of the burial was a specially designed *huipil* created by Francisca Palafox, a master weaver from Oaxaca. This indigenous garment
utilized materials common in pre-Hispanic Mexico and featured symbols that represented both Pastrana's life and Sinaloa's landscape, as
well as the dates of her birth and death. The treatment of the coffin
itself was both symbolic and utilitarian. It was covered in concrete
and housed in a tomb with walls more than a meter thick to prevent
any future disturbance. This was a necessary gesture for a body that
had been so systematically instrumentalized and objectified, and literally torn asunder; it represented an attempt, finally, to protect and
honor Pastrana.

In all of these actions Barbata has reasserted the significance of Pastrana's place of origin, the physical locus of her identity, against the
deracination imposed by aesthetic transcendence. This gesture marks
the return, or homecoming, of Pastrana's body and also the reclaiming
of a notion of artistic practice as imbedded in, and responsible to, specific situations, histories, and contexts. In this respect the Pastrana

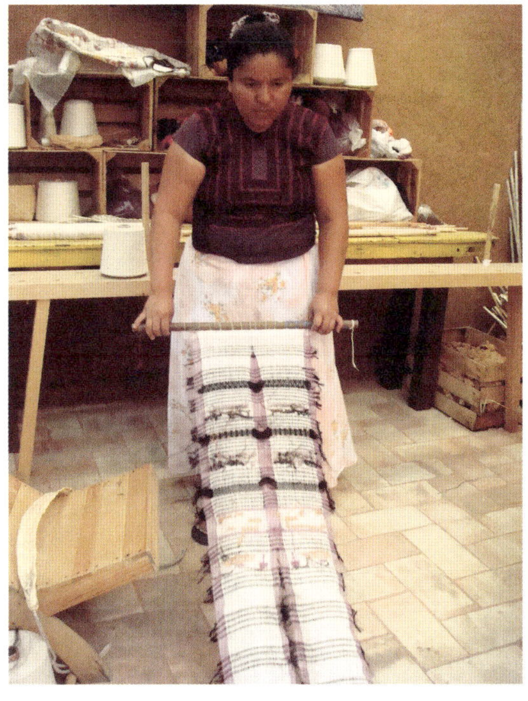

Master weaver Francisca Palafox in her studio,
making a ceremonial *huipil* for Julia Pastrana,
Oaxaca, 2012

project is consistent with Barbata's earlier work, whether with the Yanomami of Venezuela, young Trinidadians, or the stilt walkers of West Africa and the Caribbean. In each case we find Barbata engaged with an artistic practice that is imbedded in the specific lifeworld of a given group, and addressing the challenges and conflicts it faces in its encounters with modernity, ranging from economic disenfranchisement to the disavowal of local or regional cultural practices under the homogenizing assault of global mass media. We might describe this engagement as a form of contingent solidarity, produced in the experience of the work.

Barbata's approach, which enlists collaborators as agents of creative practice, stands in marked contrast to the concept of the viewer

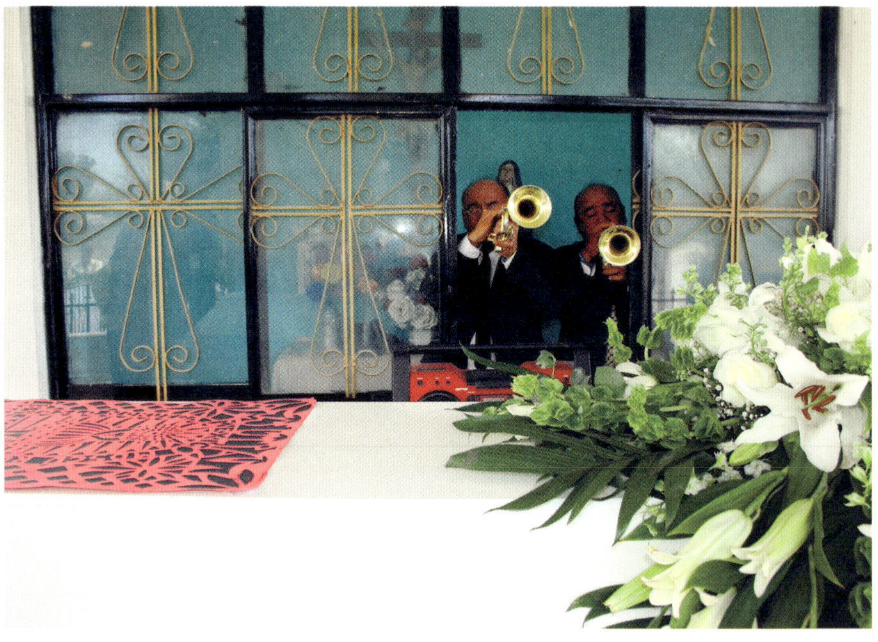

Julia Pastrana's casket entering cemetery for burial, 2012

as a generic subject of ideological programming evident in much contemporary avant-garde art. Here the viewer becomes the target of a displaced form of aggression, directed at particular hegemonic systems. All too often the concept of "critique" in contemporary art operates at the level of a quasi-infantile provocation that does nothing to address the actual mechanisms of political oppression at psychological, discursive, or institutional levels. This displacement is coupled with a form of temporal deferral typical in the traditions of modernist aesthetics, in which a work's lack of intelligibility, its refusal to engage viewers in the practical concerns of daily life, is seen as an index of its critical resistance. Here the work of art, in all its perplexing opacity or confrontational audacity, serves merely to hold open a space out of which some future, utopian society, may one day emerge. Until then, all art can do is refuse to provide the solace of aesthetic resolution, acting instead as a prickly reminder of society's failure to transform itself in a sufficiently revolutionary manner.[6] In neither case is the artist content to engage viewers, collaborators, or participants in their actually existing position as situated agents, each carrying a unique subjective itinerary, political investment, and mode of agency. Instead, solidarity (the community that will experience the Kantian *sensus communis* or Theodor Adorno's revolution yet-to-be) can only be experienced as a premonition, through individual encounters with works of art.

Barbata's mode of engagement, as part of the more general emergence of dialogical art practices over the past two decades, signals a shift in this discursive system, the implications of which have yet to be fully grasped in the fields of art criticism or history.[7] The Pastrana project represents a revealing variant of this approach. It imagines a form of solidarity that is not projected into a hypothetical future, but rather into a very real past. It acknowledges our obligation to those at whose expense the present has come into being. It expresses what philosophers have termed an "anamnetic" solidarity (from Plato's concept of anamnesis, the belief that our present knowledge of the world is founded on the past experience of our immortal soul). This concept has been taken up periodically within the traditions of Western philosophy to allude to forms of identification and solidarity directed toward those who have come before us. Thus, the German theologian Johann Baptist Metz writes of an anamnetic solidarity "in memory with the dead and the conquered." The goal of this solidarity, according to Metz, is to "break the grip of history as a history of triumph and conquest" through the evocation of a "dangerous memory."[8] In the ceremony of returning the body of Julia Pastrana to Sinaloa, Barbata suggests that art's obligation, its answerability to specific situations, contexts, and histories, is neither virtual nor hypothetical. Rather, it is an obligation to the past, and to a past, in Pastrana's case, that was structured through forms of violent and damaging objectification. For viewers today Pastrana serves as a potent reminder of the dangerous memories that lie buried beneath the otherwise triumphant histories of modernity and modernization.

NOTES

1   Accessed online at nytimes.com on January 8, 2014. http://query.nytimes.com/gst
    /abstract.html?res=F20715FD385410738DDDA80A94DB405B8684F0D3

2   Karl Julius Ferdinand Schnaase, *Niederländische Brief* (Stuttgart: J. G. Cotta, 1834),
    377–78. My thanks to Martin Krenn in Vienna for his help with this rather challenging
    translation.

3   "There is a contradiction in the idea that beauty is eternal, and yet only appears in various
    changing forms that are always connected with the religion of the time yet are also sepa-
    rate from it, offering a free overview of history. Art (or if you prefer, the concept of beauty)
    is in constant development, not for itself alone, but in connection with religion. Both com-
    bine to create the essence of humanity, and they complement each other; each needs the
    other to help it progress into the future. Therefore, both alternatives are part of the same
    history; one rests, while the other advances . . . The story forms a continuous evolution, in
    which nature and the spirit appear at any stage in ever-purer harmony. In the raw state of
    mankind both only occur as a tendency; it lies within a blurred mixture not bound together
    in deeper merger [closer union]. However, the higher harmony presupposes the purity of
    each set of oppositions.

    "In the further development [of art] therefore, each of the two freely produced ele-
    ments initially separates from the other, but this separation is always untenable, until at
    last each reaches its fullest maturity and independence, [through] the other, and with it
    creates the highest forms of harmony. Art and religion both exist on the spiritual level of
    humanity, but they behave here as the body and mind in man himself. They complement
    each other, but they are in opposition; if there is too much of one, the other suffers; only
    when they are united at the highest level of production is the highest life reached" (ibid.,
    378).

4   The term *Kunstwollen* is used by art historian Alois Riegl to describe a will or drive exer-
    cised by art itself. The meaning of the single work is only produced through the capacity
    of the art historian to organize the semantic fragments of past and present objects and to
    reconstruct the relationship between them as the symptom of a larger formal dialogue
    through which the *Kunstwollen* itself speaks. The synoptic specialist is thereby natural-
    ized as the only legitimate psychological condition of viewing. In a similar manner Schna-
    ase writes of feeling "in each section of the past, its present together with its future . . . ,"
    glimpsing "in the beauty of each individual period its connection with the others" (ibid.).

5   The project involved years of meetings and correspondence, and the efforts of almost a
    dozen different agencies and offices, including the Office of Foreign Affairs of Mexico, the
    Embassy of Mexico in Belgium, the University of Oslo, the Ministry of Health of Norway,
    Albin International Repatriation Services Ltd., funerary services in Oslo, México City,
    and Culiacán, Sinaloa, the Institute of Culture of Sinaloa, and the office of the governor
    of Sinaloa.

6   The work of art, as Adorno writes, is "an advance on a praxis that has not yet begun."
    T. W. Adorno, *Aesthetic Theory*, ed. Gretel Adorno and Rolf Tiedemann, trans. C. Lenhardt
    (London: Routledge, 1984), 123.

7   I have written about this approach in terms of Mikhail Bakhtin's concept of "answerabil-
    ity." See my entry "Dialogical Art" in *Encyclopedia of Aesthetics*, 2nd ed., ed. Michael Kelly
    (Oxford: Oxford University Press, 2014).

8   Johann Baptist Metz, *Faith in History and Society*, ed. and trans. David Smith (London:
    Burns and Oates, 1980), 184–5, 189–97. See also Heinz Streib, "The Religious Educator
    as Story-Teller: Lessons from Paul Ricoeur's Work," *Religious Education* 93, no. 3 (1998),
    314–31.

Miß Julia Pastrana.

Der Leser erschrecke nicht über die
Abbildung eines Geschöpfes, das man
der Kleidung nach für ein menschliches,
dem Kopfe nach für ein tief unter dem
Affengeschlechte stehendes Wesen zu hal=
ten geneigt ist. Es war nicht die kranke
Einbildungskraft eines Malers, welche
solche Züge auf das Papier hinwarf;
es ist die Natur selbst, die in einer
ihrer seltsamsten Launen dies Wesen
ins Leben stellte und zu ihren vielen
Räthseln ein unauflösliches mehr hin=
zufügte. Würde der Kopf mit einem
undurchdringlichen Schleier umhüllt, so
könnte uns wenig Absonderliches auf=
fallen. Die Glieder sind ebenmäßig
ausgebildet, die Hände und Füße so=
gar zierlich. Hals und Schultern haben
schöne Formen, nur sind sie mit langen
schwarzen Haaren, wie überhaupt der
ganze Körper, dicht bedeckt. Was aber
dieser Hals trägt, könnte Einem vor
Entsetzen die Haare zu Berge treiben.
Es ist kein Kopf, o bewahre! wir
nennen's nur so, weil man sich eben
auf einem Halse jeweilen einen Kopf
denkt; es ist bloß eine Zusammensetzung des
Häßlichsten, was an den Köpfen aller wilden
Thiere zu finden ist. Die Kinnbacken treten an
ihm hervor wie beim Pavian; die Stirn ist kaum
zwei Finger breit und trägt ein verschiebbares
Fettpolster, das über den kleinen schwarzen Augen
noch durch lange Borstenbüschel verunziert wird.
Die Nase ist nur ein schwammiger Fleischklum=
pen mit weit aufgesperrten Flügeln und ohne
Nasenbein. Ueber den ganzen Schädel zieht sich
eine fast zolldicke Haut, die überall mit längeren
oder kürzeren schwarzen Haaren dicht besetzt ist.
An den Backenknochen, um das Kinn, über der
Oberlippe, zu den Seiten der Nasenflügel und
unter den Ohren drängen sich diese Haare zu
einem starken Barte zusammen. Das Häßlichste
des ganzen Gesichtes ist aber der unförmlich
große Mund, der mit seinen wulstigen Lippen
mehr als einen Zoll weiter hervorsteht als das
Kinn. Von den Zähnen in demselben sehen

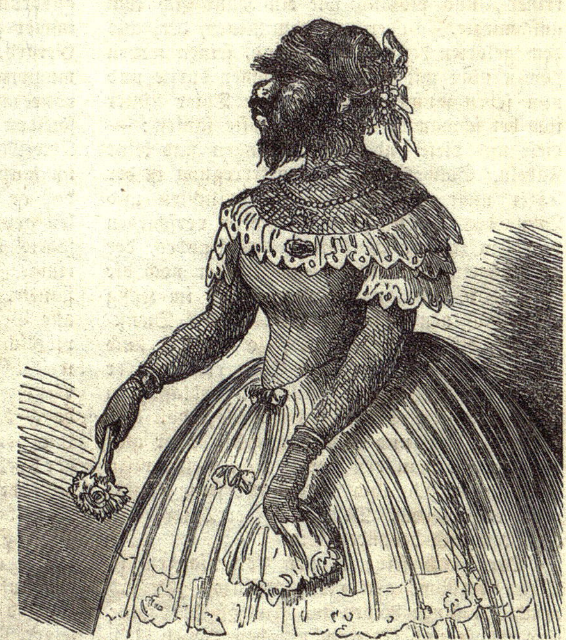

wenige Menschenzähnen ähnlich; die Zunge ist
eine große Fleischmasse ohne irgend eine bestimmte
Form. Und dieses Menschenungeheuer nennt sich
Fräulein Julia Pastrana! Klingt es nicht fast
als Hohn allen kokosnußölsodaseifeabgewaschenen
Fräuleins gegenüber? Dennoch besitzt Julia Pa=
strana manche Fertigkeiten, die man am wenig=
sten bei ihr suchen würde. Sie spricht englisch
und spanisch, singt recht ordentlich, spielt etwas
Klavier, tanzt ausgezeichnet und ist auch in
weiblichen Arbeiten nicht unbewandert. Natürlich
fragt sich ein Jeder, der sie sieht oder auch nur
von ihr hört, wer und wo die Eltern derselben
gewesen seien. Daß sie von einem wilden In=
dianerstamme Meriko's herstammt, ist mit Ge=
wißheit festgestellt; was aber nähere Angaben
betrifft, so bestehen darüber nur zweifelhafte Ge=
rüchte, die um so unwahrscheinlicher werden, je
mehr Bären und Affen darin eine Rolle spielen.
Julia Pastrana läßt sich schon seit einigen Jahren

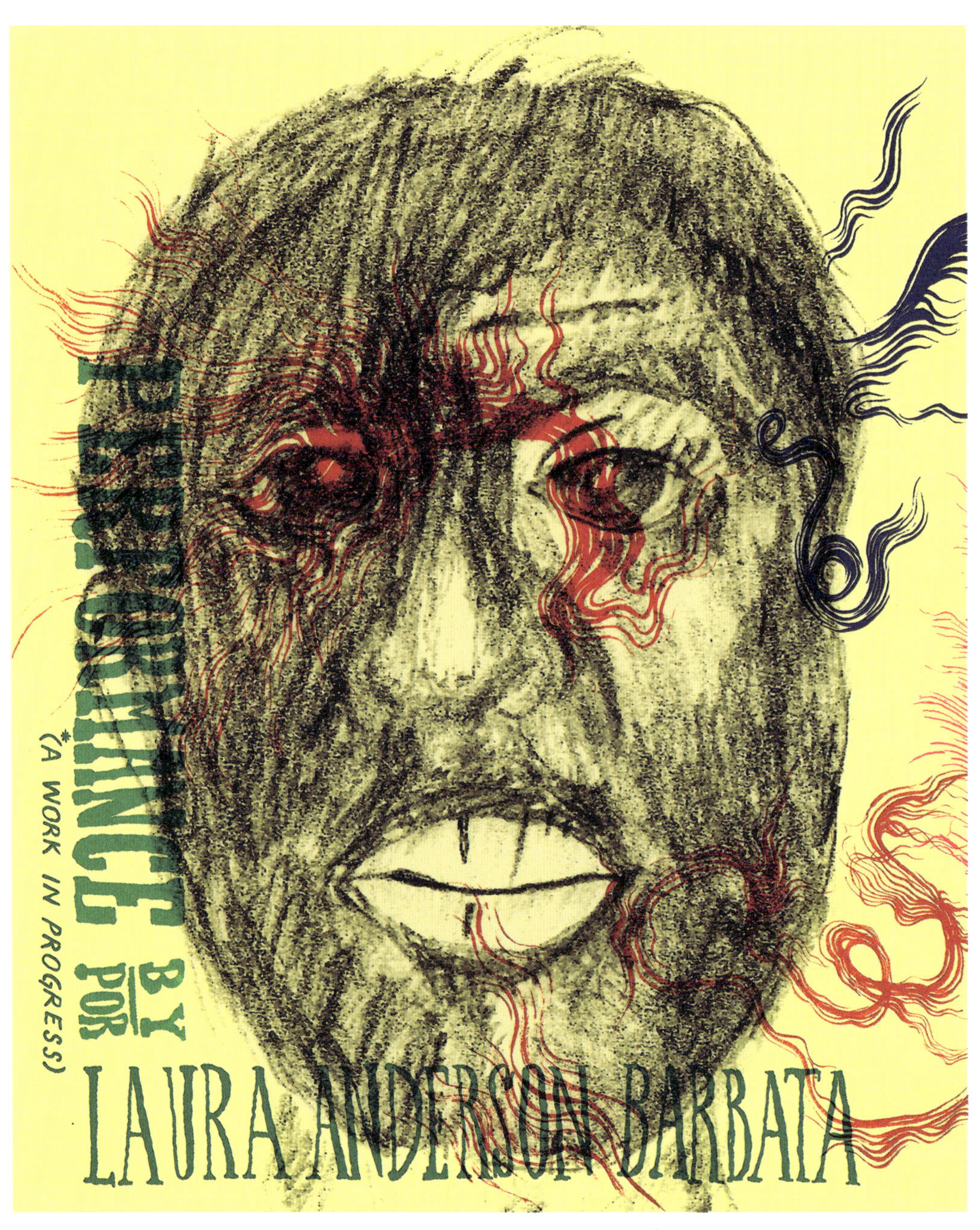

Laura Anderson Barbata, Erik Tlaseca, and Jesús Fajardo, back cover,
La Extraordinaria Historia de Julia Pastrana, zine no. 1, 2015; risograph

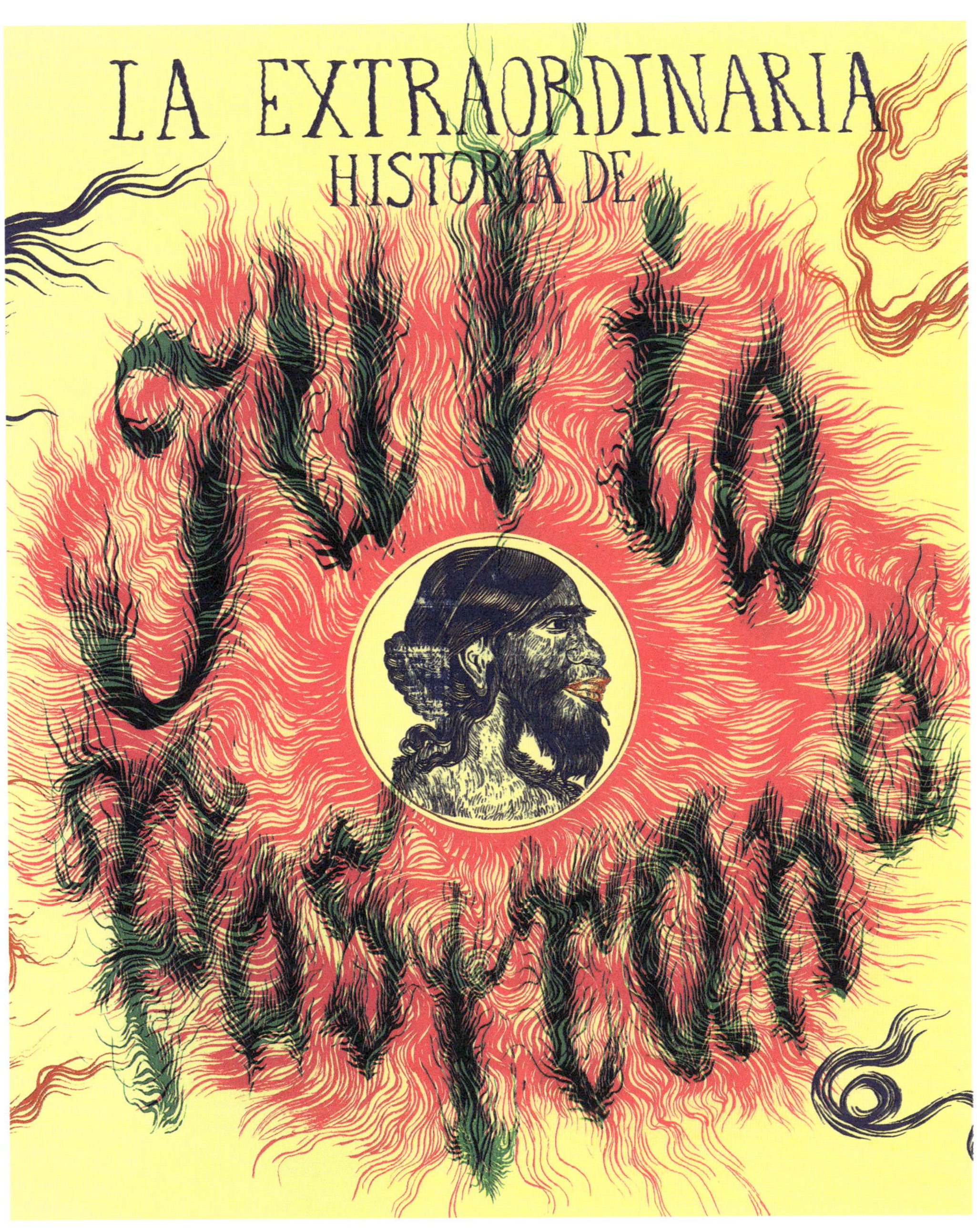

Laura Anderson Barbata and Erik Tlaseca, front cover,
La Extraordinaria Historia de Julia Pastrana, zine no. 1, 2015; risograph

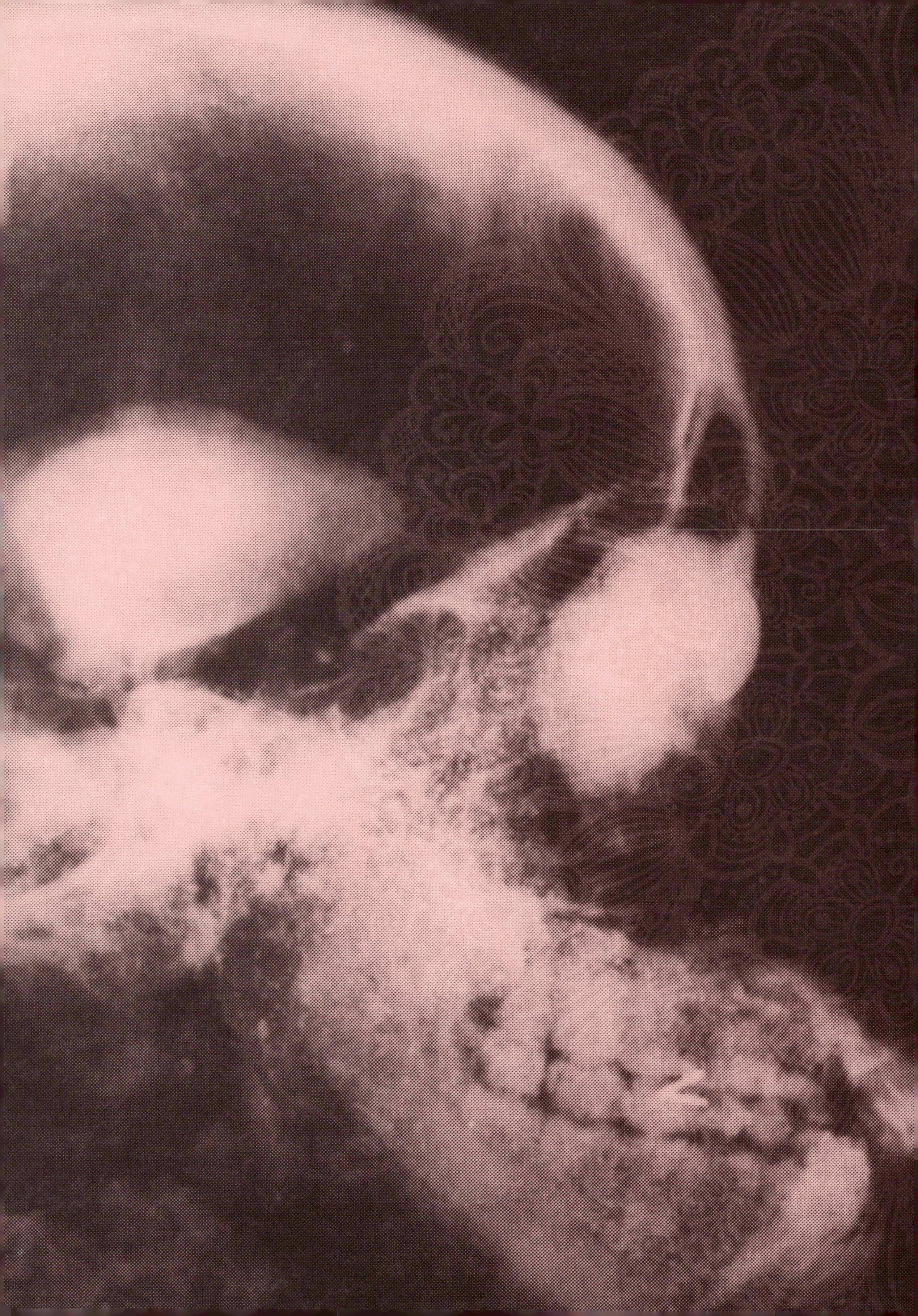

The Repatriation of Julia Pastrana: Scientific and Ethical Dilemmas

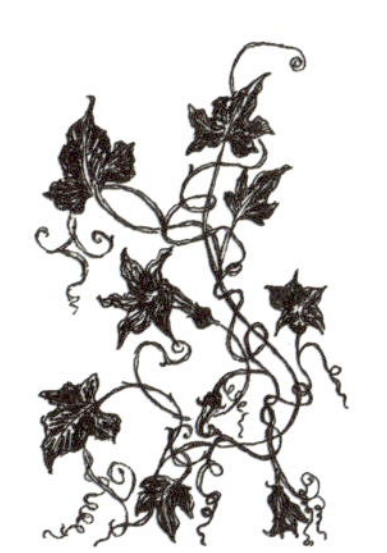

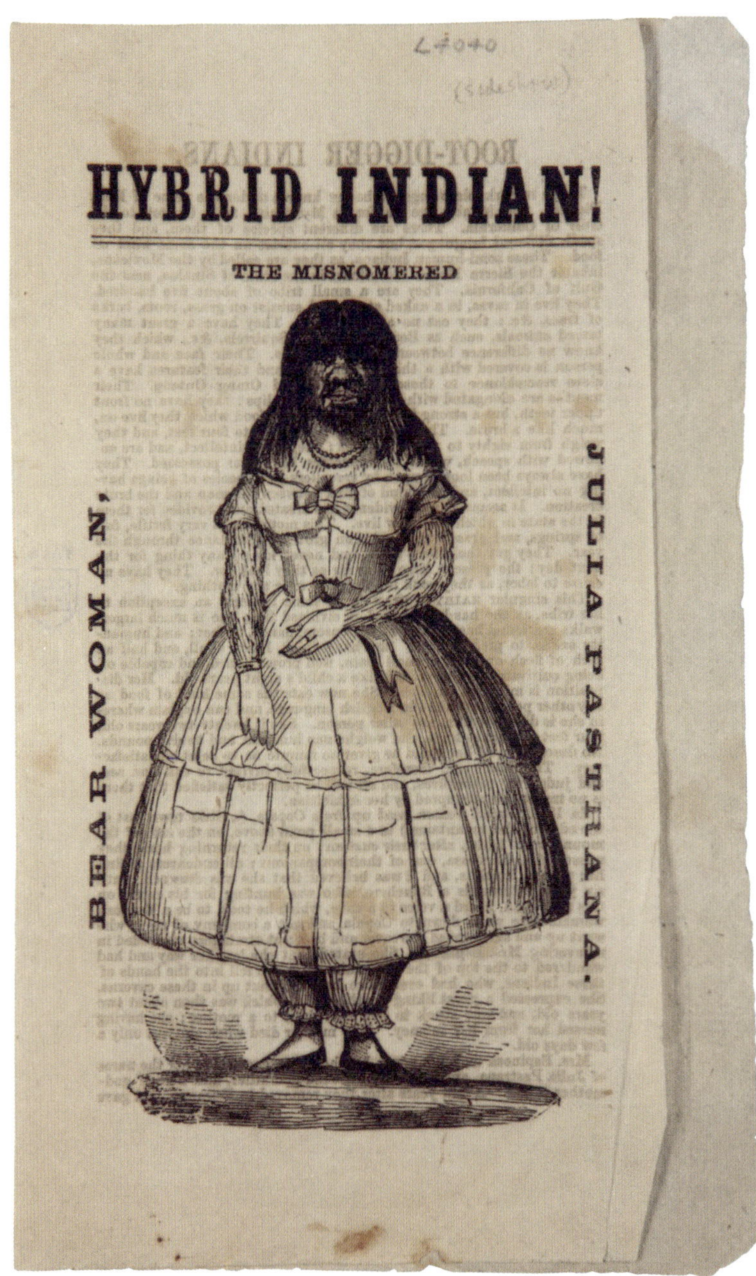

Hybrid Indian! The Misnomered Bear Woman, Julia Pastrana; flyer, 1855

The Repatriation of Julia Pastrana: Scientific and Ethical Dilemmas

NICHOLAS MÁRQUEZ-GRANT

Introduction

The repatriation of the bodies of deceased persons to their countries of origin is not a straightforward process. When archaeological or historical human remains are considered, some of which are retained in museums or academic institutions, their return to their countries of origin requires much dialogue between the different parties involved, particularly between those requesting the repatriation and the curating institutions.

In the case of Julia Pastrana,[1] the Norwegian National Committee for Research Ethics on Human Remains[2] became involved in the decision to repatriate her body following the request of Mexican authorities, via artist Laura Anderson Barbata. The media attention to this case, along with the support of the Norwegian National Committee and subsequent approval by the University of Oslo, enabled the return of Julia's remains from Oslo to her place of origin, Sinaloa, Mexico, in February 2013.

This essay deals with some of the ethical and logistical issues of repatriation, including the debate about balancing scientific interest in retaining her body and the legitimate request for reburial. In addition, from the perspective of physical anthropology, the text also addresses the dilemmas that anthropologists may face with future such cases. Only archaeological and historical remains are considered here, largely those that predate the twentieth century. Forensic anthropology, and remains that are less than one hundred years old for which recent legislation may apply (e.g., the Human Tissue Act of 2004 in England and Wales),[3] are not discussed.

What Do Bones Tell Us? The Study of Human Remains and the Reconstruction of the Past

Anthropologists may examine skeletons, mummified remains,[4] skeletal fragments, or artifacts of human tissue.[5] As anthropologist Clark Spencer Larsen puts it: "The study of human remains from archaeological sites facilitates the interpretation of lifetime events such as disease, physiological stress, injury and violent death, physical activities, tooth use and diet, and the demographic history of once living populations."[6]

Human remains can provide information about living conditions and lifestyles in the past. For example, a skeletal assemblage can yield data on dental disease, which may relate to dietary practices during a particular period. Obtaining this biological perspective on diet, health, and disease, and demography contributes to our understanding of the past in general as well as particular periods or historical events, and complements other sources of information, such as historical documents.[7]

Scientists might aim to establish whether a skeleton is that of a male or female, for example by examining traits of the adult pelvis and the skull.[8] Age at death can also be ascertained, although this may be challenging. Indicators of the age of the person can include dental development in nonadult remains, skeletal maturation and bone growth, and more degenerative changes in adult skeletons.[9] Information on age and sex can enable demographic reconstruction, such as understanding mortality patterns. It can also be used to interpret funerary practices: are males and females buried in specific parts of the cemetery? Is the cemetery arranged according to age group? Are certain grave goods buried with certain individuals?[10] Changes to the body or skeleton after death can also be a reflection of funerary practices. For example, the position of the body when it was found, and whether there is any staining on the skeleton (e.g., green staining from copper objects), can provide information about the deposition.[11] Likewise, the ritual of cremation will affect the skeleton in certain ways, and examining cremated bones may provide further information about funerary practices, the temperature and process of cremation, etc.[12]

Information on physical attributes may also be obtained. Although it is a controversial topic, cranial shape, or morphology, can be used to assess ancestry (incorrectly known as "race") in order to examine the biological distance between populations and to understand patterns of migration. Stature, which can be obtained by measuring a long bone, such as the femur, and applying a formula can also be informative at a population level to learn trends in height through time, and to see the potential influence of socioeconomic and environmental factors. Although genetics plays a major role, an increase in height tends to be associated with better welfare, health, and nutrition.[13]

Teeth provide a wealth of information.[14] They may be used for estimating age at death and, alongside the mandible, complement the evaluation of sex and ancestry. In addition, evidence from teeth may help understand some habits, for example pipe smoking, which may result in notched teeth. Dental disease, and oral pathology overall, can provide information on diet, oral hygiene, and dental care. The presence of dental caries can convey information about the diet of the population, such as high carbohydrate intake. Dental calculus (tartar) can supply information on food consumption, and periodontitis and periapical cavities (e.g., abscesses) give other data about oral hygiene. Enamel hypoplasia (defined here as an abnormal bone formation of the dental enamel, reflective of growth interruption due to malnutrition, infection, or psychological stress) can provide some information on conditions during childhood and may be used to deduce physiological stress and living conditions.[15]

Although paleopathology[16] (partly defined as the study of diseases from ancient human remains) can be challenging, it yields a wealth of information not only about past living conditions and medical care but also about the origin and evolution of conditions today, which may benefit present-day medicine. Although not all diseases leave traces on bones, evidence can be found for most groups, including congenital, neoplastic, metabolic, traumatic, infectious, and joint diseases. Among the infectious lesions, leprosy, syphilis, and tuberculosis can be found on skeletal remains. Some of the most commonly found conditions are osteoarthritis and trauma. Patterns of osteoarthritis may furnish information on physical conditions or activities, and muscle attachment sites can be used as indicators of activity.[17] Trauma, especially fractures, may be related not only to accidental injury but also to levels of violence in a population.[18]

Scientific methods have advanced in recent decades, and such studies are becoming increasingly multidisciplinary. Chemical analysis of isotopes can provide dating of human remains, characterizing diet as well as provenance.[19] DNA analysis can assist with understanding migration, population origin, and detection of disease.[20] Human remains, although mainly skeletonized in past populations, may also be preserved or mummified, and this opens up new opportunities for study, including the analysis of tattoos, hair, and stomach contents.[21] Such analyses should be undertaken with the utmost care and respect for the deceased, as some of them are destructive; guidelines regarding destructive sampling have been prepared.[22] Due to these recent and undoubted future developments, the retention of human remains for further investigation is recommended.

Ethical Issues Surrounding the Excavation, Analysis, Retention, and Display of Ancient or Historical Human Remains

The issue of excavation, study, curation, and display of human remains is a sensitive one. In recent years, with an increase in the number of debates surrounding this issue, several books have been published.[23] Roberts points out the basic questions: is it ethical to excavate human remains? Is it ethical to analyze them, to curate them, and to display them?[24]

Many of the claims for repatriation and reburial have come from indigenous groups requesting the return of the remains of their ancestors, which were taken especially under the practices of colonialism in the nineteenth century and retained largely in British and US institutions. Since then, the sensitivity surrounding human remains has come to include examples that are thousands of years old, such as those found at Avebury[25] in the UK, as well as at Kennewick, Washington, in the United States.[26]

Human remains can be found in single graves, in mass graves at archaeological sites, as parts of relics, and in a number of other contexts, for example those used as ornaments in ossuaries or exposed in catacombs.[27] The ethical issues surrounding human remains pertain not only to complete skeletons, but also to parts of skeletons, isolated bones or fragments of bones, and any other tissue.

Each country, and each jurisdiction within it, will have its own archaeological legislation, although only a limited number have specific rules dealing with human remains.[28] Among some of the legislative milestones, the 1989 Vermillion Accord on Human Remains, from the First World Archaeological Congress in South Dakota, can be noted.[29] Here the emphasis was on respect for the remains, the descendants and community of the deceased, and the scientific value of the study to society. This same year also saw the National Museum of the American Indian Act (NMAIA), followed in 1990 (and 1995) by the Native American Graves Protection and Repatriation Act (NAGPRA), two statutes that addressed the protection of remains and the cemeteries of indigenous groups.[30] Also significant was the 1992 Valetta

Convention for the protection of archaeological heritage, which promoted the conservation of and research on the archaeological heritage of Europe.[31] Two further codes of ethics are worth mentioning, one drawn up by the International Council of Museums (ICOM) in 2001[32] and also the Tamaki Makaurau accord adopted in 2006 at the World Archaeological Congress in Osaka, Japan (Fforde).[33]

A number of cases have been contested in the past, and some continue to be a matter of debate, regarding repatriation and reburial versus retention, study, and display. One of the most famous cases is that of Kennewick Man,[34] which has been very important to understanding life in North America about nine thousand years ago, but claims by indigenous groups have halted analysis. This case has continued for many years, since no strong argument could be made by current Native American groups. However, a recent DNA study has identified an ancestral link.[35] Some archaeological excavations have been stopped after protests, for example in medieval Jewish cemeteries in Spain and the UK,[36] as well as the eighteenth-century African American cemetery found in Manhattan in 1991.[37] Human remains as museum displays, especially when the name and wishes of the deceased are known, such as in the case of Charles Byrne, still arouse public controversy.[38]

Retention versus Repatriation and Reburial: Case Studies

The claim for reburial and repatriation of human remains from institutions such as museums and universities often involves cases hundreds or thousands of years old. Claims, some of which are stronger than others, are made primarily on the basis of religious, ancestral, cultural, and genetic grounds. The requests examine the balance between the rights and dignity of the deceased; the opinions and rights of the public; applicable legislation; ancestral, genetic, or religious links by those requesting the repatriation; and the scientific value of the remains for understanding the past, interpreting medical conditions, or for general education and research.[39]

Claims regarding Australian (including Tasmanian) aboriginal and Hawaiian skulls held at UK institutions are known to have taken place.[40] In the case of Avebury in the United Kingdom, a prehistoric skeleton on display at a museum has been claimed as related to present-day paganism and the druids by the Council of British Druid Orders (CoBDO), who are pressuring for burial of the remains. However, the claim is not strong enough at present, and such cases are difficult to prove if more than five hundred years old.[41]

Another widely noted example is the controversy surrounding the display of the body of a bushman at the Museu Darder in Catalonia, Spain, dating to around 1830 and thought to have been brought to Spain in 1888. In 1991 public opinion raised concerns about the display,[42] and after several years of debate and international attention, including at the United Nations, the body was returned to Botswana in 2000.[43] Another case, perhaps better known due to its display at Musée de l'Homme in Paris, was that of Saartjie (Sarah) Baartman (1789–1815), whose body was exhibited until the 1970s. Claims for the return of the body for burial in South Africa were supported by the international community, including personal assistance by Nelson Mandela. Baartman's remains were finally laid to rest in a protected tomb in South Africa in 2002.[44]

Other cases worldwide are notable and worth mentioning. Truganini, a Tasmanian female, specifically wanted to be buried; but when she died in 1876 her body, a scientific curiosity at the time, was dissected and sent to different countries for analysis and teaching. She was finally cremated in 1976.[45] South America has also had its controversial cases, for example the repatriation of Chief Charrua Vaimaca Peru from Paris to Uruguay in 2002.[46] He was a French prisoner taken in 1833 to France, where he died and his body examined and put on display. In 2000 the Uruguayan parliament approved a law promoting the claim that the remains should be returned as requested by the indigenous groups, and that this was of national importance. Many more examples exist worldwide, including Maori remains to be returned to New Zealand[47] and Sami remains in Finland, Sweden, and

Norway to be returned to Sami communities.[48] Of course, reburial has also taken place for reasons other than religious, genetic, or cultural affiliation. Sometimes it is undertaken due to lack of storage space, due to legislation, or even to lack of interest in a particular period.

The arguments in support of retention mainly stem from the lack of legitimate claims for repatriation and reburial, and from scientific needs. The latter are especially relevant in light of future research techniques that may be developed. Buikstra and Gordon[49] assessed the new research that had been carried out on older specimens and proved that a reexamination of the material provided revised results and changed the interpretation. Maintaining good curation practices has certainly been a major factor in the retention of remains, and a number of papers and books have been written on the subject.[50] Remains can also be used for teaching future scientists.[51] Other considerations involve developments such as the laser scanning of bones, enhanced photographic records, 3D printing, and the uses of social media, all of which will involve their own ethical considerations.[52]

The Case of Julia Pastrana: An Anthropologist's Personal Involvement and Scientific Dilemma

I had some involvement, although minimal compared to the main actors, in the process of repatriating the body of Julia Pastrana. It began with a series of interviews I had given to journalist Silvia Isabel Gámez in the Mexican newspaper *Reforma* back in 2011.[53] She later put me in touch with Mexican artist Laura Anderson Barbata, who I had met during a visit to Mexico in 2012 and with whom I have maintained a strong friendship. One of the reasons for the initial contact by Gámez was to obtain a scientific perspective on the issue of repatriation, partly stemming from my interest in legislation and ethics at the time.[54] I was asked for my opinion on the process of repatriation from Norway to Mexico, whether I would support such a request, and whether I could assist with scientific opinions, witness the transfer of the body, and provide advice on logistics, knowledge I had gained in my work as a forensic anthropologist. The first thing was to find out a bit more about Pastrana, her life, her death, and the circumstances that led to her body being at the University of Oslo.

I had already come across her name in a book I read in 1999, as a PhD student at the then Institute of Biological Anthropology, University of Oxford. This was *The Living Races of Mankind*,[55] which contained a few illustrations of Pastrana and other individuals with similar hereditary conditions. Through further research I learned that she was born in Mexico, and that her talents included singing, dancing, and playing a musical instrument. She traveled in North America as well as Europe for performances, although her rise to fame was primarily due to her physical characteristics. According to the literature she had generalized hypertrichosis terminalis and severe gingival hyperplasia,[56] which meant a disproportionately large and protruding jaw.[57] Charles Darwin, in *The Variation of Animals and Plants under Domestication*, described her as "a remarkably fine woman, but she had a thick masculine beard and a hairy forehead; she was photographed, and her stuffed skin was exhibited as a show . . . We ought to remember her for her success and talents during life, rather than her condition and mummification after death" (1868, ch. 25).

The circumstances of her death documented in the literature[58] were that when on tour in Moscow in 1860 she gave birth to a child with a similar condition. Both child and mother soon died due to complications during childbirth. The bodies were examined and embalmed by Professor J. Sokolov, from the University of Moscow.[59] They were reclaimed by Theodore Lent, Julia's husband and agent, were exhibited by him, and after his death continued to be on public view in Norway until 1921. After a number of further ownerships, the bodies ceased to be exhibited due to an outcry during a tour of the United States in the 1970s. They were stored in a building in Oslo, although there was a break-in in 1976, when the child's remains were damaged, and a further robbery in 1979, when Julia's body was stolen. The body was found years later and identified in 1990 at the Forensic Institute of Oslo, which then passed it on to the department of anatomy at the university. The child's remains were never found. On February 7, 2013, the University of Oslo handed Julia's body over to the Mexican authorities, a process for which I was a witness, and she was buried in her place of birth on February 12.

For a number of years the efforts to return Pastrana's body to Mexico were led by artist Laura Anderson Barbata and others working with her. Media attention also played an important part. When journalist Silvia Gámez sought my opinion,[60] she asked me what steps could be taken to ensure repatriation, what were the legislative and scientific protocols, and whether I knew of any similar cases. The following questions came to mind:

- *Who is requesting the repatriation and/or (re)burial?*
- *What are the grounds of the claimants and the reasons for repatriation?*
- *If the body is to be retained by an academic institution and access granted for research, what will we learn about living conditions and history during a particular period?*
- *Are the medical conditions unique?*
- *Does study help in our understanding of the evolution of health and disease?*
- *What do we know about the pathological condition of Julia's body today, and are there similar cases?*
- *If she is repatriated, can we retain tissue samples for future study?*
- *What were the circumstances that led to the body being at the University of Oslo?*
- *Has repatriation been denied in the past? For what reasons?*
- *Do the reasons for retention involve research and education?*
- *Is the body curated in adequate facilities?*
- *Has the body been available for research by bona fide scientists?*
- *Has this research been published in recent years?*
- *Has the body been exhibited for educational purposes?*

- *Was she ever buried?*
- *Which weighs more in this case: respect and dignity for
  the deceased or retention for research purposes, to better
  understand nineteenth-century history and the evolution
  of the disease?*

Further questions occurred to me, ones that perhaps may serve as a guide for anthropologists considering similar cases:

- *On what grounds would I support the body being retained?
  In what way would this advance science?*
- *Would Pastrana have wanted to return to Mexico? Would she
  have wanted to be buried?*
- *What is the legislation in Norway in this regard? Who has
  the power to decide: the university, the scientists, the government? Is there legislation regarding "ownership" of human
  remains?*
- *If the body is repatriated, can prior research be done using
  CT scans, radiographs, photographs, and other nondestruc-
  tive techniques? Should a sample of DNA be taken for future
  analysis? Would this data be available for study by bona fide
  researchers in the future?*
- *If repatriation takes place, how can damage to the body be
  avoided during transportation?*
- *How can we ensure that there are no financial gains as a
  result of repatriation, no exhibition, no cremation, but a
  funeral and a dignified burial in a protected grave?*

Regardless of what my peers in the scientific community may have advised, my opinion as a scientist was to support repatriation. I was there to offer scientific advice if required. In this case, I felt that the dignity and respect due to someone who had never been buried took precedence over any scientific advantage. However, especially as a specialist in human remains and as an archaeologist who works to reconstruct the past, I felt that as much data from the remains as possible should be recorded prior to repatriation. I made sure that this recommendation was conveyed to the Mexican individuals making the request.

Repatriation in this case was not related specifically to a request by a direct descendant, family member, indigenous group, or community. Neither were there religious grounds. Some of these considerations would have made the decision easier, not only at a personal level but also at an institutional level. On the other hand, if retention was to be favored, could the institution provide access to research as well as good conservation, curation, and storage of the remains? Also, though future research might provide further information about Pastrana's particular medical condition, was this necessary?

My rationale was due to a number of considerations. In the first place would be the need for information about her death and how her body came to the university. Pastrana had never been buried, unlike some individuals who are buried, exhumed for one reason or another, and later claimed for reburial. The main justification for retention of her body would be to help understand the history and evolution of her medical condition. With regard to scientific knowledge, there is a wealth of information and historical accounts about nineteenth-century Mexico as well as regarding individuals with rare conditions of her type.[61] The nineteenth century lies in contrast to earlier periods, where much less is known about diet, lifestyle, health status, demography, living conditions, social organization, economy, violence, etc. Regarding the medical condition: Julia Pastrana was not the only individual known to have this condition in the nineteenth century.[62] Her condition has been studied by a number of scientists,[63] and there are cases today of individuals with the same condition.[64] Due to the techniques at the time and the way her body had been embalmed and prepared for exhibition after death, available information is more limited than that which can be obtained for populations today. Therefore retaining her remains for this reason would, in my opinion, be of limited value, as new studies have focused on living patients. Nevertheless, prior to any possible repatriation my recommendation was to allow radiographs, photography, and scientific recording to take place, including obtaining samples for future DNA analysis if required.

One of the philosophical dilemmas of this case was that we don't know how Julia felt, what her wishes were about her remains, what her attitudes toward burial were, or how religious she was. We don't know whether she missed Mexico. I wondered whether there would be a letter, a diary, a poem or other writing from her expressing her feelings, which would complement the support for repatriation.

Another concern that I had was whether her remains would be protected after their return. It would be unfortunate if after recommending her return the body was damaged further than it already had been. I emphasized that on its return, the body should be respected, treated with dignity, not exhibited or used for commercial or financial gain, and placed in a protected grave to be maintained for years. In addition, I specified that the body should not be cremated.

From the perspective of my academic circle, I had to consider what my peers and colleagues would think about my support for this repatriation; I was happy with my justifiable answer. Finally, a more philosophical question: what did I think as a person? Would I want my remains retained by an institution? Would I want the remains of my relatives stored and not buried, if there was no clear wish from them prior to death?

The decision of the University of Oslo was very respectful, and they should be congratulated for listening to the request initiated by the Mexican individuals mentioned above, led by Laura Anderson Barbata. The assessment by the Norwegian National Committee for the Evaluation of Research on Human Remains and their recommendation was also crucial. According to their website,[65] this advisory board received four letters concerning the case of Pastrana: one from Barbata; one from journalist Silvia Isabel Gámez; one from Mario López Valdez, governor of the state of Sinaloa; and one from Per Holck, professor of medicine at the University of Oslo, Norway. The conclusion of the

Norwegian National Committee was that Julia Pastrana's remains should be buried, that a nationally coordinated return to Mexico was a responsible way of carrying out the burial, and that samples might be taken of the remains, provided this was followed up by an initiative to inform relevant research groups of their existence. In addition, the committee stated that their ethical evaluation of Julia Pastrana's case took into account three main points: (1) Julia Pastrana was a well-known, individually identified person; (2) her life and death were relatively close in time to the present day; and (3) the attention Pastrana received while alive, and the treatment of her remains after her death, to a great extent relied on interest about her appearance, which the committee found ethically unacceptable. The committee also considered Pastrana's wishes, and although they stated that these were not known, it would seem quite unlikely that she would have wanted her body to remain a specimen in an anatomical collection.

The Repatriation of Julia Pastrana's Body

In a ceremony described elsewhere in this book, the repatriation of the body of Julia Pastrana took place on February 7, 2013. Alongside Laura Anderson Barbata and on behalf of the state of Sinaloa, a group of scientists witnessed the handing of custody from the University of Oslo to the Mexican authorities. Laura and I arrived at 9:10 a.m. (I recorded the time of events as part of the documentation) at the mortuary of the university, and in a private chapel (Ullevål University Hospital) oversaw this process and the closure of the coffin. The body, covered by a sheet up to the head, lay inside a wooden coffin. Not out of curiosity but simply to ensure integrity and ascertain the extent of the remains being handed over, we asked for the sheet to be removed. We saw that footwear was still present, attached by bolts to the body.[66] We decided to detach the bolts, which were on metal rods extending into the lower limbs, and remove the shoes, yet leave them inside the coffin. A brief recording was made of the preservation of the body,[67] and we witnessed the coffin being sealed and placed in

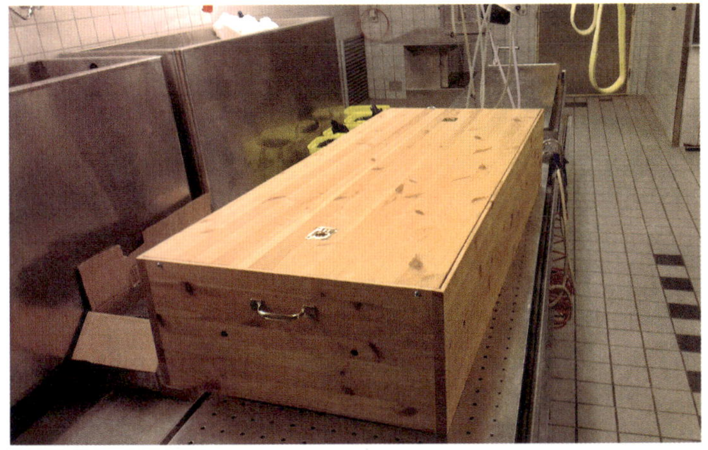

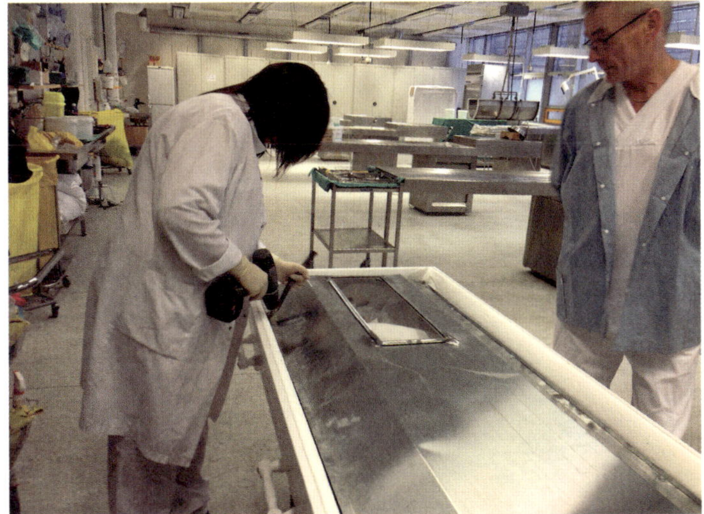

Container for Julia Pastrana, Anatomical Institute,
University of Oslo, 2013

Zinc coffin being sealed for Julia Pastrana's repatriation, 2013

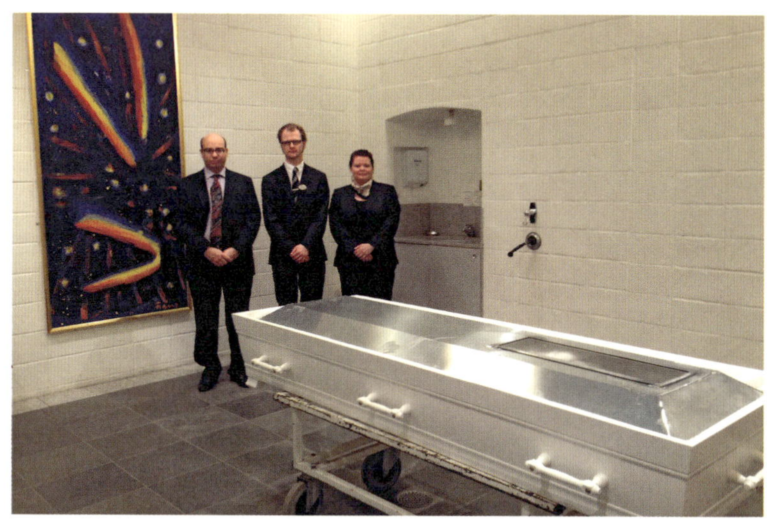

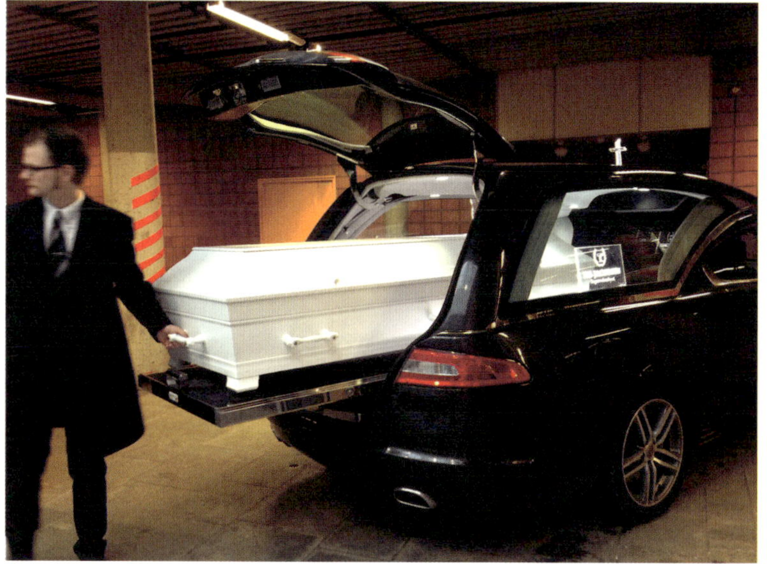

Dr. Nicholas Márquez-Grant (left) and attendants from
T. S. Jacobsen funeral agency with Julia Pastrana's coffin, 2013

Julia Pastrana's coffin being transported to the chapel
at Rikshospitalet, Oslo University Hospital, 2013

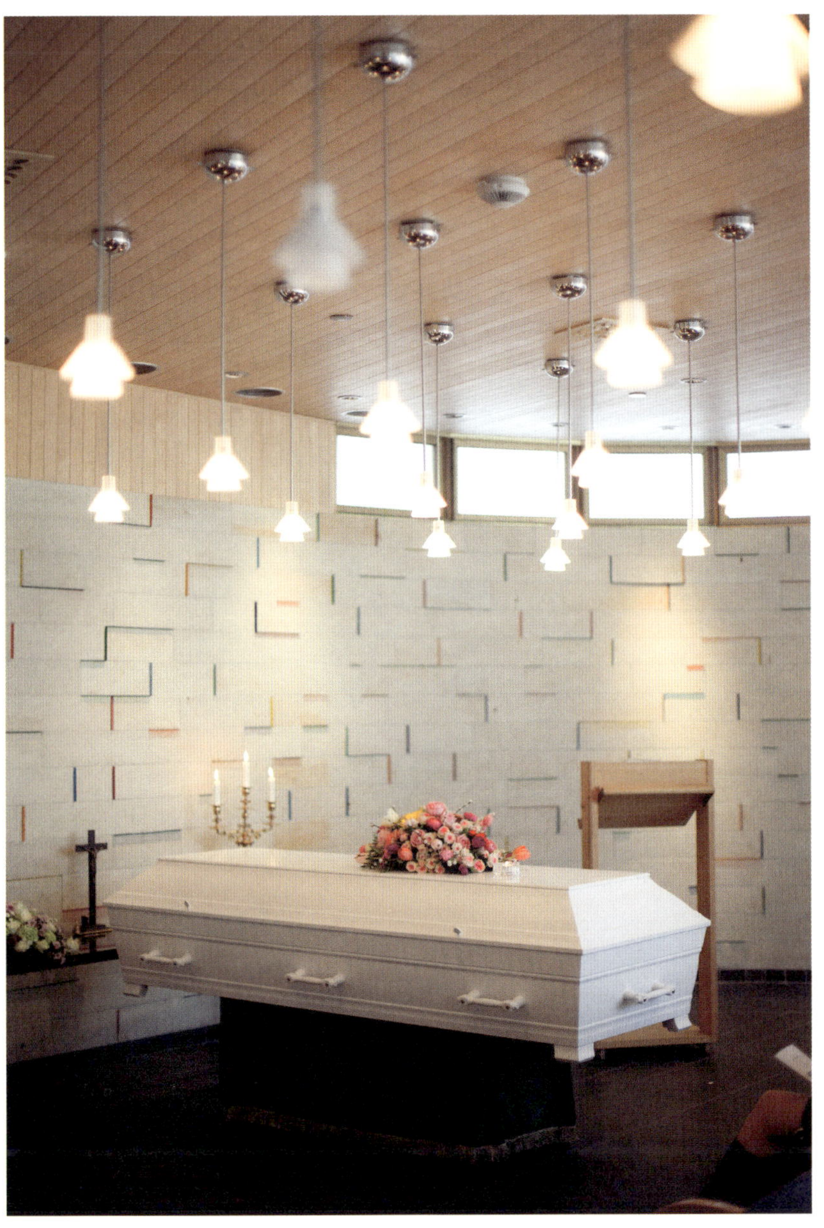

Julia Pastrana's coffin in chapel at Rikshospitalet,
Oslo University Hospital, 2013

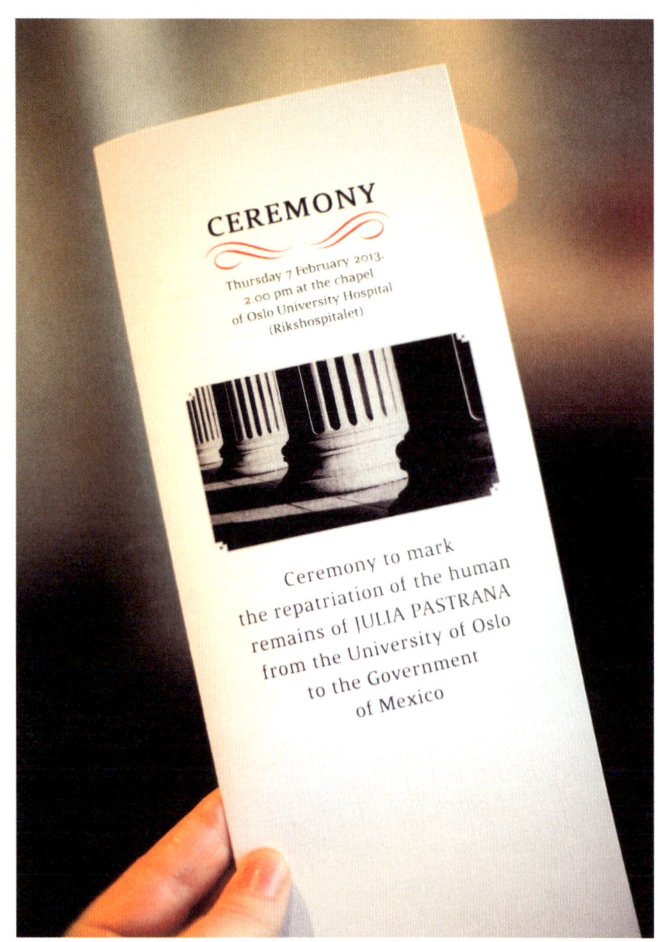

Program for repatriation ceremony at the chapel
at Rikshospitalet, Oslo University Hospital, 2013

a transportation container by an international funeral company. The coffin was then taken to the local chapel, where a ceremony was held, attended by the vice rector of the University of Oslo and the dean of the faculty of medicine, as well as the Mexican ambassador. Scientists, artists, and members of the public, as well as disability groups, were on hand during this occasion of dignified remembrance. The body was later taken to Mexico by a professional repatriation company. Laura Anderson Barbata was present with local authorities and the public to witness the final burial of Julia Pastrana in Sinaloa.

Conclusion

This paper has provided a personal account, from a scientific perspective, of seeing both the value of the study of human remains and the value of their repatriation. It has allowed me to highlight how scientific information obtained from remains can help us understand aspects of our present and our future, and how these individuals become our teachers. As scientists and members of the public we are privileged to be able to learn from them.

As a scientist, I was asked to give my opinion regarding repatriation, a topic which is debatable in my field today and tends to be assessed on a case-by-case basis. This was not to be taken lightly, and it led to my asking a number of questions that may serve other scientists in future cases. After much consideration and analysis, I supported the repatriation of the body of Julia Pastrana and was able to help from a scientific perspective when required. This experience has been extremely rewarding for me.

One consideration, in my personal opinion and from the point of view of scientific institutions, is that the increased return of remains from other cultures may limit studies of human variation as well as the resources to train future forensic anthropologists. However, at times scientists do not convey proper information to the public; outreach programs should be undertaken so the public can understand the value of such study.

I am not aware of any political gains from this repatriation of Julia Pastrana's body. In fact, cases like this show us something about ourselves as individuals, demonstrating that no matter what the circumstances, people will fight for the respect and dignity of the deceased.

Rest in peace, Julia Pastrana, and may your successes be remembered in the future, as I am sure they will have been remembered by the people you made happy during your lifetime. *Descansa en paz, Julia.*

NOTES

1 A. E. W. Miles, "Julia Pastrana: The Bearded Lady," *Proceedings of the Royal Society of Medicine* 67 (1974): 8–12; J. Browne and S. Messenger, "Victorian Spectacle: Julia Pastrana, the Bearded and Hairy Female," *Endeavour* 27 (2003): 155–59; Stern 2008.

2 https://www.etikkom.no/en/our-work/about-us/the-national-committee-for-research-ethics-on-human-remains/ (accessed June 2016); see also B. J. Sellevold, "Norway/Norge," in N. Márquez-Grant and L. Fibiger, eds., *The Routledge Handbook of Archaeological Human Remains and Legislation* (Abingdon: Routledge, 2011), 317–28; H. Fossheim, *More Than Just Bones: Ethics and Research on Human Remains* (Oslo: Norwegian National Research Ethics Committee, 2012).

3 http://www.legislation.gov.uk/ukpga/2004/30/contents (accessed June 2016).

4 D. R. Brothwell, *The Bog Man and the Archaeology of People* (London: British Museum Publications, 1986); T. Ammitzbøll et al., "The People," in J. P. Hart Hansen et al., eds., *The Greenland Mummies* (Montreal: McGill-Queen's University Press, 1991), 64–101; J. H. Taylor, "The Collection of Egyptian Mummies in the British Museum," in A. Fletcher et al., eds., *Regarding the Dead: Human Remains in the British Museum* (London: British Museum, 1991), 103–14.

5 D. Antoine, "Curating Human Remains in Museum Collections," in A. Fletcher et al., eds. (2014), 3–9.

6 C. S. Larsen, *Bioarchaeology: Interpreting Behavior from the Human Skeleton* (Cambridge: Cambridge University Press), 1.

7 See general overview in Y. M. İşcan and K. A. R. Kenney, *Reconstruction of Life from the Skeleton* (New York: Alan R. Liss, 1989); A. Chamberlain, *Demography in Archaeology* (Cambridge: Cambridge University Press) 2006; S. Mays, *The Archaeology of Human Bones*, 2nd ed. (Abingdon: Routledge, 2010); C. A. Roberts, *Human Remains in Archaeology: A Handbook* (York: Council for British Archaeology, 2009); C. A. Roberts, *The Archaeology of Disease*, 3rd. ed. (Stroud: The History Press, 2010); C. Roberts and M. Cox, *Health and Disease in Britain: From Prehistory to the Present Day* (Stroud: Sutton, 2003).

8 See an overview of methods in D. H. Ubelaker, *Human Skeletal Remains: Excavation, Analysis, Interpretation*, 3rd. ed. (Washington, D.C.: Taraxacum, 1989); J. E. Buikstra and D. H. Ubelaker, eds., *Standards for Data Collection from Human Skeletal Remains* (Magnolia, AK: Archaeological Survey Research Series No. 44, 1994); D. Komar and J. Buikstra, *Forensic Anthropology: Contemporary Theory and Practice* (New York: Oxford University Press, 2008); M. T. A. Tersigni-Tarrant and N. R. Shirley, *Forensic Anthropology: An Introduction* (Boca Raton, FL: CRC Press, 2013).

9   See M. Cox, "Ageing Adults from the Human Skeleton," in M. Cox and S. Mays, eds.,
    Human Osteology in Archaeology and Forensic Science (London: Greenwich Medical
    Media, 2000), 61–81; L. Scheuer and S. Black, *Developmental Juvenile Osteology* (London:
    Academic Press, 2000); A. Schmitt et al., *Forensic Anthropology and Medicine: Comple-
    mentary Sciences from Recovery to Cause of Death* (Totowa, NJ: Human Press, 2005);
    K. E. Latham and M. Finnegan, *Age Estimation of the Human Skeleton* (Springfield, IL:
    Charles C. Thomas, 2010); D. Dirkmaat, *A Companion to Forensic Anthropology*
    (Chichester: Wiley-Blackwell, 2012).

10 See M. Parker-Pearson, *The Archaeology of Death and Burial* (Stroud: Sutton, 1999);
    T. Taylor, *The Buried Soul: How Humans Invented Death* (London: Fourth Estate, 2002);
    E. M. Murphy, ed., *Deviant Burial in the Archaeological Record* (Oxford: Oxbow, 2008).

11 W. D. Haglund and M. H. Sorg, eds., *Forensic Taphonomy: The Postmortem Fate of Human
    Remains* (Boca Raton, FL: CRC Press, 1996); W. D. Haglund and M. H. Sorg, eds., *Advances
    in Forensic Taphonomy: Method, Theory, and Archaeological Perspective* (Boca Raton, FL:
    CRC Press, 2001); J. T. Pokines and S. A. Symes, *Manual of Forensic Taphonomy* (Boca
    Raton, FL: CRC Press, 2013).

12 S. I. Fairgrieve, *Forensic Cremation Recovery and Analysis* (Boca Raton, FL: CRC Press,
    2007); C. W. Schmidt and S. Symes, eds., *Analysis of Burned Human Remains*, 2nd. ed.
    (London: Academic Press, 2015); T. Thompson, ed., *The Archaeology of Cremation: Burned
    Human Remains in Funerary Studies* (Oxford: Oxbow Books, 2015).

13 C. B. Ruff, "Variation in Human Body Size and Shape," *Annual Review of Anthropology* 31
    (2002): 211–32; C. Padez, "Secular Trend in Stature in the Portuguese Population (1904–
    2000)," *Annals of Human Biology* 30 (2003): 262–78; Roberts and Cox 2003.

14 S. Hillson, *Dental Anthropology* (Cambridge: Cambridge University Press, 1996); J. D. Irish
    and G. R. Scott, *A Companion to Dental Anthropology* (Chichester: Wiley-Blackwell, 2015).

15 K. Dobney and A. Goodman, "Epidemiological Studies of Dental Enamel Hypoplasias in
    Mexico and Bradford," in H. Bush and M. Zvelebil, eds., *Health in Past Societies: Biocul-
    tural Interpretations of Human Skeletal Remains in Archaeological Contexts,* BAR Inter-
    national Series 567 (Oxford: Archaeopress, 1991), 81–100; T. King et al., "Linear Enamel
    Hypoplasias as Indicators of Systemic Physiological Stress," *American Journal of Physical
    Anthropology* 128 (2005): 547–59; E. Maclellan, "Linear Enamel Hypoplasia: What Can It
    Say about the Condition of Childhood?" *Totem: The University of Western Ontario Journal
    of Anthropology*, 13, no. 1 (2005), available at http://ir.lib.uwo.ca/totem/vol13/iss1/7;
    H. M. Wong, "Aetiological Factors for Developmental Defects of Enamel," *Austin Journal
    of Anatomy* 1 (2014): 1003, available at http://austinpublishinggroup.com/anatomy
    /fulltext/download.php?file=Anatomy-v1-id1003.pdf.

16 A. C. Aufderheide and C. Rodríguez-Martín, *The Cambridge Encyclopedia of Human Paleo-
    pathology* (Cambridge: Cambridge University Press, 1998); D. J. Ortner, *Identification of
    Pathological Conditions in Human Skeletal Remains*, 2nd. ed. (San Diego: Academic Press,
    2003); T. Waldron, *Palaeopathology* (Cambridge: Cambridge University Press, 2009);
    Roberts 2010; R. W. Mann and D. R. Hunt, *Photographic Regional Atlas of Bone Disease:
    A Guide to Pathologic and Normal Variation in the Human Skeleton*, 3rd. ed. (Springfield,
    IL: Charles C. Thomas, 2013).

17 R. D. Jurmain, "Degenerative Changes in Peripheral Joints as Indicators of Mechanical
    Stress," *International Journal of Osteoarchaeology* 1 (1991): 247–52; C. J. Knüsel, "On the
    Biomechanical and Osteoarthritic Differences between Hunter-Gatherers and
    Agriculturalists," *American Journal of Physical Anthropology* 91(1993): 523–25;
    R. Jurmain, *Stories from the Skeleton: Behavioral Reconstruction in Human Osteology*
    (Abingdon: Routledge, 2012).

18 N. C. Lovell, "Trauma Analysis in Paleopathology," *Yearbook of Physical Anthropology* 40 (1997): 139–70; V. L. Wedel and A. Galloway, eds., *Broken Bones: Anthropological Analysis of Blunt Force Trauma* (Springfield, IL: Charles C. Thomas, 2013); C. Knüsel and M. Smith, eds., *The Routledge Handbook of the Bioarchaeology of Human Conflict* (Abingdon: Routledge, 2013).

19 M. A. Katzenberg, "Stable Isotope Analysis," in M. A. Katzenberg and S. R. Saunders, eds., *Biological Anthropology of the Human Skeleton* (New York: Wiley-Liss, 2000); M. Schoeninger and K. Moore, "Stable Bone Isotope Studies in Archaeology," *Journal of World Prehistory* 6 (1992): 247–96; B. L. Beard and C. M. Johnson, "Strontium Isotope Composition of Skeletal Material Can Determine the Birthplace and Geographic Mobility of Humans and Animals," *Journal of Forensic Sciences* 45 (2000): 1049–61; W. Meier-Augenstein and I. Fraser, "Forensic Stable Isotope Analysis Leads to Identification of a Mutilated Murder Victim," *Science & Justice* 48 (2008): 153–59.

20 H. D. Donoghue et al., "PCR Primers That Can Detect Low Levels of Mycobacterium Leprae DNA," *Journal of Medical Microbiology* 50 (2001): 177–82; I. Hershkovitz et al., "Detection and Molecular Characterization of 9,000-Year-Old Mycobacterium Tuberculosis from a Neolithic Settlement in the Eastern Mediterranean," *PLoS One* 3 (10) (2008); e3426, doi: 10.1371/journal.pone.0003426; M. Haber et al., "Ancient DNA and the Rewriting of Human History," *Genome Biology* 17 (2016): 1, doi: 10.1186/s13059-015-0866-z; B. Llamas et al., "Ancient Mitochondrial DNA Provides High-Resolution Time Scale of the Peopling of the Americas," *Science Advances* 2 (4) (2016): e1501385, doi: 10.1126/sciadv.1501385.

21 A. C. Aufderheide, *The Scientific Study of Mummies* (Duluth: University of Minnesota, 2011).

22 E.g., APABE, *Science and the Dead: A Guideline for the Destructive Sampling of Archaeological Human Remains for Scientific Analysis* (2013), available at http://www.archaeologyuk.org/apabe/pdf/Science_and_the_Dead.pdf.

23 C. Fforde, *Collecting the Dead: Archaeology and the Reburial Issues* (London: Duckworth, 2004); J. Lohman and K. J. Goodnow, eds., *Human Remains & Museum Practice* (Oxford: Berghahn Books, 2006); D. Sayer, *Ethics and Burial Archaeology* (London: Duckworth, 2010); J. M. Alberti et al., "Should We Display the Dead?" *Museum and Society* 7 (2009): 133–49; Tiffany Jenkins, *Contesting Human Remains in Museum Collections: The Crisis of Cultural Authority* (Abingdon: Taylor and Francis, 2010); H. Fossheim, *More Than Just Bones: Ethics and Research on Human Remains* (Oslo: Norwegian National Research Ethics Committee, 2012).

24 Roberts 2009: 17.

25 https://historicengland.org.uk/advice/technical-advice/archaeological-science/human-remains-advice/avebury-reburial-results/ (accessed June 2016).

26 D. W. Owsley and R. L. Jantz, *Identification of Pathological Conditions in Human Skeletal Remains* (San Diego: Academic Press, 2014); M. Rasmussen et al., "The Ancestry and Affiliations of Kennewick Man," *Nature* 523 (2015): 455–58.

27 See P. Koudounaris, *Memento Mori: The Dead among Us* (London: Thames and Hudson, 2015).

28 N. Márquez-Grant and L. Fibiger 2013; N. Márquez-Grant et al., "Physical Anthropology and Osteoarchaeology in Europe," *International Journal of Osteoarchaeology* (2016), doi: 10.1002/oa.2520.

29 http://worldarch.org/code-of-ethics/; http://ethics.iit.edu/ecodes/node/3914 (both accessed June 2016).

30 D. H. Ubelaker, "United States of America," in N. Márquez-Grant and L. Fibiger 2011.

31 Márquez-Grant et al. 2016; see also https://rm.coe.int/CoERMPublicCommonSearch
    Services/DisplayDCTMContent?documentId=090000168007bd25 (accessed June 2016).

32 See 2006 Code of Ethics: http://archives.icom.museum/ethics.html (accessed June 2016).

33 See also: http://ethics.iit.edu/ecodes/node/4414 (accessed June 2016).

34 Owsley and Jantz 2014.

35 Rasmussen et al. 2015.

36 J. L. Jiménez and C. Mata, "Creencias religiosas versus gestión del patrimonio arque-
    ológico," *Trabajos de Prehistoria* 58 (2001): 27–40; M. L. Endere, "Patrimonios en disputa:
    acervos nacionales, investigación arqueológica y reclamos étnicos sobre restos humanos,"
    Trabajos de Prehistoria 57 (2000): 5–17; P. V. Addeyman, "Circumstances of Excavation
    and Research," in J. M. Lilley et al., eds., *The Jewish Burial Ground at Jewbury*, The
    Archaeology of York, vol. 12 (York: York Archaeological Trust, 1994), 298–300; D. Sayer,
    Ethics and Burial Archaeology (London: Duckworth, 2010).

37 J. E. Howson, "The Foley Square Project: An 18th-Century Cemetery in New York City,"
    African American Archaeology, Newsletter no. 6 (Spring 1992): 3–4; T. W. Epperson, "The
    Politics of 'Race' and Cultural Identity at the African Burial Ground Excavations, New York
    City," *World Archaeological Bulletin* 7 (1997): 108–17; see also https://www.nps.gov/afbg
    /learn/historyculture/index.htm (accessed June 2016).

38 L. Doyal and T. Muinzer, "Should the Skeleton of 'The Irish Giant' Be Buried at Sea?"
    British Medical Journal 343 (2011): d7597; see also recent debate surrounding the
    remains of Joseph Merrick (the Elephant Man): http://www.bbc.co.uk/news/uk-england
    -leicestershire-36478601 (accessed June 2016).

39 J. Buikstra, "A Specialist in Ancient Cemetery Studies Looks at the Reburial Issue," *Early
    Man* 3 (1981): 26–27; Lohman and Goodnow 2006; V. Cassman et al., eds., *Human Remains:
    Guides for Museums and Academic Institutions* (Lanham, MD: Altamira Press, 2007);
    Jenkins 2010.

40 Fforde 2004; C. S. Larsen and P. L. Walker, "The Ethics of Bioarchaeology," in T. R.
    Turner, ed., *Biological Anthropology and Ethics: From Repatriation to Genetic Identity*
    (Albany: SUNY Press, 2005), 111–19; P. M. Lambert, "Ethics and Issues in the Use of
    Human Skeletal Remains," in A. L. Grauer, ed., *Companion to Paleopathology* (Chichester:
    Wiley-Blackwell, 2016), 17–33; see also https://internationalrepatriation.files.wordpress
    .com/2013/04/2015-international-repatriation-guide-final.pdf (accessed June 2016).

41 Department for Culture, Media, and Sport, *Guidance for the Care of Human Remains
    in Museums* (London: DCMS, 2005), available at: https://www.britishmuseum.org/pdf
    /DCMS%20Guide.pdf; G. Moshenska, "The Reburial Issue in Britain," *Antiquity* 83 (2009):
    815–20; Sayer 2010 and references therein; see also https://content.historicengland.org
    .uk/content/docs/consultations/avebury-reburial-request-summary.pdf (accessed June
    2016).

42 D. Jaume et al., "Racism, Archaeology, and Museums: The Strange Case of the Stuffed Man
    from the Museu Darder," *World Archaeological Bulletin* 6 (1992): 113–18.

43 C. Davies, *The Return of El Negro* (Johannesburg: Penguin Books, 2003).

44 J. Bredekamp, "The Politics of Human Remains: The Case of Sarah Bartmann," in Lohman
    and Goodnow, 25–32.

45 Fforde 2004: 100.

46 M. Sans, "Uruguay," in Márquez-Grant and Fibiger 2011.

47 See Fforde 2004; N. Tayles and S. Halcrow, "New Zelanda/Aotearoa," in Márquez-Grant
    and Fibiger 2011.

48 T. Ahlström et al., "Sweden/Sverige," in Márquez-Grant and Fibiger 2011; Núñez et al.,
    "Finland/Suomi," in Márquez-Grant and Fibiger 2011.

49 J. E. Buikstra and C. C. Gordon, "The Study and Restudy of Human Skeletal Series: The Importance of Long-Term Curation," *Annals of the New York Academy of Sciences* 376 (1981): 449–65.

50 Cassman et al. 2007; Jenkins 2010; P. L. Walker, "Bioarchaeological Ethics," in Katzenberg and Saunders; C. Roberts and S. Mays, "Study and Restudy of Curated Skeletal Collections in Bioarchaeology," *International Journal of Osteoarchaeology* 21 (2011): 626–30; M. Giesen, ed., *Curating Human Remains: Caring for the Dead in the United Kingdom* (Martlesham: Boydell Press, 2013); Fletcher et al. 2014.

51 Buikstra 1981.

52 R. Beckett and G. Conlogue, *Paleoimaging* (Boca Raton, FL: CRC Press, 2009); Killgrove 2015.

53 http://reforma.vlex.com.mx/vid/apoyan-regreso-mujer-mono-329622715 (accessed June 2016).

54 Márquez-Grant and Fibiger 2011.

55 H. N. Hutchinson et al., *The Living Races of Mankind* (London: Hutchinson, 1901).

56 J. Bondeson and A. E. W. Miles, "Julia Pastrana, the Nondescript: An Example of Congenital, Generalized Hypertrichosis Terminalis with Gingival Hyperplasia," *American Journal of Medical Genetics* 47 (1993): 198–212.

57 See S. Canún et al., "Hypertrichosis Terminalis, Gingival Hyperplasia, and a Characteristic Face: A New Distinct Entity," *American Journal of Medical Genetics*, 116A (2003): 278–83; H. H. Afifi et al., "De Novo 17q24.2–q24.3 Microdeletion Presenting with Generalized Hypertrichosis Terminalis, Gingival Fibromatous Hyperplasia, and Distinctive Facial Features," *American Journal of Medical Genetics*, Part A, 167A (2015): 2418–24.

58 J. Sokolov, "Julia Pastrana and Her Child," tr. M. Ralston, *The Lancet*, May 3 (1862): 467–69; J. Bondeson, *A Cabinet of Medical Curiosities* (London: I. B.Tauris, 1997); Browne and Messenger 2003; C. H. Gylseth and L. O. Toverud, *Julia Pastrana: The Tragic Story of the Victorian Ape Woman* (Stroud: Sutton, 2003); and other contributions in this volume.

59 Sokolov 1862.

60 See a summary in http://reforma.vlex.com.mx/vid/apoyan-regreso-mujer-mono-329622715 (accessed June 2016).

61 E.g., Bondeson 1997; R. Bogdan, *Freak Show: Presenting Human Oddities for Amusement and Profit* (Chicago: The University of Chicago Press, 1988); N. Durbach, *Spectacle of Deformity: Freak Shows and Modern British Culture* (Oakland: University of California Press, 2009).

62 See Hutchinson et al. 1901; Bondeson and Miles 1996.

63 E.g., Bondeson and Miles 1993.

64 Canún et al. 2003; see more recently publications by Afifi et al. 2015; C. WenChie et al., "Congenital Generalized Hypertrichosis Terminalis," *European Journal of Dermatology* 25 (2015): 223–27.

65 https://www.etikkom.no/hvem-er-vi-og-hva-gjor-vi/komiteenes-arbeid/Uttalelser/Skjelettutvalget/Statement-concerning-the-remains-of-Julia-Pastrana/ (accessed June 2016).

66 See also this reported in http://www.nytimes.com/2013/02/12/arts/design/julia-pastrana-who-died-in-1860-to-be-buried-in-mexico.html?_r=0 (accessed June 2016).

67 A few lines were recorded by the author, and this information is available on request to bona fide researchers.

do labor on vault at court house, 4 75
John Gager. digging vault, 3 10
Morgan & Downs, plank for vault, 3 80
J. Beery. planking the same, 4 50
King & Zeigler, spikes for same, 38
J. W. Stevenson, repairing table, 2 00
Elections, 195 00
W. Trevitt, field notes U.S. survey, 350 27
Lawyers, 50 00
Coroners. 11 25
Constables, 329 93
Jurors. 685 64
Prosecuting Attorney, 210 00
   do   in Probate court, 113 32
   do   Record 3 50
Sheriff's fees and salary, 235 12
John Bell, P. J. salary and fees, 185 50
L Gelpin, P. J. fees, 4 31
D. Capper Co. Clerk fees, 302 86
C. H. Greene, do 54 23
Justices, 100 77
Witnesses, 744 91
County Commissioners, 158 00
Auditor's fees, &c., 2,032 44

   Total expenditures, 10,562 92
Receipts above expenditures, 863 41

INTEREST FUND—Receipts.

Amount on hand June 1, 1854. 333 59
   Contra.
Paid Interest orders, 319 70
" Amount transferred to Co. fund, 13 88

BRIDGE FUND—Receipts.

Amount on hand June 1, 1854, 175 82
   do. collected on duplicate of 1854. 2,479 02

   Total receipts, 2,654 84
   Expenditures.
Paid Bridge orders, 2,108 51

   Balance in Treasury, 546 33

SECTION 16—Receipts.

Rec'd of principal from all sources 1,446 24
   do   Interest   " 773 03

   Total receipts, 2,219 27
   Contra.
Paid State of principal, 1,446 24
" Township by distribution, 432 78

   Total expenditures, 1,879 02
Balance in treasury, 340 95

INFIRMARY FUND—Receipts.

Amount in Treasury June 1, 1854. 599 40
" collected on duplicate of 1854, 770 30

   Total receipts, 1,369 70
   Contra.

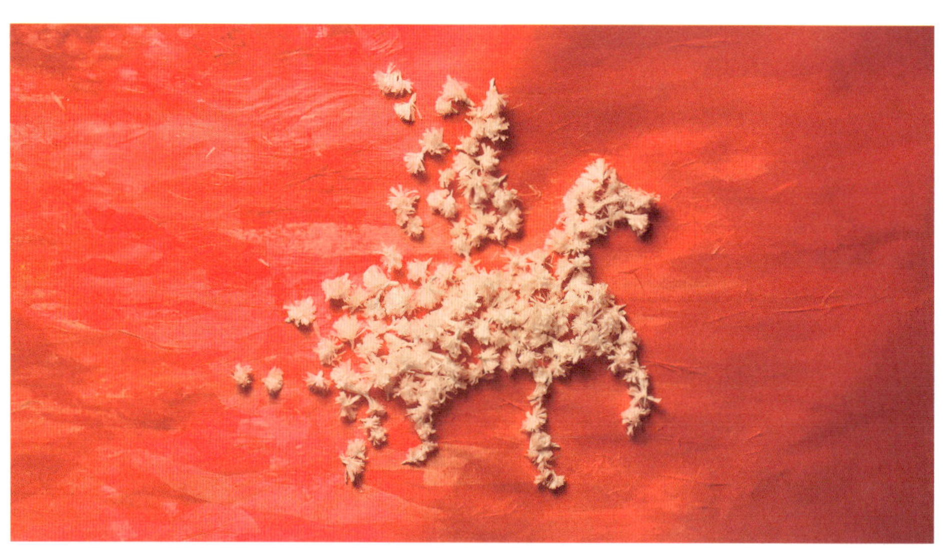

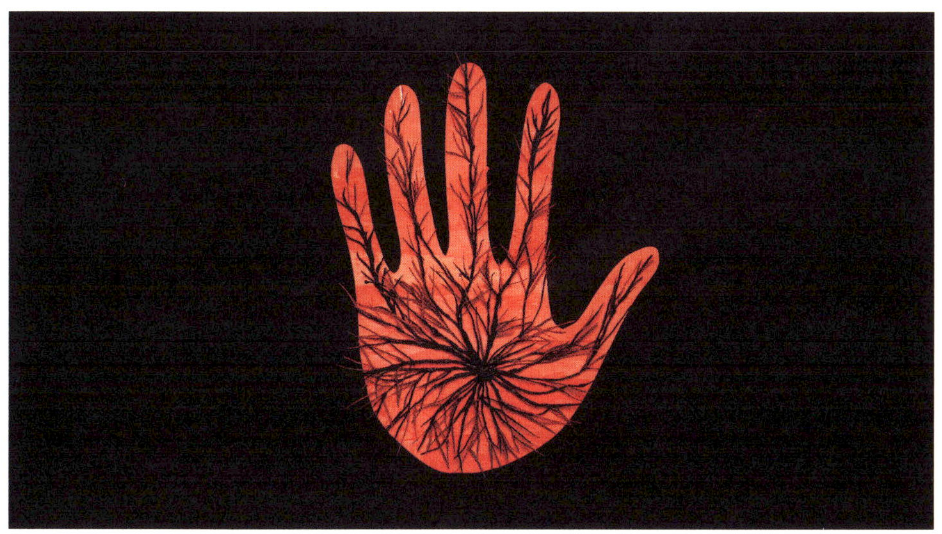

Laura Anderson Barbata and Rafael Esquer,
Julia Pastrana, su vuelta y sus raíces, 2013; animation stills

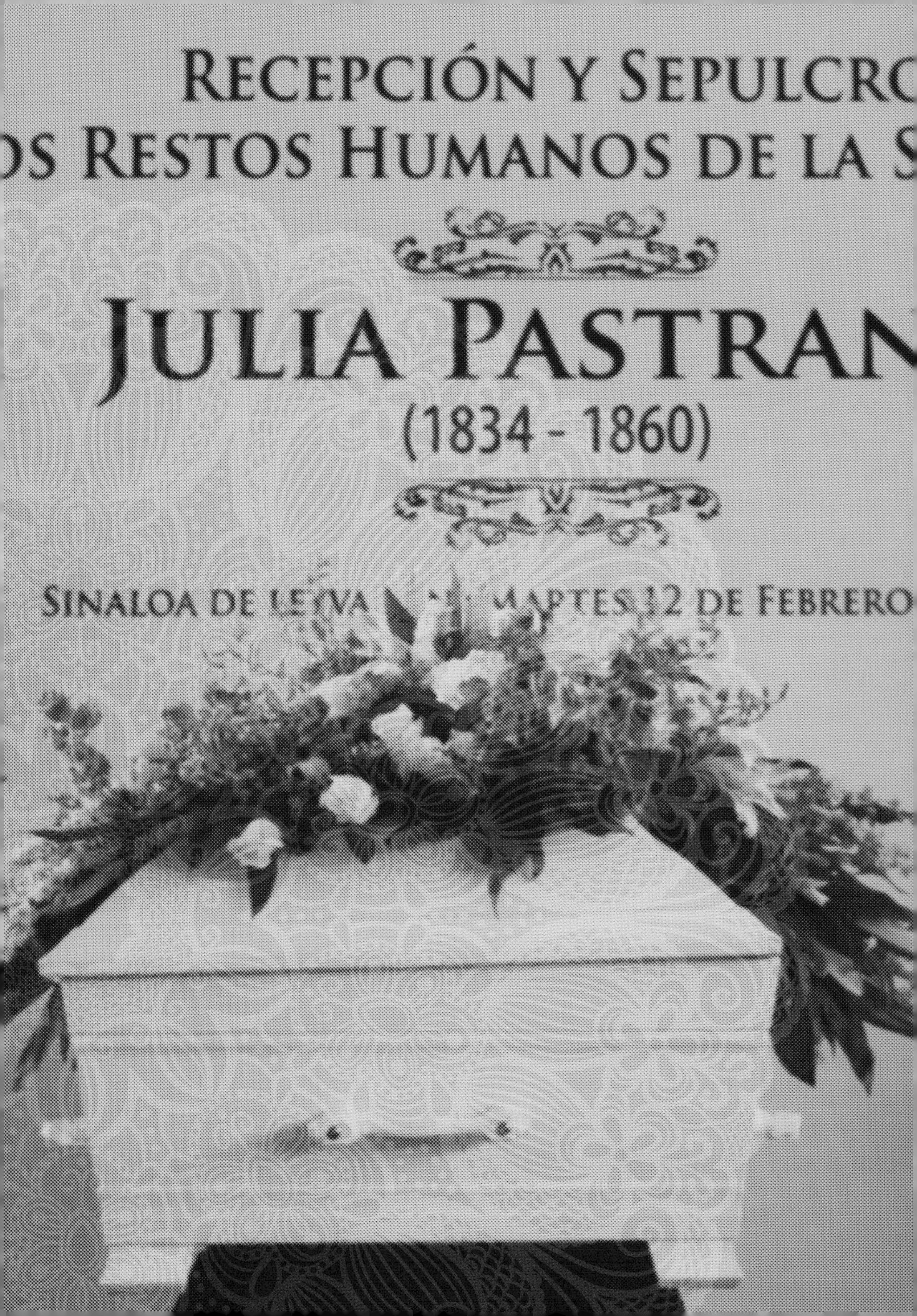

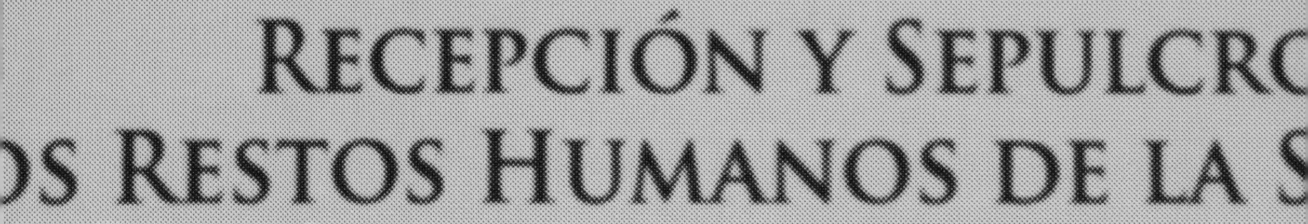
RECEPCIÓN Y SEPULCRO
OS RESTOS HUMANOS DE LA S

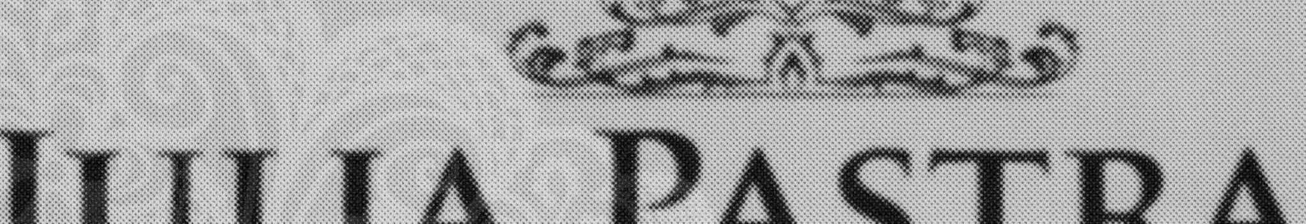
JULIA PASTRAN
(1834 - 1860)

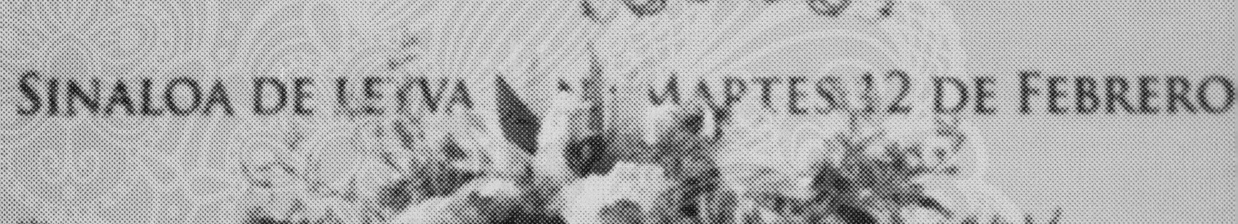
SINALOA DE LEIVA MARTES 12 DE FEBRERO

The Repatriation Pilgrimage of Julia Pastrana

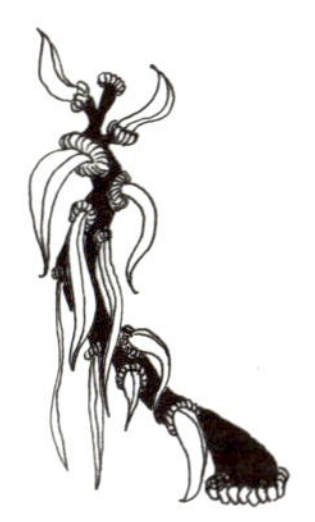

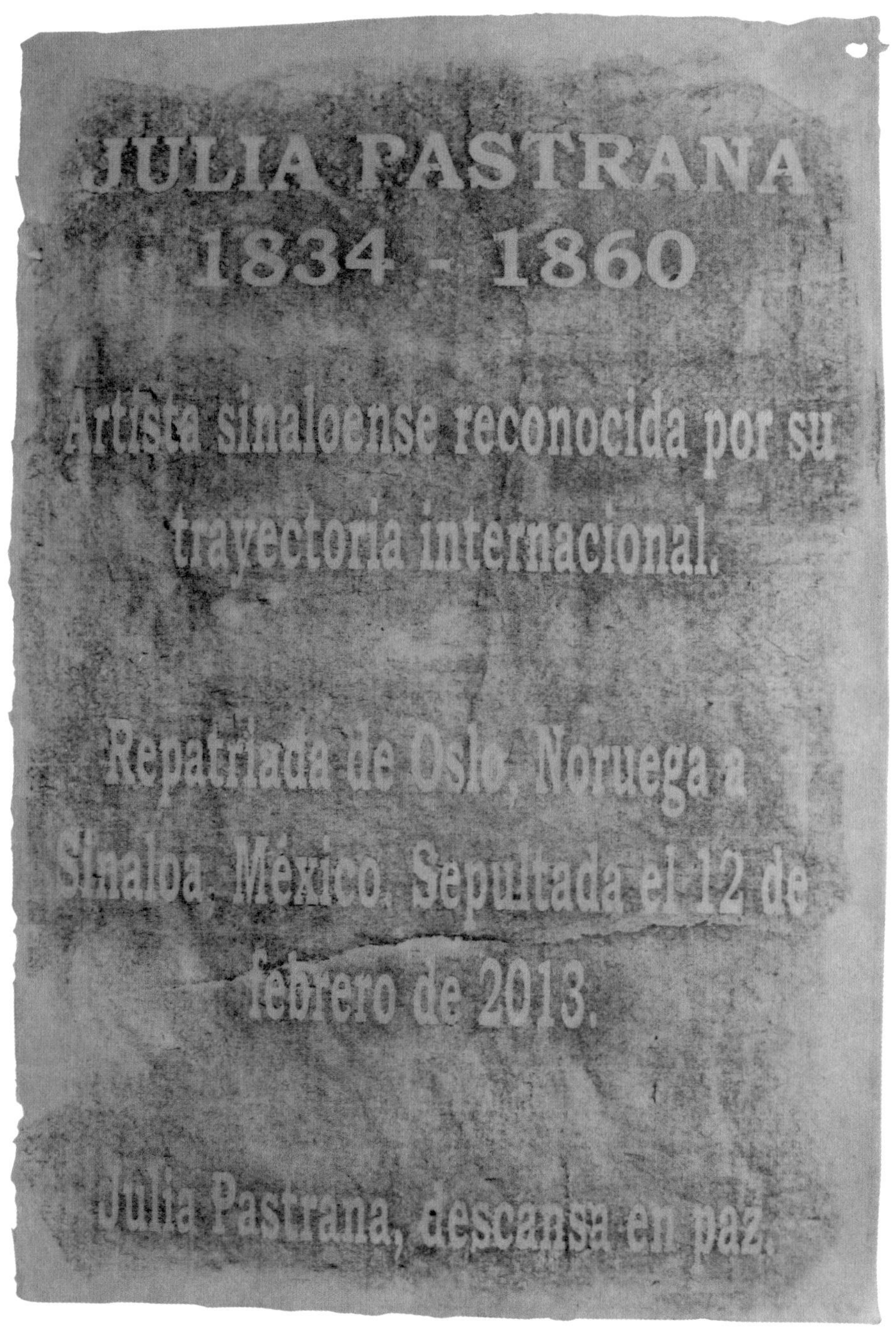

Julia Pastrana's tombstone; rubbing by Laura Anderson Barbata, 2013

The Repatriation Pilgrimage of Julia Pastrana

LAURA ANDERSON BARBATA

In 2003 Amphibian Stage Productions, a theater company directed by my sister Kathleen Culebro, invited me to collaborate with designs for a play that they were about to premiere in New York: *The True History of the Tragic Life and the Triumphant Death of Julia Pastrana, the Ugliest Woman in the World*, by Shaun Prendergast. This is how I learned about Julia Pastrana. The story opens with a view of a stage where Pastrana is about to perform, set in the period of the 1850s, for which I created the designs. At the moment when she is to appear onstage, the lights go out and the play unfolds in complete darkness, creating an auditory and olfactory experience in which actors move around the audience, narrating the life of Julia as she traveled through Europe, a performer in a freak show, until her death in Moscow. It also briefly recounts the fate of her mummified body, and that of her baby, until they were added to the Schreiner Collection of human remains in the anatomy department of the University of Oslo. Upon hearing her story, everyone in the audience was moved and outraged. My sister organized a petition for repatriation to be sent to the Mexican Embassy in Norway, for which she gathered hundreds of signatures, including my own. I felt that my duty as a Mexican artist, and as a woman, was to do everything possible to have Pastrana

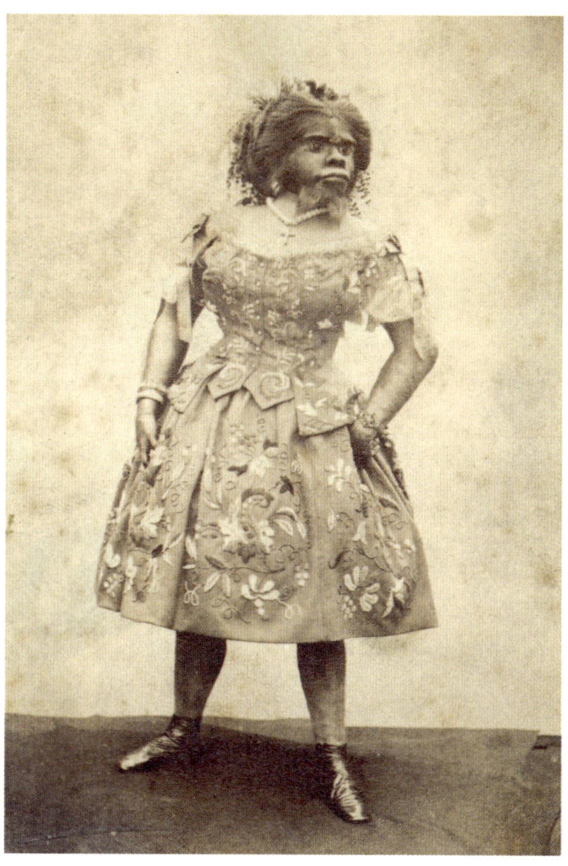

Photograph of the embalmed Julia Pastrana, c. 1860–70

removed from the anatomy collection and returned to Mexico, her place of birth—where she was at the time practically unknown—to receive a proper burial.

There are times when signing a petition is not enough. Petitions are primarily catalysts for awareness building; they offer us options for supporting a cause and ask us to what extent we are willing to act. I felt that Julia needed to recover her dignity by finding a place in her own history, as well as in our memory. If I did not help this to happen, she would remain indefinitely stored in a university collection with an inventory number and an inconclusive existence.

The following year I was invited to visit the north of Norway and to meet with indigenous Sami artists and intellectuals, with whom I had my first exchanges concerning the collection of human remains. The Schreiner Collection has hundreds of Sami skulls, many obtained under questionable circumstances, and the people I met had initiated their own repatriation requests.

Invited by the Office of Contemporary Art (OCA) in Norway for an artist residency in 2005, I began correspondence with the curator of the Schreiner Collection, Dr. Per Holck. My intention at first was to understand with absolute clarity the motives and justifications that allowed the institution to keep Julia Pastrana in their collection. Holck's answers to my queries were abrupt, brief, and even curt; his posture toward me made it clear that her repatriation would be a long and complicated process. However, his responses also indicated areas that were vague and poorly reasoned, which allowed me to press for more precise explanations and information. I thought that if I asked for answers in the right way, this would allow Dr. Holck and his department to see Julia in a new light—an empathic one, beyond the purely scientific view. In the course of my pursuit I approached the Norwegian National Committee for Research Ethics in the Social Sciences and the Humanities (NESH), where I met many people working in the fields of justice, law, ethics, and human rights, who advised me on the procedures and arguments to request the removal of Julia Pastrana from the anatomy collection. This was a lengthy process, and one that took a great deal of time, because it involved numerous meetings and back-and-forth communication, mostly in the form of physical letters, not email.

During this process in Oslo, I felt the urgency of altering the way Julia Pastrana was seen and treated to one that was more humane. It was my belief that if I could shift the understanding of Pastrana as part of a large institution to Julia as an individual, it would promote compassion and empathy as well as a change in conduct toward her. It was important for me to know that I was doing all I could to contribute to the restoration of her dignity. It was frustrating to rely

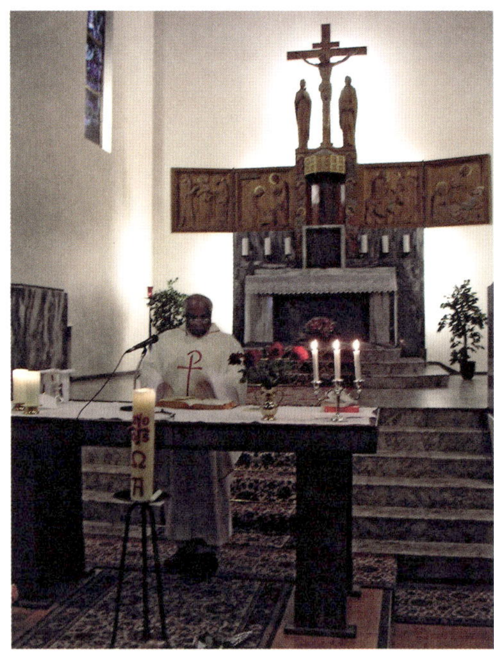

Memorial mass for Julia Pastrana, St. Joseph
Chapel, Oslo, Norway, 2005

solely on the decisions of committees and organizations to advance
this cause, and I knew there were simple things I could do publicly to
immediately acknowledge Pastrana's humanity, despite the fact that
she was still being stored in a box in a basement. Thus, I found ways
to address these issues on a personal and intimate level, unrestrained
by official protocols. I knew that after her death in Moscow she had
been immediately mummified, almost certainly without a religious
ceremony, even though she was a practicing Catholic. I assumed that
no obituary was published after her death. It seemed to me that these
were the first steps I could take to begin restoring the rights she had
been denied. My actions were from one individual to another, but I
also wanted to share them openly with anyone interested in joining
me. With this in mind, on September 10, 2005, I published an obituary
for Julia Pastrana in the local newspaper *Aftenposten*, and announced

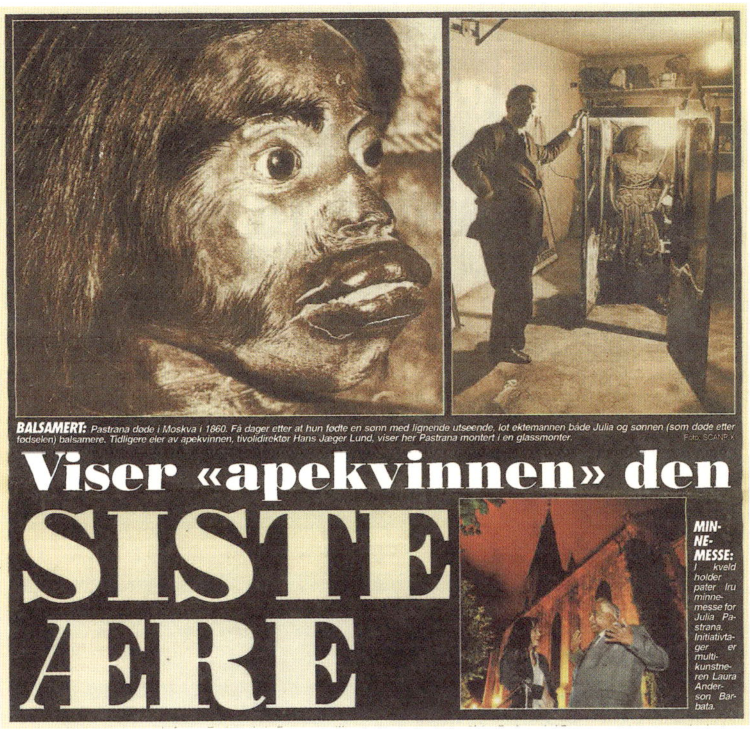

Newspaper article, *VG*, Oslo, Norway, September 12, 2005

a memorial mass at St. Joseph's Chapel, the Catholic church in Oslo, to be celebrated two days later. The mass was organized with the help of Christiane Erharter of OCA, and Per Boye Hanson, who at the time was the chair of OCA. It would be officiated by Father Iruthayanathan Pethuruppillai, with whom I had previously met to discuss Pastrana. He was very supportive and proposed specific readings and prayers. I invited a few friends, many of them artists, and my advisors. I did not expect many people to attend; what was important for me was to take the first step toward changing the treatment of Julia Pastrana.

Much to my surprise, this action went further; it touched many people on a deep level and confused others. A few hours before the mass I received a call urging me to go to St. Joseph's, because reporters were asking Father Iru about Pastrana, his motives, and the meaning of the ceremony about to take place. Father Iru was perplexed. There was clearly a morbid tone to the questions. The following day *VG* newspaper published a full-page article on Pastrana and the mass, with half a page featuring an insensitive close-up photo of Julia's face in a mummified state, another large photo of Julia and her baby inside the glass case that had been used to exhibit them, and a fantastical photo of Father Iru and me with the church behind us, lit as if in flames, a blood-red sky above us. Despite this morbid display, the general mood was quite positive on the day of the service. Hundreds of people attended the mass, most of whom I had never met. People introduced themselves to me; there were clowns, students, activists, artists, some even bringing flowers, and they were grateful to join in this moment of recognizing Julia's humanity. Beside the altar we had a photo of Julia, the only one known to exist of her alive, a candle, and a vase with white flowers. It was a beautiful and discreet memorial.

My residency in Oslo ended, and I returned to New York and Mexico, continuing exchanges with NESH on a regular basis. In 2008, following their counsel, I contacted the National Committee for Research Ethics on Human Remains and presented a petition for the committee to consider the repatriation of Julia Pastrana for burial. Their letter of response was lost for almost a year by the US Postal Service. It finally reached me, torn and badly damaged, inside a plastic bag with a note of apology from the USPS. (Oddly, everything related to Pastrana always seemed to end this way; these documents appeared to be suffering the same fate as her body, getting lost in limbo and in the process further damaged.) But I do not give up easily, and I was determined to continue looking for ways in which to advance my pursuit.

The document stated, much to my dismay, that even though the committee agreed that Pastrana probably would not have chosen to be kept in a collection, I did not have familial ties and thus did not qualify to petition for her burial. This added a new layer of complications. I contacted a number of specialists in the hope of finding a relative of Pastrana's in Mexico through DNA testing, but they led me to understand that this would be an unreliable route. Even if someone manifests the same genetic characteristics, it is no guarantee of kinship, and without having access to Pastrana's DNA such kinship would be impossible to prove. The Schreiner Collection claimed that their principal motive in keeping Julia Pastrana's body was to contribute to science and genetic research. But in fact, from the time she was placed in the collection until she was repatriated, no requests had been received to study her, and no DNA sample had been taken. (It was only after the date was confirmed for her repatriation that the university obtained a DNA sample for their archives.)

At this stage, I understood that the justification for requesting Julia's repatriation had to be founded on ethical, moral, and human-rights grounds. These would form stronger arguments than genetic ties, since it is our moral duty to defend the well-being and ethical treatment of all human beings, regardless of kinship, nationality, race, gender, religion, age, or condition. By this time, in 2011, the local newspaper *Reforma* had published a number of articles by the journalist Silvia Gámez, who publicized the story of Julia Pastrana in Mexico, gaining wide coverage and interest on a national level. After more research—mostly devoted to ethics, human-rights laws, national and international rights, museum and collection exhibition practices and guidelines, and previous examples of repatriation requests—I was able to prepare a strong case, supported by public opinion in Mexico, that provided clear justifications for repatriation. Yet I felt that to make the petition indisputable—irrefutable—I would not only need to enlist the interest and support of the government of Mexico, I would have to identify an official, with legal authority, who would lobby for the case beyond the bureaucratic duties of his or her office, to guarantee that it would be followed through to success. Who this person should be became evident as I reviewed my own history.

I grew up in the beautiful city of Mazatlán on the Pacific coast in Sinaloa, the state where Julia was born. Sinaloa, with a rich indigenous and colonial history, is home to communities that maintain their cultural and linguistic traditions. It is the breadbasket of Mexico, providing the country with rice, vegetables, wheat, and beans; it boasts a rich seacoast and fishing industry, with beautiful beaches and ports that have been central to the development of the country. It is also a state that has been deeply wounded by the violence of drug cartels and the war on drugs. I decided to contact the governor of Sinaloa, to make him aware of Julia Pastrana, the rights she had been denied both during her life and after her death, and the need for her, as a Mexican citizen, to be repatriated to her birth state. I also believed that her return would allow people in Sinaloa to participate collectively in an effort to bring peace to one of their own citizens.

In mid-2012 I drafted my final petition, met with Governor Mario López Valdez, and presented the case of Pastrana as having both national and international humanitarian importance. I specifically mentioned the case of Sarah Baartman, who was repatriated and buried in South Africa in 2002 through the efforts of President Nelson Mandela. The governor immediately understood the relevance of this case and initiated a formal government petition for Pastrana's repatriation. His petition was executed by the Mexican secretariat of foreign affairs, who intervened on behalf of Mexico and the State of Sinaloa and submitted it to authorities at the University of Oslo and government agencies of Norway.

Thus formal letters of request for Pastrana's repatriation were sent to Norway from the governor of Sinaloa, from the Mexican secretariat of foreign affairs, and from me. These documents went through a complex pilgrimage, in part because Mexico at the time did not have diplomatic representation in Norway, and also because this case involved unique circumstances and challenges: Pastrana did not have a birth or a death certificate, and without these she could not legally be treated as a human being by any authority, funerary service, or repatriation service company, and could not cross any national boundary.

These petitions, when received in Norway, set off a series of events that required authorization from the various organizations and institutions that had authority over Pastrana's fate. After much dialogue between these institutions, both in Mexico and Norway, the Schreiner

ESTADOS UNIDOS MEXICANOS
ESTADO LIBRE Y SOBERANO DE SINALOA

SINALOA
02906497

REGISTRO CIVIL
ACTA DE DEFUNCION

No. DE CONTROL
02906497

No. DE CONTROL
CU0120100196

CRIP

OFICIALIA No. 012	LIBRO No. 01	ACTA No. 00196	FECHA DE REGISTRO:	11 / FEBRERO / 2013
LOCALIDAD: CULIACAN		MUNICIPIO: CULIACAN		ENTIDAD FEDERATIVA: SINALOA

FINADO

NOMBRE:	JULIA	PASTRANA	.....	EDAD: 26 AÑOS
	NOMBRE(S)	PRIMER APELLIDO	SEGUNDO APELLIDO	

ESTADO CIVIL: CASADO(A)	NACIONALIDAD MEXICANA	SEXO: FEMENINO

DOMICILIO: .....

	MOSCU	.....	.....	RUSIA
	LOCALIDAD	MUNICIPIO	ENTIDAD FEDERATIVA	PAIS

FECHA DE NACIMIENTO: 1834

LUGAR DE NACIMIENTO:	OCORONI	SINALOA	SINALOA	MEXICO
	LOCALIDAD	MUNICIPIO	ENTIDAD FEDERATIVA	PAIS

DATOS DEL ACTA DE NACIMIENTO

OFICIALIA No. 999	LIBRO No. 99	ACTA No 09999	FECHA DE REGISTRO:	.....
LOCALIDAD :		MUNICIPIO:		ENTIDAD FEDERATIVA: .....

NOMBRE DEL CONYUGE:	THEODORE	LENT (FINADO)	.....	NACIONALIDAD: ESTADOUNIDENSE
	NOMBRE(S)	PRIMER APELLIDO	SEGUNDO APELLIDO	
NOMBRE DEL PADRE:	.....	.....	.....	NACIONALIDAD: .....
	NOMBRE(S)	PRIMER APELLIDO	SEGUNDO APELLIDO	
NOMBRE DE LA MADRE:	.....	.....	.....	NACIONALIDAD: .....
	NOMBRE(S)	PRIMER APELLIDO	SEGUNDO APELLIDO	

FALLECIMIENTO

DESTINO DEL CADAVER:	INHUMACION	NOMBRE DEL PANTEON O CREMATORIO:	PANTEON HISTORICO

UBICACION:	SINALOA DE LEYVA, SINALOA.	ORDEN No.: .....

FECHA DE DEFUNCION:	25 DE MARZO DE 1860	HORA: .....

LUGAR:	.....	CERTIFICADO No.: .....

DONDE FALLECIO: MOSCU, RUSIA.

CAUSA(S) DE LA MUERTE: FIEBRE PUERPERAL 5 DIAS.

TIPO DE DEFUNCION: NATURAL

NOMBRE DEL MEDICO QUE CERTIFICO LA DEFUNCION: .....

DOMICILIO: .....

No. DE CEDULA PROFESIONAL: .....

DECLARANTES

NOMBRE:	LAURA ANDERSON BARBATA		EDAD: 54 AÑOS
DOMICILIO:	C. CASANDRA, 17, COL. DELICIAS, CUERNAVACA, MORELOS.		
NACIONALIDAD: MEXICANA	OCUPACION: ARTISTA VISUAL	PARENTESCO: NINGUNO	

TESTIGOS

NOMBRE:	MARIA LUISA MIRANDA MONRREAL		EDAD: 55 AÑOS
DOMICILIO:	C. ISLA MAGDALENA, 704 NORTE, FRACC. LAS ISLAS, AHOME, SINALOA.		
NACIONALIDAD: MEXICANA	OCUPACION: FUNCIONARIO(A) PUBLICO(A)	PARENTESCO: NINGUNO	
NOMBRE:	GILBERTO JAVIER LOPEZ ALANIS		EDAD: 68 AÑOS
DOMICILIO:	ANDADOR DE LAS AMERICAS, 2676, FRACC. VILLA UNIVERSIDAD, CULIACAN, SINALOA.		
NACIONALIDAD: MEXICANA	OCUPACION: HISTORIADOR	PARENTESCO: NINGUNO	

FIRMAS

TESTIGO

DECLARANTE

TESTIGO

SE DIO LECTURA A LA PRESENTE ACTA Y CONFORMES CON SU CONTENIDO LA RATIFICAN Y FIRMAN QUIENES EN ELLA INTERVINIERON Y SABEN HACERLO, Y QUIENES NO, IMPRIMEN SUS HUELLA DIGITAL. DOY FE.

EL C. OFICIAL 12 DEL REGISTRO CIVIL

C. LIC. WALKIRIA AZARETTE SANCHEZ JUAREZ
NOMBRE

FIRMA

LA PRESENTE ACTA TIENE ANEXAS LAS ANOTACIONES SIGUIENTES:
.....

ARCHIVO

Julia Pastrana's death certificate, February 11, 2013

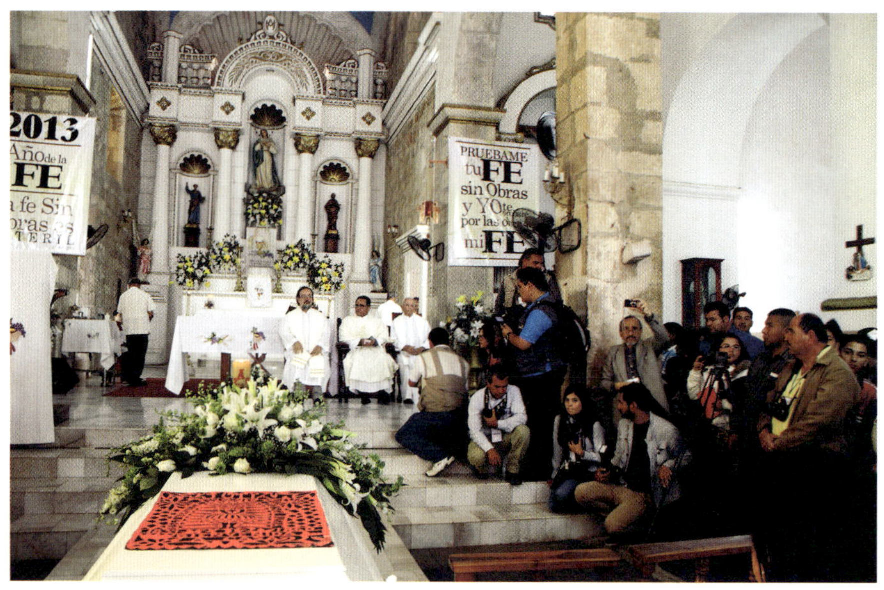

Catholic mass for Julia Pastrana, Church of San Felipe y Santiago,
Sinaloa, Mexico, February 12, 2013

Collection agreed to transfer custody of Pastrana to Mexico for repatriation, with the condition that she receive a Catholic funeral and burial. Julia was a practicing Catholic, so this was a welcome condition, one that allowed the authorities to change their discourse and to a degree make amends with the past. It was a radical change that acknowledged Julia's rights and humanity after many years of neglect and denial in their care.

Careful and complex planning followed, in which numerous representatives from Norway, England, France, and Mexico were assigned to facilitate the process. Dr. Nicholas Márquez-Grant, a forensic anthropologist from the University of Oxford, and I were witnesses when Julia's body was removed from the storage box where she had been kept for many years and placed in a zinc-lined white coffin that was sealed at the Ullevål University Hospital (see p. 117). She was then taken to the chapel in the hospital and attended by T. S. Jacobsen Funeral Agency of Oslo. On February 7, 2013, the University

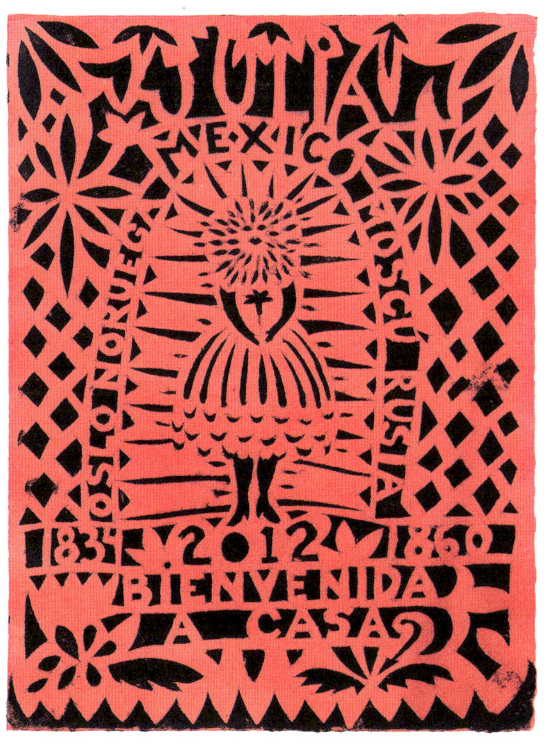

Bienvenida a casa, 2012; handmade paper work
created to welcome Julia Pastrana to Mexico
for her burial; ed. 11

of Oslo officially transferred custody of Julia Pastrana to Mexico. Ambassador Martha Barcena Coqui of the Mexican Embassy in Denmark represented Mexico, and I represented the State of Sinaloa. The University of Oslo held a private service for Pastrana at the chapel at Rikshospitalet, Oslo University Hospital, with speeches by the vice rector Ragnhild Hennum, Dr. Jan G. Bjaalie, head of the Institute of Basic Medical Science, Ambassador Martha Barcena Coqui, and myself. Among the guests were scholars, artists, members of the press, and the curator of the Schreiner Collection, Dr. Per Holck, who I was meeting in person for the first time.[1]

After the ceremony Julia was transported to the Oslo International Airport, where she was put aboard a series of commercial flights:

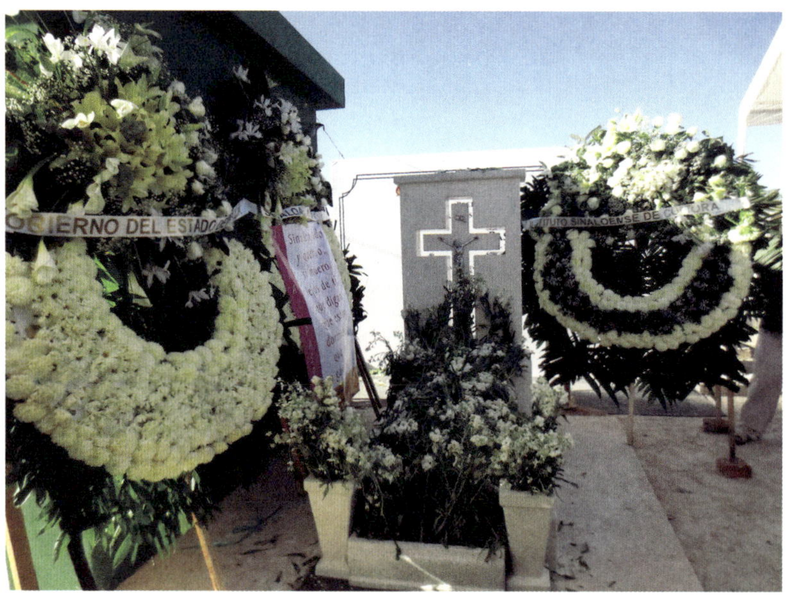

Julia Pastrana's tomb on the day of her burial, 2013

Oslo to Paris, Paris to Mexico City, and Mexico City to Culiacán, the state capital of Sinaloa. At every city where she landed, and at every border crossing, there were representatives to expedite the travel process of this undocumented celebrity. In Sinaloa, the director of the department of culture, Maria Luisa Miranda, organized all the events that followed. Julia Pastrana was received with a small private ceremony and kept overnight at the governor's private airport; her sealed coffin was protected by guards around the clock. The next day, she was taken in a hearse to Sinaloa de Leyva, the city north of Culiacán closest to where it is believed she was born. (Historians in Mexico claim that she was from Santiago de Ocoroni.) Upon our arrival in Sinaloa de Leyva, there was another official ceremony of welcome with the mayor and governor; speeches followed, including one from me. After the ceremony, which included local funerary traditions, Julia's closed coffin was taken in a procession to the cathedral, where a mass was offered.

After the mass the procession traveled to the Panteón Histórico cemetery, accompanied by traditional tambora music and mariachis. These ceremonies, typical of Sinaloa, are the way prominent people are buried in this area of the country. Hundreds of people from neighboring villages, and as far as Santiago de Ocoroni, held signs, using the moment to make a statement in defense of human rights, against violence toward women, and to demand rights for indigenous people. Thousands of white flowers had been sent from all over the world, responding to a call to donate a flower that would be placed on her tomb. To protect her grave from further violations, the plot was carefully prepared in advance. It was twice as deep as a normal grave and surrounded by walls one meter thick. Once her casket had been lowered into the ground and partially covered with white flowers, it was covered with concrete. A white marble tombstone was placed on top and completely covered with flowers and wreaths. Her epitaph reads:

Julia Pastrana
1834–1860
Sinaloan artist recognized for her international trajectory
Buried the 12th of February 2013
Repatriated from Oslo, Norway, to Sinaloa, Mexico
Julia Pastrana, rest in peace

The repatriation and burial of Julia Pastrana was the result of a collective effort. Every institution and individual with whom I discussed Pastrana had an important role to play and contributed to the success of the endeavor. I could not have achieved this without them. Her repatriation represents the writing of a new chapter in the social advances of Mexico and the countries that harbored her. A pending debt to Julia is settled with her return. This allows for the redefinition of a past that belongs exclusively to her but pains all of society: the people of Sinaloa, the people of Mexico, women, people with differences, and all of those who value the human condition, promote respect, and defend human rights and justice. It is the acknowledgment of a person as well

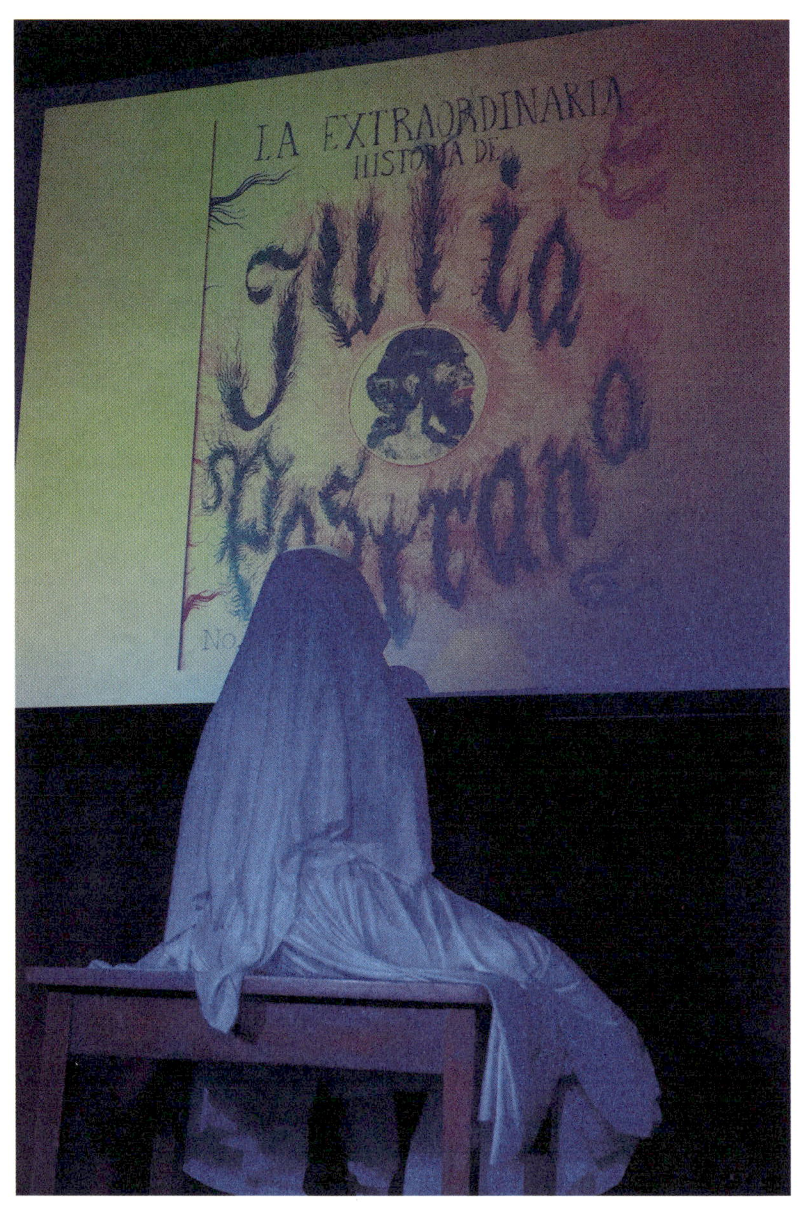

Laura Anderson Barbata and Fem Appeal, *La Extraordinaria Historia de Julia Pastrana*; Cobra Club, New York, 2016

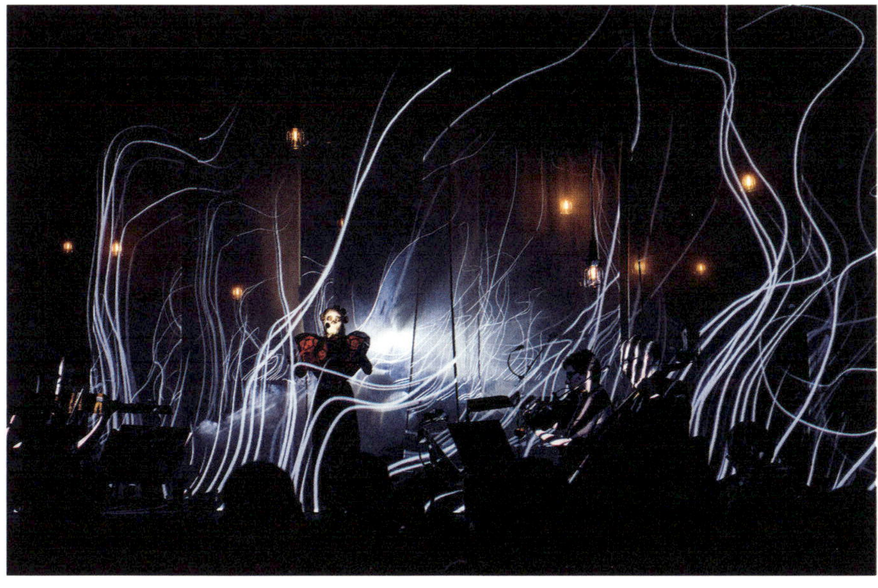

Dia de los Muertos, Apparatjik with Concha Buika and Void, Bergen, Norway, 2016

as of an artist, a mezzo-soprano who sang in four languages and was a graceful dancer.

Julia Pastrana returns to Sinaloa and is received with an artistic and ceremonial act to welcome her, to pay homage to her and to bring an end to her long pilgrimage. With hundreds of flowers sent from all over the world, people expressed their joy to see this painful chapter come to a close. It was a collective exercise by an extensive network of individuals and institutions who believe in justice, in hope, and that it is possible to create a better future, one that is just and where it is possible to live in a country filled with flowers and peace.

Julia Pastrana is now buried, her pilgrimage has ended, her body will no longer be exhibited and exploited. But my responsibility is not over. Julia Pastrana's story is a reminder that what happened to her is not an experience that is exclusively from the past. Today there are far too many cases of exploitation, abuse, neglect, cruelty, and discrimination. Julia Pastrana is a reminder that we urgently need to champion women's rights, indigenous rights, children's rights, and eliminate human trafficking. We must end gender discrimination, defend the rights of people with differences, protect religious choices, and end the voracious dehumanization of people in the name of political, commercial, religious, and scientific purposes. I believe it is our responsibility, now more than ever, to lobby for an ethical treatment of all people with all of the means we have available. From wherever we stand we can contribute to the advancement of these ideals. For me, it means that I continue working on topics related to her, the injustices she lived, and how they are still relevant today. Among the works I am engaged in are: an evolving performance piece with the collaboration of burlesque artist Fem Appeal, and a series of zines, made in collaboration with Erik Tlaseca, that address different topics related to Julia Pastrana, such as repatriation of human remains, museum ethics, exhibition practices, the objectification of people and women, human trafficking, beauty and the commercialization of women's bodies, feminism, animal rights, love, and circus arts. In addition, we are also developing an opera about Julia Pastrana in collaboration with the artist collective Apparatjik, Concha Buika, and Void.

We still have much to learn from Julia Pastrana. While her body now rests in peace in Sinaloa, Mexico, her memory must be kept alive to remind us of all that still needs to be done.

NOTE

1 I was allowed to invite guests, so I included those who had guided, advised, supported, and encouraged me in Oslo: Ute Meta Bauer, former director of OCA, Norway; Dr. Hilde Nagell, former director of National Committee for Research Ethics in the Social Sciences and the Humanities (NESH); Dr. Oddbjorn Sormoen, former chair of the National Committee for Research Ethics on Human Remains, Oslo; Dr. Berit Sellevold, the Norwegian Institute for Cultural Heritage Research; Dr. Halvor Hanisch, University of Oslo; Dr. Nicholas Márquez-Grant, University of Oxford; Kjersti Horn, director of the National Theater in Oslo; Gavin Jantjies, senior curator, Museum of Contemporary Art, Oslo; Sandrine Conte, documentary filmmaker; Magne Furuholmen and Jonas Bjerre, from Apparatjik.

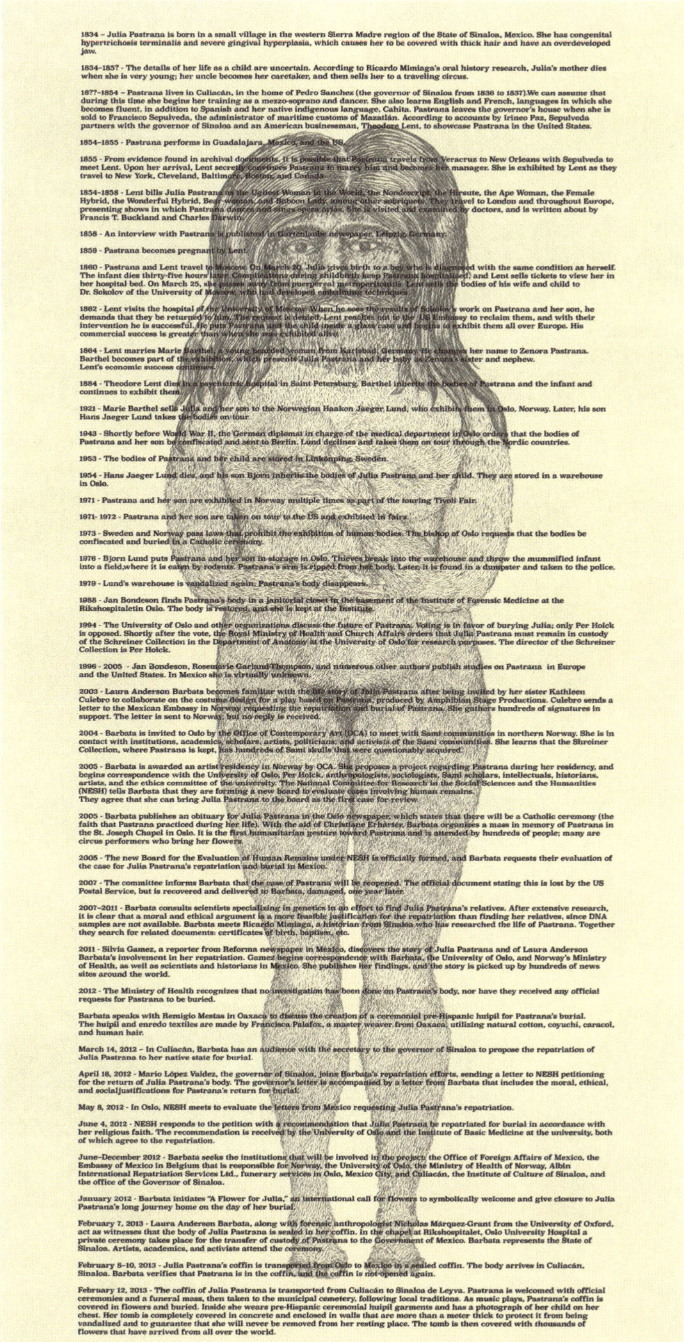

1834 – Julia Pastrana is born in a small village in the western Sierra Madre region of the State of Sinaloa, Mexico. She has congenital hypertrichosis terminalis and severe gingival hyperplasia, which causes her to be covered with thick hair and have an overdeveloped jaw.

1834–185? - The details of her life as a child are uncertain. According to Ricardo Mimiaga's oral history research, Julia's mother dies when she is very young; her uncle becomes her caretaker, and then sells her to a traveling circus.

18??–1854 – Pastrana lives in Culiacán, in the home of Pedro Sanchez (the governor of Sinaloa from 1836 to 1837).We can assume that during this time she begins her training as a mezzo-soprano and dancer. She also learns English and French, languages in which she becomes fluent, in addition to Spanish and her native indigenous language, Cahita. Pastrana leaves the governor's house when she is sold to Francisco Sepulveda, the administrator of maritime customs of Mazatlán. According to accounts by Irineo Paz, Sepulveda partners with the governor of Sinaloa and an American businessman, Theodore Lent, to showcase Pastrana in the United States.

1854–1855 - Pastrana performs in Guadalajara, Mexico, and the US.

1855 - From evidence found in archival documents, it is possible that Pastrana travels from Veracruz to New Orleans with Sepulveda to meet Lent. Upon her arrival, Lent secretly convinces Pastrana to marry him and becomes her manager. She is exhibited by Lent as they travel to New York, Cleveland, Baltimore, Boston, and Canada.

1854–1858 - Lent bills Julia Pastrana as the Ugliest Woman in the World, the Nondescript, the Hirsute, the Ape Woman, the Female Hybrid, the Wonderful Hybrid, Bear-woman, and Baboon Lady, among other sobriquets. They travel to London and throughout Europe, presenting shows in which Pastrana dances and sings opera arias. She is visited and examined by doctors, and is written about by Francis T. Buckland and Charles Darwin.

1858 - An interview with Pastrana is published in Gartenlaube newspaper, Leipzig, Germany.

1859 - Pastrana becomes pregnant by Lent.

1860 - Pastrana and Lent travel to Moscow. On March 20, Julia gives birth to a boy who is diagnosed with the same condition as herself. The infant dies thirty-five hours later. Complications during childbirth keep Pastrana hospitalized, and Lent sells tickets to view her in her hospital bed. On March 25, she passes away from puerpereal metroperitonitis. Lent sells the bodies of his wife and child to Dr. Sokolov of the University of Moscow, who had developed embalming techniques.

1862 - Lent visits the hospital of the University of Moscow. When he sees the results of Sokolov's work on Pastrana and her son, he demands that they be returned to him. The request is denied. Lent reaches out to the US Embassy to reclaim them, and with their intervention he is successful. He puts Pastrana and the child inside a glass case and begins to exhibit them all over Europe. His commercial success is greater than when she was exhibited alive.

1864 - Lent marries Marie Barthel, a young bearded woman from Karlsbad, Germany. He changes her name to Zenora Pastrana. Barthel becomes part of the exhibition, which presents Julia Pastrana and her baby as Zenora's sister and nephew. Lent's economic success continues.

1884 - Theodore Lent dies in a psychiatric hospital in Saint Petersburg. Barthel inherits the bodies of Pastrana and the infant and continues to exhibit them.

1921 - Marie Barthel sells Julia and her son to the Norwegian Haakon Jaeger Lund, who exhibits them in Oslo, Norway. Later, his son Hans Jaeger Lund takes the bodies on tour.

1943 - Shortly before World War II, the German diplomat in charge of the medical department in Oslo orders that the bodies of Pastrana and her son be confiscated and sent to Berlin. Lund declines and takes them on tour through the Nordic countries.

1953 - The bodies of Pastrana and her child are stored in Linköping, Sweden.

1954 - Hans Jaeger Lund dies, and his son Bjorn inherits the bodies of Julia Pastrana and her child. They are stored in a warehouse in Oslo.

1971 - Pastrana and her son are exhibited in Norway multiple times as part of the touring Tivoli Fair.

1971- 1972 - Pastrana and her son are taken on tour to the US and exhibited in fairs.

1973 - Sweden and Norway pass laws that prohibit the exhibition of human bodies. The bishop of Oslo requests that the bodies be confiscated and buried in a Catholic ceremony.

1976 - Bjorn Lund puts Pastrana and her son in storage in Oslo. Thieves break into the warehouse and throw the mummified infant into a field, where it is eaten by rodents. Pastrana's arm is ripped from her body. Later, it is found in a dumpster and taken to the police.

1979 - Lund's warehouse is vandalized again. Pastrana's body disappears.

1988 - Jan Bondeson finds Pastrana's body in a janitorial closet in the basement of the Institute of Forensic Medicine at the Rikshospitaletin Oslo. The body is restored, and she is kept at the Institute.

1994 - The University of Oslo and other organizations discuss the future of Pastrana. Voting is in favor of burying Julia; only Per Holck is opposed. Shortly after the vote, the Royal Ministry of Health and Church Affairs orders that Julia Pastrana must remain in custody of the Schreiner Collection in the Department of Anatomy at the University of Oslo for research purposes. The director of the Schreiner Collection is Per Holck.

1996 - 2005 - Jan Bondeson, Rosemarie Garland-Thompson, and numerous other authors publish studies on Pastrana in Europe and the United States. In Mexico she is virtually unknown.

2003 - Laura Anderson Barbata becomes familiar with the life story of Julia Pastrana after being invited by her sister Kathleen Culebro to collaborate on the costume design for a play based on Pastrana, produced by Amphibian Stage Productions. Culebro sends a letter to the Mexican Embassy in Norway requesting the repatriation and burial of Pastrana. She gathers hundreds of signatures in support. The letter is sent to Norway, but no reply is received.

2004 - Barbata is invited to Oslo by the Office of Contemporary Art (OCA) to meet with Sami communities in northern Norway. She is in contact with institutions, academics, scholars, artists, politicians, and activists of the Sami communities. She learns that the Shreiner Collection, where Pastrana is kept, has hundreds of Sami skulls that were questionably acquired.

2005 - Barbata is awarded an artist residency in Norway by OCA. She proposes a project regarding Pastrana during her residency, and begins correspondence with the University of Oslo, Per Holck, anthropologists, sociologists, Sami scholars, intellectuals, historians, artists, and the ethics committee of the university. The National Committee for Research in the Social Sciences and the Humanities (NESH) tells Barbata that they are forming a new board to evaluate cases involving human remains. They agree that she can bring Julia Pastrana to the board as the first case for review.

2005 - Barbata publishes an obituary for Julia Pastrana in the Oslo newspaper, which states that there will be a Catholic ceremony (the faith that Pastrana practiced during her life). With the aid of Christiane Erharter, Barbata organizes a mass in memory of Pastrana in the St. Joseph Chapel in Oslo. It is the first humanitarian gesture toward Pastrana and is attended by hundreds of people; many are circus performers who bring her flowers.

2005 - The new Board for the Evaluation of Human Remains under NESH is officially formed, and Barbata requests their evaluation of the case for Julia Pastrana's repatriation and burial in Mexico.

2007 - The committee informs Barbata that the case of Pastrana will be reopened. The official document stating this is lost by the US Postal Service, but is recovered and delivered to Barbata, damaged, one year later.

2007–2011 - Barbata consults scientists specializing in genetics in an effort to find Julia Pastrana's relatives. After extensive research, it is clear that a moral and ethical argument is a more feasible justification for the repatriation than finding her relatives, since DNA samples are not available. Barbata meets Ricardo Mimiaga, a historian from Sinaloa who has researched the life of Pastrana. Together they search for related documents: certificates of birth, baptism, etc.

2011 - Silvia Gamez, a reporter from Reforma newspaper in Mexico, discovers the story of Julia Pastrana and of Laura Anderson Barbata's involvement in her repatriation. Gamez begins correspondence with Barbata, the University of Oslo, and Norway's Ministry of Health, as well as scientists and historians in Mexico. She publishes her findings, and the story is picked up by hundreds of news sites around the world.

2012 - The Ministry of Health recognizes that no investigation has been done on Pastrana's body, nor have they received any official requests for Pastrana to be buried.

Barbata speaks with Remigio Mestas in Oaxaca to discuss the creation of a ceremonial pre-Hispanic huipil for Pastrana's burial. The huipil and enredo textiles are made by Francisca Palafox, a master weaver from Oaxaca, utilizing natural cotton, coyuchi, caracol, and human hair.

March 14, 2012 – In Culiacán, Barbata has an audience with the secretary to the governor of Sinaloa to propose the repatriation of Julia Pastrana to her native state for burial.

April 16, 2012 - Mario López Valdez, the governor of Sinaloa, joins Barbata's repatriation efforts, sending a letter to NESH petitioning for the return of Julia Pastrana's body. The governor's letter is accompanied by a letter from Barbata that includes the moral, ethical, and socialjustifications for Pastrana's return for burial.

May 8, 2012 - In Oslo, NESH meets to evaluate the letters from Mexico requesting Julia Pastrana's repatriation.

June 4, 2012 - NESH responds to the petition with a recommendation that Julia Pastrana be repatriated for burial in accordance with her religious faith. The recommendation is received by the University of Oslo and the Institute of Basic Medicine at the university, both of which agree to the repatriation.

June–December 2012 - Barbata seeks the institutions that will be involved in the project: the Office of Foreign Affairs of Mexico, the Embassy of Mexico in Belgium that is responsible for Norway, the University of Oslo, the Ministry of Health of Norway, Albin International Repatriation Services Ltd., funerary services in Oslo, Mexico City, and Culiacán, the Institute of Culture of Sinaloa, and the office of the Governor of Sinaloa.

January 2012 - Barbata initiates "A Flower for Julia," an international call for flowers to symbolically welcome and give closure to Julia Pastrana's long journey home on the day of her burial.

February 7, 2013 - Laura Anderson Barbata, along with forensic anthropologist Nicholas Márquez-Grant from the University of Oxford, act as witnesses that the body of Julia Pastrana is sealed in her coffin. In the chapel at Rikshospitalet, Oslo University Hospital a private ceremony takes place for the transfer of custody of Pastrana to the Government of Mexico. Barbata represents the State of Sinaloa. Artists, academics, and activists attend the ceremony.

February 8–10, 2013 - Julia Pastrana's coffin is transported from Oslo to Mexico in a sealed coffin. The body arrives in Culiacán, Sinaloa. Barbata verifies that Pastrana is in the coffin, and the coffin is not opened again.

February 12, 2013 - The coffin of Julia Pastrana is transported from Culiacán to Sinaloa de Leyva. Pastrana is welcomed with official ceremonies and a funeral mass, then taken to the municipal cemetery, following local traditions. As music plays, Pastrana's coffin is covered in flowers and buried. Inside she wears pre-Hispanic ceremonial huipil garments and has a photograph of her child on her chest. Her tomb is completely covered in concrete and enclosed in walls that are more than a meter thick to protect it from being vandalized and to guarantee that she will never be removed from her resting place. The tomb is then covered with thousands of flowers that have arrived from all over the world.

Laura Anderson Barbata, *More Than Words Could Tell*, 2017; ink on paper

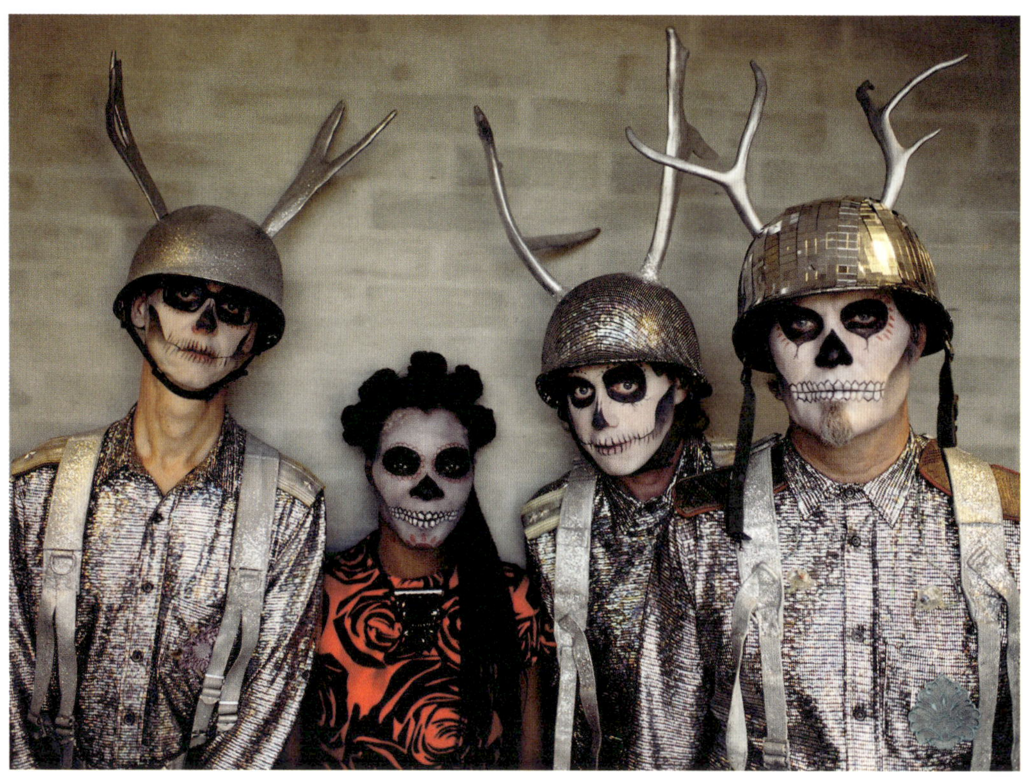

Dia de los Muertos, Apparatjik with Concha Buika and Void, Bergen, Norway, 2016

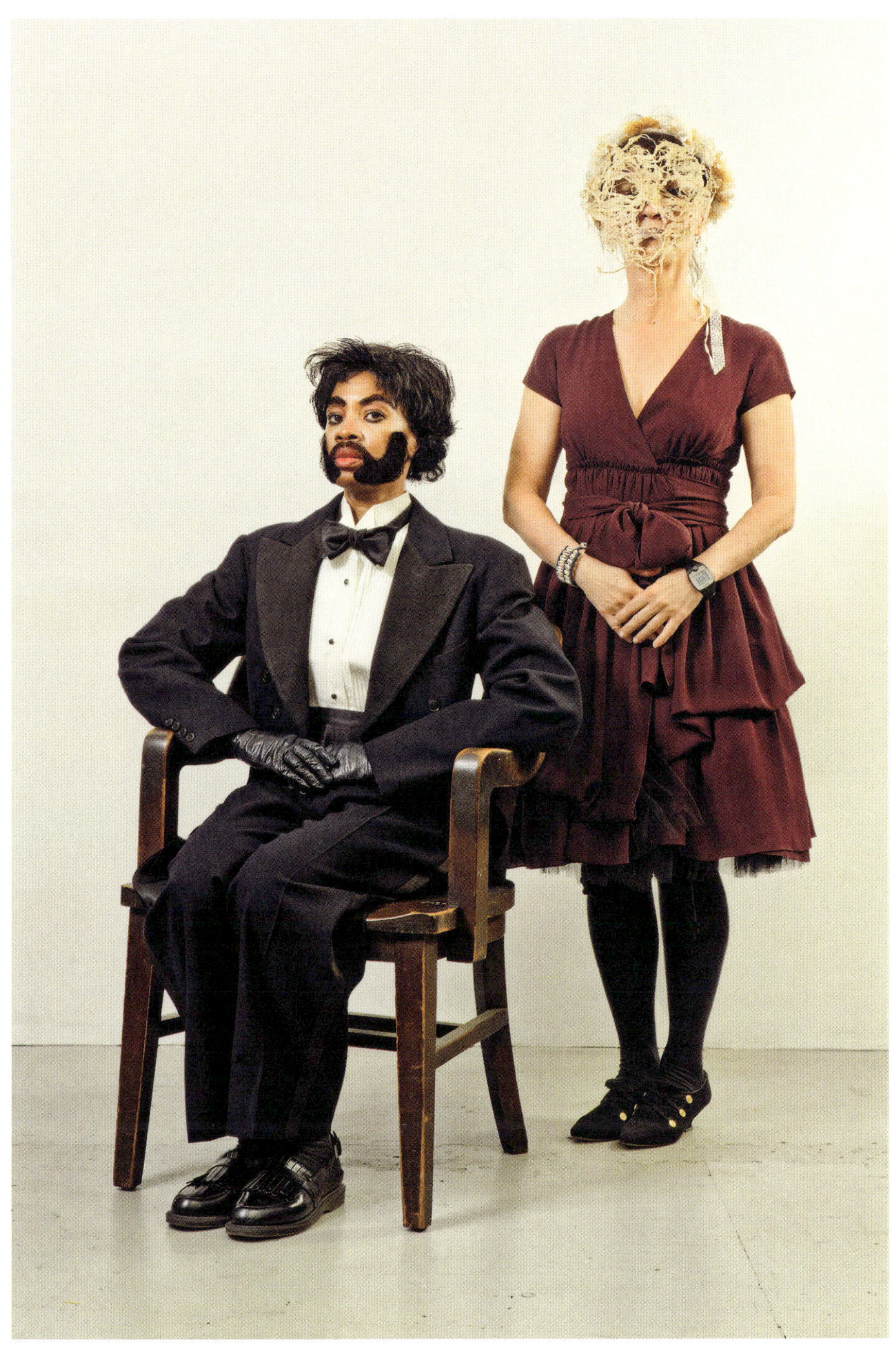

Laura Anderson Barbata and Fem Appeal, *Lent y Julia*, 2016; photograph on fiber paper

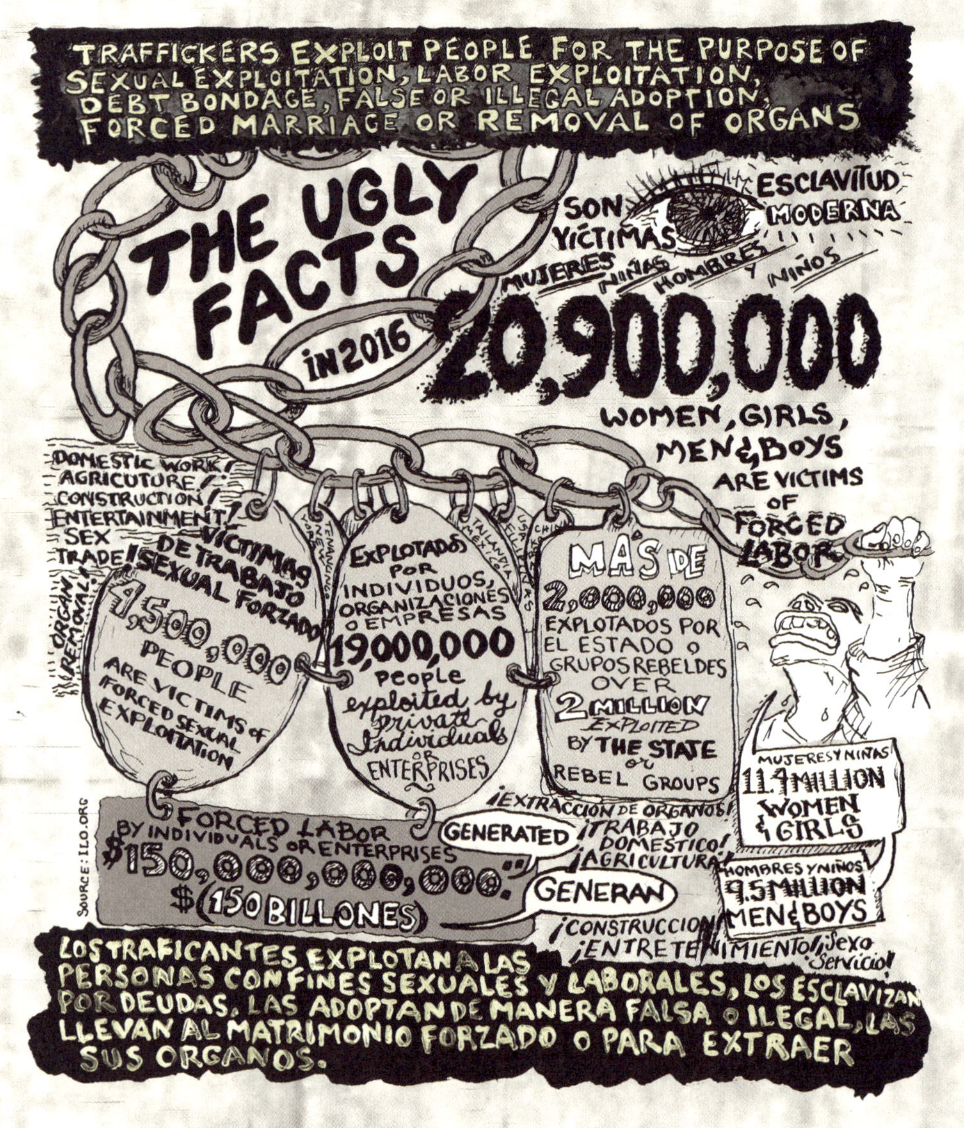

Laura Anderson Barbata and Erik Tlaseca, page from *La Extraordinaria Historia de Julia Pastrana,* zine no. 3, 2016; risograph

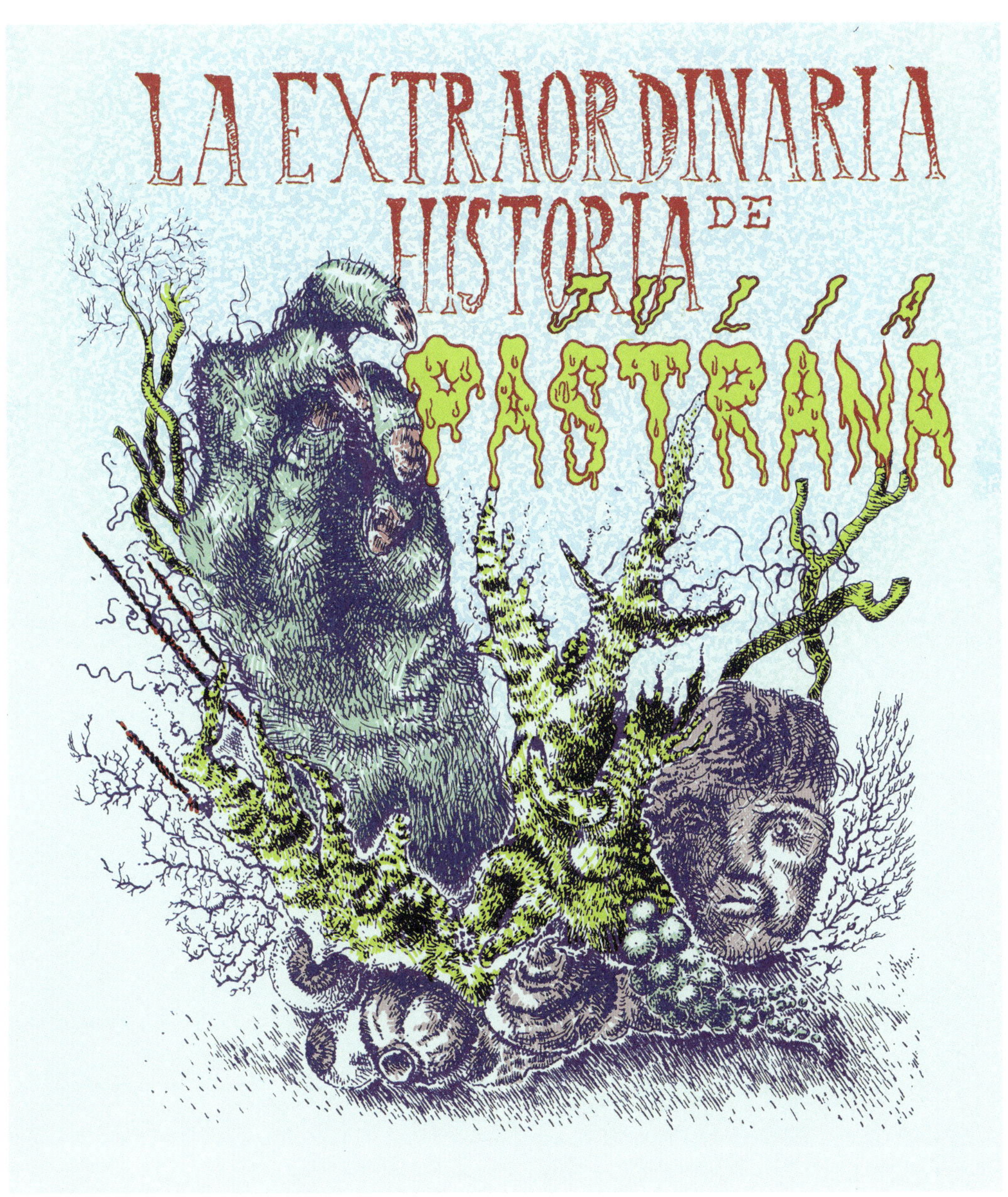

Laura Anderson Barbata and Erik Tlaseca, front cover, *La Extraordinaria Historia de Julia Pastrana,* zine no. 2, 2016; risograph

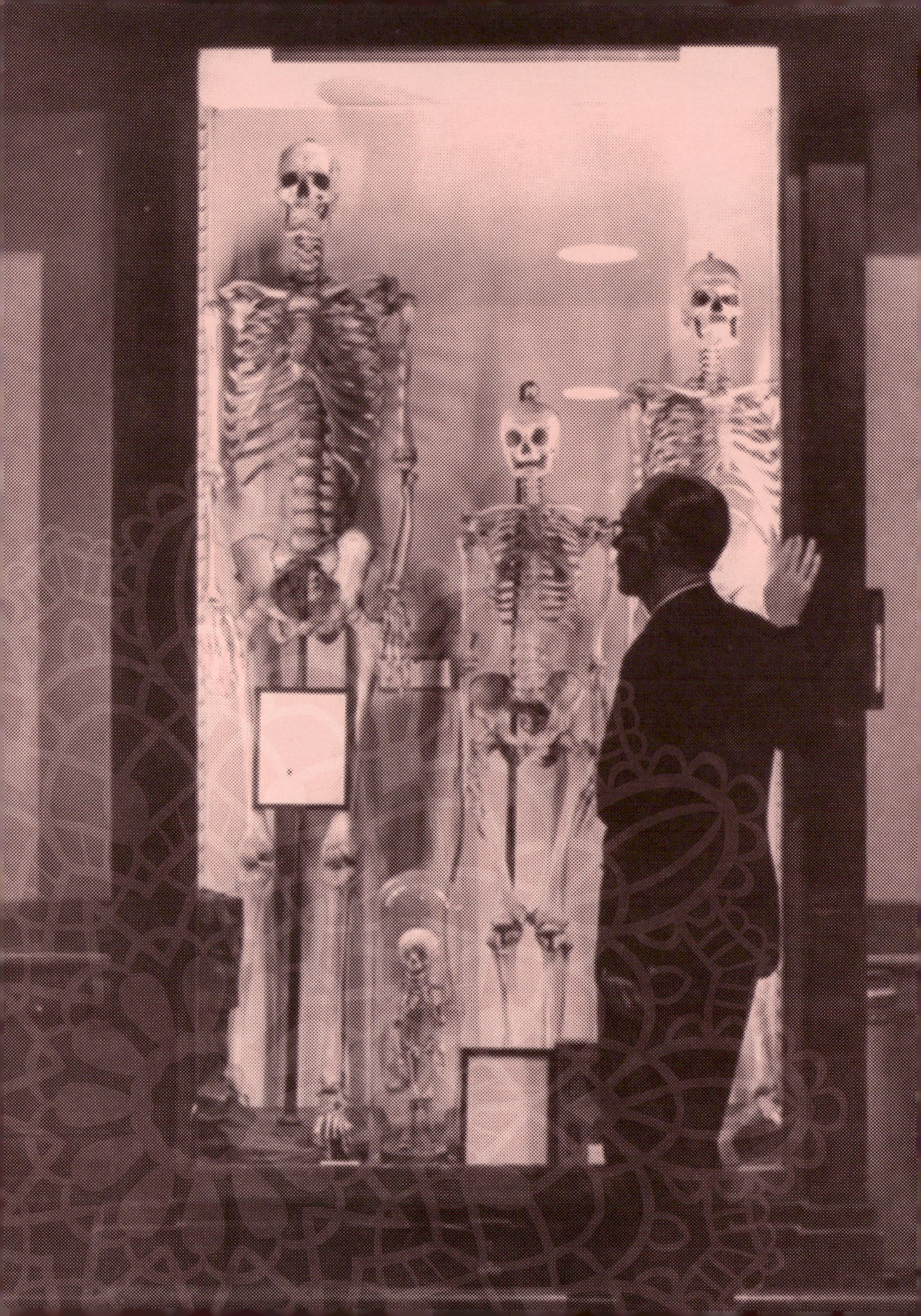

Lives on Show, Bodies behind Glass: Julia Pastrana's Parallels in Museum Collections

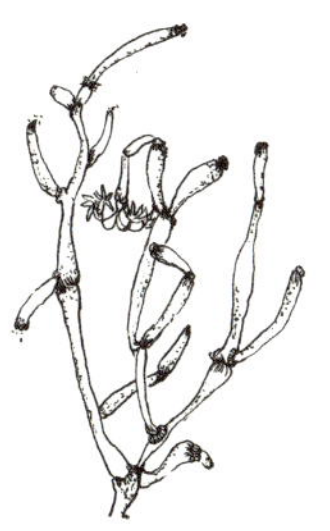

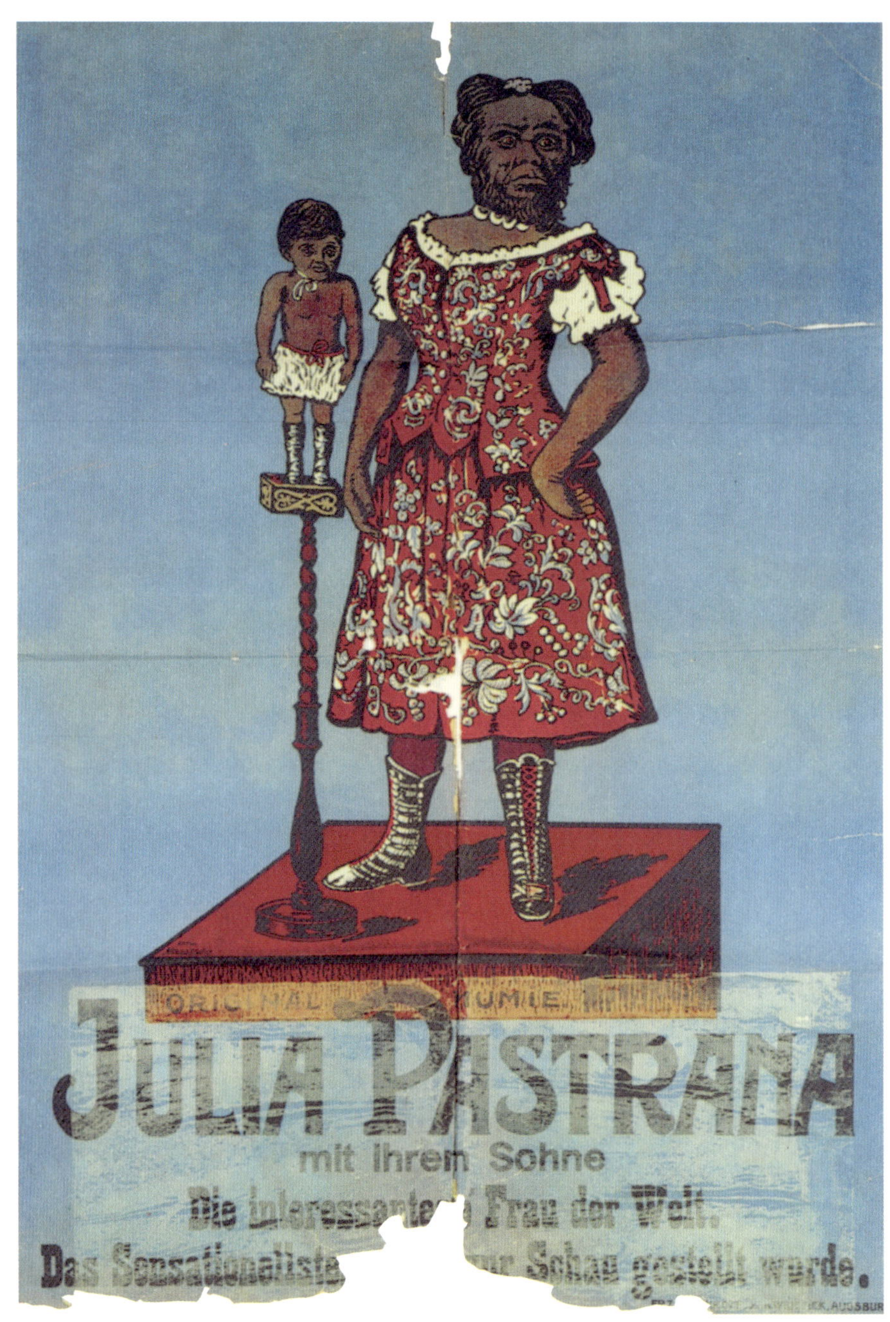

Poster of Julia Pastrana and her son, c. 1862–80

Lives on Show,
Bodies behind Glass:
Julia Pastrana's Parallels
in Museum Collections

BESS LOVEJOY

Julia Pastrana was exhibited in both life and death, but she is far from the only person to have ended up in a museum collection. In fact, the storehouses of many medical and natural history museums are so full of bodies and body parts—mummies, skulls, shrunken heads—that it would not be inappropriate to approach them with the reverence normally reserved for a cemetery. Of course, cemeteries are generally meant to create a communal home for the departed, while museums often collect (or have historically collected) humans based on a search for the remarkable or anomalous, and with an eye to hierarchical classification.

Pastrana, like many of the other bodies mentioned here, was "collected" not to welcome her into the eternal family of humanity, but to emphasize her divergence. A similar logic is at work with a number of other bodies that have been exhibited over the past several centuries. While some have received repatriations and reburials, others have been lost or remain on display, a challenge to a society that likes to imagine it has moved beyond dehumanizing difference.

Perhaps the most well known of these examples is Sara, or Saartjie, Baartman, born in the 1770s in the Camdeboo valley, about four hundred miles from Cape Town, South Africa.[1] Her multiple names hint at the issues surrounding her identity: though many scholars refer to her by the Cape Dutch "Saartjie," this use of the diminutive (meaning "little Sara") encodes not only a sense of endearment among family and friends but also colonialist power relationships. For this reason, some prefer to call her Sara Baartman, the name she was baptized with in 1811.[2] Her fame, however, came under an altogether different moniker: the Hottentot Venus.

"Hottentot," a racial category invented by Europeans, was generally placed very low on the Great Chain of Being, just barely above the apes.[3] The word is derogatory Dutch for "to stammer," a reference to the clicking of the Khoisan language.[4] Baartman herself was of the Gonaqua people, a subgroup of the Khoekhoe. She grew up on a colonialist's farm, but after being orphaned, left the frontier with a free black trader known as Pieter Cesars.[5] Cesars brought her to Cape Town, where she worked as a servant in various households, had at least one notable relationship (with a military drummer), and bore several children, none of whom seem to have survived infancy.

Her most fateful posting was as the wet nurse for the children of Hendrik Cesars, Pieter's brother.[6] It was around this time that she came to the attention of British military surgeon Alexander Dunlop, who may have employed Cesars, and who grew interested in exhibiting Baartman as a way to supplement his military pay. As a Gonaqua woman, Baartman belonged to a group that had been highly eroticized in the European imagination for centuries—seen as innocent, primitive, and lusty all at once.[7] She was also described as being both pretty and charming, and talented on her *ramkie*, a type of African guitar.

Dunlop may have first seen Baartman when Hendrik Cesars began to show her, as a kind of erotic tourist attraction, at a naval hospital. At any rate, Dunlop and Cesars hatched a plan to bring Baartman to Europe, where the colonialist imagination was hungry for examples of the African Other, particularly in its female form. It's not clear what promises were made to Baartman, but she may have been urged along by tales of the fame, money, and adventure awaiting her on English shores. By comparison, the confines of her life of servitude in Cape

Erik Tlaseca, illustration of Sarah Baartman from
La Extraordinaria Historia de Julia Pastrana,
zine no. 2, 2016; risograph

Town may have seemed narrow and grubby. She reportedly asked Cesars's wife before leaving, "Who will give me anything here?"[8]

Baartman arrived on British soil in May 1810.[9] In London she was transformed into the Hottentot Venus, billed in promotional advertisements as a "most correct and perfect specimen of that race . . . with all the rude ornaments usually worn by those people." Dunlop and Cesars set up the exhibition in Piccadilly, then ground zero for the trade in human curiosities (and not far from where the "Sicilian Fairy," Caroline Crachami, was exhibited a decade and a half later). During her shows, Baartman was covered in a custom-made one-piece silk body stocking dripping with beaded necklaces and feathers, which she wore while singing, swaying, and playing folk songs on her *ramkie*.

She became the biggest theatrical sensation of the winter of 1810. As the writer Rachel Holmes has noted, her exhibition tapped not only into the fevered British fantasies about the "dark continent" of African female sexuality, but also into a more general British obsession with posteriors. While not unusual in the African context—indeed, Baartman's physique likely wouldn't seem strange to anyone living in a diverse US city today—she was seen as having a notably large bottom. Holmes writes:

> *From low to high culture of all forms, Britain was a nation obsessed by buttocks, bums, arses, posteriors, derrières, and every possible metaphor, joke, or pun that could be squeezed from this fundamental cultural obsession. . . . Much of Saartjie's success was the result of a simple phenomenon: with her shimmying, voluptuous bottom, she perfectly captured the zeitgeist of late-Georgian Britain.* [10]

Baartman was also rumored to possess the famed "Hottentot apron," an elongated labia whose size was theorized to represent the gargantuan sexual appetites in the females of her people. While on the one hand the concoction of such theories by European men of science served to reinforce a racist and colonialist order (in which "primitive" sexual appetites were connected to moral and intellectual inferiority), the shadow side of such imaginings fed erotic obsessions, evident in pornographic writings and drawings of the time. All of this made Saartjie/Sara/Venus a particularly potent show.

Tragically, the rumors of her imagined extended labia may have contributed to Baartman's demise. The exhibit at Piccadilly closed in May 1811, and for the next three years she toured Britain, appearing in fairs around the English countryside as well as in Ireland. The historical record grows dim after 1812, but in September 1814 Baartman reappeared in Paris,[11] where she fell (or was nudged) into the orbit of

Georges Cuvier, then a professor of comparative anatomy at the city's Museum of Natural History and often considered Europe's foremost scientist.

In Paris, Baartman at first reportedly seemed cheerful onstage, but as the fall progressed, Cesars—in a desperate bid to increase his earnings—extended her showings to punishingly long hours. Baartman began suffering from recurrent bouts of the flu, exacerbated by a nascent alcoholism. As she sickened, Cesars departed for South Africa (Dunlop had long since left the scene), and a showman named Reaux took over her engagements. With Baartman barely recovered from the flu, Reaux began showing her in twelve-hour shifts.

Reaux was well placed, in the most macabre sense, to preside over Baartman's exhibitions. According to Holmes, he was an entertainer and animal trainer who also served as one in the Museum of Natural History's network of "animal resurrectionists," supplying corpses for the institution's cabinets. With Baartman growing ever more exhausted and brandy dependent, Reaux apparently calculated that she'd be worth more to him dead than alive.

In the spring of 1815, he arranged for a special three-day showing of Baartman before a panel of scientists and artists at the Museum of Natural History.[12] Cuvier had been to see the Hottentot Venus exhibition in Paris and been greatly intrigued; he helped Reaux organize the group of zoologists, anatomists, and others who assembled to sketch Baartman at the museum. Cuvier himself was largely interested in the question of the Hottentot apron, and had expected that Baartman would pose naked, but she refused. After three days of poking and prodding, she eventually shed her body stocking, but kept a handkerchief resolutely clasped between her legs.

Sadly, death would afford her no such dignity. Exhausted and alcoholic, Baartman died on the night of December 29, 1815; the precise cause of her death is unknown. Reaux immediately went to Cuvier's museum to discuss transferring her body there. A legal decree of 1813 forbade human corpses from being housed at the museum, but Étienne Geoffroy St. Hilaire, the great naturalist who oversaw the museum's menagerie, wrote to the chief of police for special permission. This was granted, on the condition that Baartman's dignity would be maintained. Yet the body was transferred with no solemnizing rites.

Cuvier began the dissection less than twenty-four hours after Baartman had died. By the time he was done, he had taken a plaster cast of her body, preserved her brains and genitals as wet specimens, modeled her genitals in wax, and prepared her skeleton for display in his Cabinet d'Anatomie Comparée, among what was then the world's largest collection of human and animal specimens. For years, the great naturalist reportedly kept the jars containing Baartman's brains and genitals outside the door to his own private apartments.[13]

Cuvier died in 1832, honored with an elaborate state funeral before his burial in Père Lachaise cemetery. Sometime between 1822 and the 1850s, according to Holmes, Baartman's skeleton, body cast, brain, and genitals were put on public display, where they stayed until the 1970s. In the early 1980s, the writer and paleontologist Stephen Jay Gould rediscovered the jars containing Baartman's remains stored among the brains of illustrious nineteenth-century white male scientists at the museum—including Cuvier's.

From that point on, Baartman's body became a new kind of symbol. No longer made to carry the connotations of outsized African female sexuality and an imagined proximity to beasts, she became representative of the wrongs of colonialism, racism, sexism, and apartheid.

In 1994, a year after apartheid ended, Nelson Mandela raised the matter of Baartman's repatriation to French president François Mitterrand.[14] At first the French refused, saying Baartman's remains would be better cared for in France. But South African officials made it clear that they wouldn't back down, and a South African paleoanthropologist named Phillip Tobias was appointed to lead the negotiations with French authorities. Talks stalled until 2000, when Ben Ngubane, then minister of arts, culture, science, and technology, intervened, with support of then-president Thabo Mbeki. (The return of El Negro from Botswana to Spain, whose story is outlined below, also helped pave the way.)

The repatriation eventually gained supporters in the French government, including research minister Roger-Gérard Schwartzenberg, who testified in the French senate that the return of Baartman's body would mark Europe's emergence "from the long night of slavery, colonialism, and racism."[15] The debate reached the highest echelons of the French government, in part because Baartman's body, deemed national patrimony, couldn't leave the country without a change in law. On February 21, 2002, the French government finally voted to release Baartman to South Africa.

Her skeleton, plaster cast, and the two bell jars were carefully packaged in a foam-lined box and placed on a South African Airways flight. The symbolic date of August 9, Women's Day in South Africa and International Indigenous People's Day, was chosen for her reburial near the banks of the Gamtoos River. A cleansing ritual and dressing ceremony in a Cape Town theater prepared her for burial before an estimated 2,500 people, on a day filled with music, dancing, and poetry. News anchor Redi Direko said, "Rarely has one figure meant so much to an entire country." After spending five years of her life on display in a degrading spectacle, and for nearly two centuries treated as museum property collected in the service of a dehumanizing ideology, Baartman was finally given a burial closer to the one she would have imagined for herself—although she scarcely could have predicted what an important symbol she'd become.

If Baartman's body was the focus of intense popular and scientific attention, the body of Qisuk—an Inuit man from northwestern Greenland who also ended up in a museum—suffered from a casual neglect as shocking as it is revealing.

Qisuk is known to history thanks to Robert Peary, an explorer obsessed with being the first to reach the North Pole (whether or not he did so is a matter of some dispute). Peary arrived in the region around Cape York, Greenland, in 1891, intent on studying the Inuit who lived at this northernmost edge of the inhabited world, and determined to find a practical route to the pole.[16] One of the strongest men in his small tribe, Qisuk began working with Peary soon after the explorer arrived, displaying superior skills as a hunter and sled dog driver.

About five years later, Franz Boas, one of the founders of anthropology, then working at the American Museum of Natural History, asked Peary if he could bring him an Eskimo for study. In his words, it would "enable us to obtain leisurely certain information which will be of the greatest scientific importance."[17] Eager to impress his patrons at the AMNH, Peary brought back not one but six Inuit: another strong hunter named Nuktaq, his wife Atangana, their adopted daughter Aviaq, a young man named Uisaakassak, the aforementioned Qisuk, and his son Minik, then about seven years old. Minik would later say: "They promised us nice warm homes in the sunshine land, and guns and knives and needles and many other things. . . . Our people were afraid to let them go, but Peary promised them that they should have Nuktaq and my father back within a year."[18]

Minik got a macabre foreshadowing of future events when he noted that five barrels of the bones of his ancestors had also been taken aboard Peary's ship, the *Hope*, much to his disapproval. But he was powerless to stop their transport. The *Hope* arrived in New York on September 30, 1897, when twenty thousand New Yorkers came to see the Inuit disembark (Peary, of course, charged admission).[19] But neither Peary nor Boas had concerned themselves with the Inuits' housing, so the group was bundled off to the museum's basement, where curious onlookers peered at them through gratings over the windows.

Not surprisingly, given this mass exposure to new germs, the group soon fell ill. On October 11, 1897, the *New York Times* reported, with casual racism, "The unfortunate little savages have caught cold or warmth, they do not know which, but assuming it was the latter their sole endeavor yesterday was to keep cool. Their efforts in this direction were a source of amusement to several scores of visitors."[20]

However, overheating wasn't the problem—tuberculosis was. By November 1, the entire group was at Bellevue Hospital.

Atangana was the first to die, but three others followed; all of the Inuit except for Minik and Uisaakassak would eventually pass away in New York. On February 17, 1898, Qisuk breathed his last. Peary, who had paid little attention to the group since they arrived, sent a telegram to the museum: "Deeply regret Eskimo's death. Confident everything was done. Entire responsibility mine."[21] Meanwhile, the hospital wrote to Boas at the museum: "The body will I suppose belong to the Museum of Natural History or Mr. Peary and they can of course do anything they wish with it." According to contemporary newspaper reports, it was decided that the medical students at Bellevue would be allowed to dissect Qisuk's body, with his skeleton to be mounted and preserved at the AMNH.[22]

Although the remains of the other Inuit in the party had similar fates, Qisuk has received somewhat more attention thanks to the story of Minik, his son, who stayed in New York City and became the focus of popular and press attention. (Uisaakassak returned to Greenland at the earliest opportunity.) For his part, Boas published only one astonishingly brief statement on the study of the six Inuit: "Many things heretefore unknown have been learned regarding their language, their traditions and their personal characteristics. Casts of their heads have been made for the museum."[23]

At first Minik was kept in the dark about the fate of his father's bones, and the museum staff even went so far as to stage a mock funeral. One cold February evening, a group of scientists and other AMNH employees gathered in the museum's gardens for an approximation of an Inuit death ritual, the part of Qisuk's body being played by a log and a mask wrapped in cloth. As far as Minik knew, his father's body was then laid to rest beneath a pile of stones in the garden.[24] In fact, Qisuk's corpse had been sent more than 150 miles upstate, to a processing facility in Lawyersville run by William Wallace, the museum superintendent. Within months, the bodies of the three other Inuit had made the trip to the Lawyersville facility and then to the osteological department of the museum. The AMNH maintains they were never on public display, but newspaper reports that erupted some years later told a different tale.

On January 6, 1907, a full-page article in *The New York World*'s magazine supplement showed a drawing of Minik reaching his hands toward the museum, next to the headline "Give Me My Father's Body." According the story—echoed by other reports in the ensuing years—Minik had come across his father's bones in a case at the museum and been horrified. The museum never formally responded to the press reports, despite the efforts of a prominent publicist, who helped Minik lobby for their return. Minik even appealed to the state legislature, and the matter was brought before President Roosevelt, to no avail. By April 1909, as press coverage of the situation intensified, the secretary of the AMNH said they knew of no request for the return of the bones. Herman Carey Bumpus, then the museum's director, declared himself "thoroughly mystified" by the whole thing. "As for the father's body," he said, "I know nothing of it. He made no demands on me for it. . . . We have no bodies here."[25] (As the historian Kenn Harper notes, Bumpus may have been employing an evasive tactic in which skeletons did not count as "bodies.")

In 1909 Minik returned to Greenland. Before he left, he told reporters: "You're a race of scientific criminals. I know I'll never get my father's bones out of the American Museum of Natural History. I am glad enough to get away before they grab my brains and stuff them into a jar."[26] (Sadly, Minik would never readjust to Inuit life, and ended up returning to New York City, only to die in New Hampshire in the 1918 flu epidemic. He is buried in the Indian Stream cemetery in Pittsburg, New Hampshire.)

Qisuk, however, stayed in the museum until 1993, in a box marked with the accession number 99/3610. He owes his removal from the museum in large measure to Harper, who in 1986 published *Give Me My Father's Body: The Life of Minik, the New York Eskimo*. Minik's story, as recounted by Harper, was discovered in 1992 by reporters

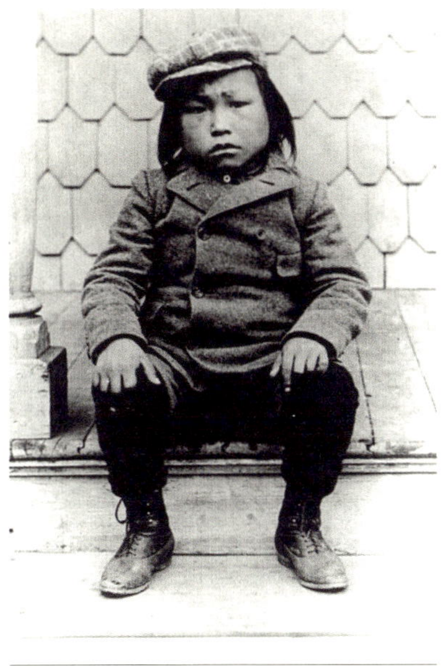

Minik Wallace in New York shortly
after his arrival, 1897

working for the *Washington Post* and for Canada's *Globe and Mail*. Their articles finally managed to garner widespread attention for the story, and for the idea of finally burying Qisuk. The granddaughter of William Wallace, then living in Saudi Arabia, also got involved in agitating for the reburial of all four Inuit still kept at the AMNH. The Native American Graves Protection and Repatriation Act had been passed in 1990, and although it didn't directly apply to these bodies from Greenland, it showed that times had changed—museums could finally be forced to recognize that those of non-European descent were still humans worthy of culturally appropriate burial rites in their own lands.

In 1992, the AMNH decided to finally lay the story, and the Inuit bones, to rest. After protracted negotiations with the village of Qaanaaq, the settlement closest to the point where Peary had disembarked, an agreement was reached for the return of the remains. On July 28, 1993, the carefully packed bones of all four Inuit were loaded onto military aircraft at an Air Force base in New Jersey and transported to Thule Air Base in northern Greenland, then flown by helicopter to Qaanaaq. The bodies were received at a small Lutheran church there, where on August 1, after a brief ceremony, they were buried in individual coffins and a common grave on a hillside with view of the sea. On August 4, 1997—one hundred years after the group had left Greenland for New York—a commemorative plaque was added to the gravesite. It began with the words *nunamingnut uteqihut*: "they have come home."[27]

In contrast to Sara Baartman and Qisuk, little is known of the early life of the preserved human known as "El Negro," who was exhibited for about eighty years in a small museum in Banyoles, in the north of Spain. He was likely a member of the Batlhaping people of Botswana, and died about 1830 of a lung infection, a few years shy of his thirtieth birthday.[28]

Shortly after his funeral, perhaps just hours after the mourners had left, he was stolen from his grave. The culprits were two French taxidermists, the brothers Edouard and Jules Verreaux. Their family shop in Paris, Maison Verreaux, was one of the first shops in the world dealing solely in natural history specimens.[29] The brothers knew Cuvier and supplied specimens to his museum. In fact, they'd been in Botswana on a collecting trip, shooting lions and crocodiles and digging up plants. They sent the body that would later become known as El Negro back to Paris alongside thousands of other specimens from their expedition.

In Paris the brothers displayed the body for several years alongside other African wonders. After they died, Barcelona naturalist Francesc Darder, who also operated a biological supply house and dabbled in taxidermy, bought much of the collection.[30] El Negro even went on display at the Barcelona World Exhibition of 1888. In 1916 Darder gave his whole collection to Banyoles in gratitude for the hospitality they had displayed while he was researching a local lake some years earlier, and an entire museum was built up around these items—with El Negro a main attraction.

The display apparently caused little protest until around 1991, when a local doctor of Haitian descent began to raise concerns during the lead-up to the 1992 Olympics in Barcelona. The doctor, Alphonse Arcelin, wrote to the national daily *El País*, demanding that the display be taken down lest it cause offense to Olympics visitors:[31] "If the man is not moved, I'm willing to ask all black athletes not to participate in competitions in a place where such a racist statement is made even worse: it is a man stolen from his grave."

The mayor and townspeople resisted, arguing that the display wasn't racist and that the body was a beloved local curio. The town council voted to keep the display in its glass box as it had always been, and councilor Carles Abella said: "El Negro is our property. It's our business and nobody else's. The talk of racism is absurd. Anyway, human rights only apply to living people, not dead."[32] Soon, "Keep El Negro" T-shirts, balloons, and badges appeared in support of the museum, whose admission numbers skyrocketed. That Easter, townspeople enjoyed El Negro–shaped chocolates. Arcelin brought his protests as far as the Olympic organizing committee in Barcelona and the Spanish foreign ministry, but made little headway, despite protests from some Olympic athletes and organizers.[33]

About five years later, the issue came before the Organization of African Unity and the Republic of Botswana, and the Spanish government eventually pressed the town to relent, though not without some ill feeling. "It was exhibited with respect," Georgina Gratacos, the curator of the Darder Museum in Banyoles, told the *New York Times*. "There wasn't any racism. This is a part of history and this interest that Europeans had largely remains unknown. It was a time when to see exotic things you had to bring them to Europe, whether they were animals or human beings." Fortunately, El Negro's reburial shows that the logic that allowed European museums to collect human remains gathered without permission now seems at best distasteful—however innocently it is painted.

Not all of El Negro returned for the state funeral in Gabarone, Botswana's capital, in 2000, only a bare, clean skull with broken teeth. It seems likely that's all that was left of the once-young Batlhaping man after his Parisian preservation and 170 years of display. His grave is now in Tsholofelo Park, Gaborone, marked by four white posts strung with chains. People come on weekends to see it, throwing coins onto the grass to wish El Negro's spirit some rest, at long last.

Born around 1721 somewhere in Eritrea, reportedly the son of an African prince, Angelo Soliman (as he would later be baptized) was abducted and sold on the slave market at age seven. He served a series of masters: an African, a marquise in Sicily, a Prince Lobkowitz, and then two princes of Liechtenstein, both of whom he traveled with in Europe, and with one of whom he also served in battle. He was a "court Moor," part of a European fashion for black servants, known for his great refinement and intelligence. After successfully integrating himself into Viennese society, he married in 1768 and became a Freemason in 1783, joining the same lodges as Mozart and Haydn. He died of a stroke in 1796, at age seventy, while out in the street. After his death a curious transformation took place:[34] despite having played a relatively distinguished role in Viennese society, he was embalmed and displayed as a "savage" in the imperial cabinet of natural curiosities.

Despite protests from both his daughter and the Catholic Church, Soliman was prepared for posthumous display on the orders of Emperor Franz II.[35] Visitors to the Physikalische Kabinett around the start of the nineteenth century would have seen Soliman's flayed skin mounted on a wooden model, standing in a glass case in a room decorated to look like a tropical forest. His stuffed corpse was adorned with beads and shells, his head crowned with red, blue, and white

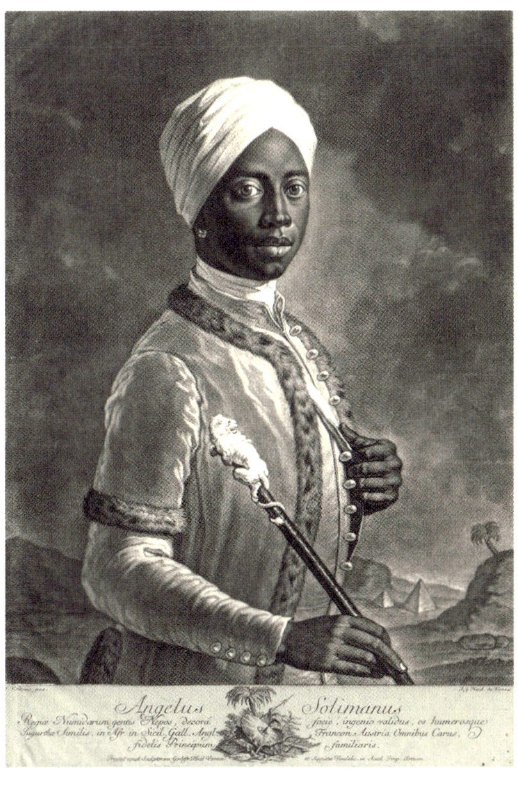

Angelo Soliman, by Gottfried Haid, based on
artwork by Johann Nepomuk Steiner, c. 1750

feathers, a far cry from the bright white caftan and turban atop a
Western vest and breeches he was known for wearing in Vienna.[36]
After about 1802, he was joined in the exhibit by the taxidermied figures of several other Africans, including a young girl, a zoo warden,
and a hospital porter. All were destroyed in the October revolution of
1848, when the troops of Prince Alfred Windischgrätz fired cannon-
balls on the imperial castle to try to quell riots in the city.

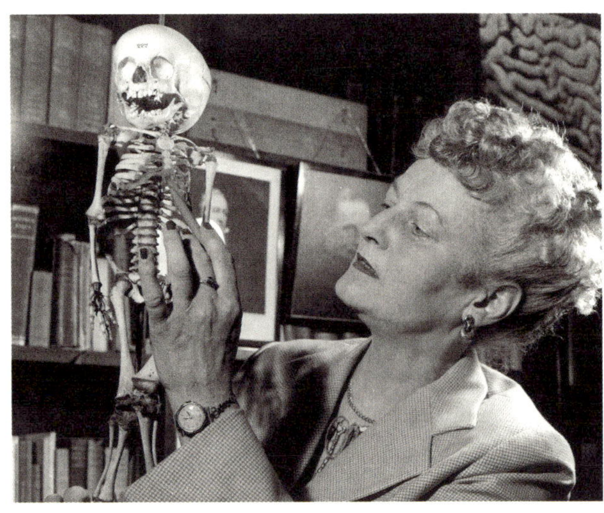

Curator Jessie Dobson holding the skeleton
of Caroline Crachami, c. 1954–71

From these successful repatriations and reburials, and one reburial that can never be, we turn to several skeletons that are still in museums. These can only be a sample, since the world's museums teem with remains collected under a wide variety of circumstances.

One of the most poignant examples of a person exhibited in life and death—still in storage—is Caroline Crachami, displayed in England around 1824 as the "Sicilian Fairy," or the "Sicilian Dwarf." She was said to have been born in Palermo and to have measured only about nineteen inches long at age nine. Some modern scholars believe she was only a toddler when she died, but her particular kind of dwarfism is rare enough to prevent an easy age-based analysis of her bones.[37]

The story that has come down to us is that her Sicilian parents moved to Dublin, where her father was hired as a musician, and where the family consulted one Dr. Gilligan about her care. He recommended a move to London, where, he felt, the (comparatively) warmer climate would be better for her health. Lacking money, the parents agreed to have Gilligan take their daughter there, with the understanding that he would exhibit her in order to defray the costs of the trip.

Crachami was a success: she became Britian's most famous dwarf, presented at court and drawing as many as two hundred paying visitors a day. Despite her tiny form, her proportions are said to have been basically the same as those of an adult woman. She was described as pale, with an "unearthly" voice, an unsteady walk, and an attraction to bright, pretty things. The *Literary Gazette and Journal* called her "the fairy of your superstition in actual life."

The climate of London does not, in fact, seem to have been salubrious for Crachami, and she died of tuberculosis in June 1824. Gilligan sold her body to Sir Everard Home, president of the Royal College of Surgeons and sergeant surgeon to the king. Home brought the body to the Royal College, much to the dismay of Crachami's father, who seems to have shown up in London just in time to find his daugher being dissected.[38] Her skeleton was on display in the middle of a room at the Hunterian zoological museum, next to the skeleton of "Irish Giant" Charles Byrne. The bones still today are accompanied by a small exhibit showing relics from her life: silk stockings, gray ballerina slippers, a ring, and a thimble, as well as wax casts of her foot, arm, and face.

Of all the people mentioned in this chapter, Charles Byrne, the "giant" who shared Crachami's glass case at the Hunterian (see p. 177), was most explicit about what he wanted done with his body after death. And he very much did not want it on display.

Born in Ireland in 1761, Byrne grew to more than seven feet seven inches tall during his young adulthood. He was exhibited in 1780s London (see p. 172), where he attracted considerable attention as a "modern living colossus."[39] He also developed alcoholism and tuberculosis, which seem to have been hazards of the exhibition life (as well as in the time period more generally). Noting his illness, the distinguished British surgeon and collector of curiosities John Hunter offered Byrne money for his corpse. Byrne refused, and was horrified

JUST ARRIVED

IN

London,

THAT

Wonderful Phenomenon of Nature,

THE CELEBRATED

Irish Giant,

Mr. O'BRIEN,

INDISPUTABLY

The Talleſt Man in the known World,

BEING NEAR

NINE FEET HIGH,

And is almoſt Forty Stone Weight.

Is a lineal Deſcendent of the old and puiſſant

King Brien Boreau,

And has, in Perſon and Appearance, all the Similitudes of that great and grand

POTENTATE.

Who will exhibit himſelf, for a ſhort Time only, next Door to the CANNON COFFEE-HOUSE, COCKSPUR-STREET, nearly oppoſite SPRING-GARDENS.

ADMITTANCE ONE SHILLING.

It is remarkable of this Family, that, however various the Revolutions in point of Fortune or Alliance, the lineal deſcendents thereof have been favored by Providence with the original Size and Stature, which have been ſo peculiar to the Family.

Mr. O'BRIEN begs leave to inform the Nobility and Gentry, that from the confined Air of London, his ſtay in the metropolis muſt be very ſhort.

Printed by P. BOYLE 14, Vine-ſtreet, Piccadilly.

Announcement for an appearance of Charles Byrne, aka O'Brien,
the Irish Giant, 1809

enough by the idea of being exhibited after death to build a lead coffin and ask some fishermen (by other accounts, an undertaker) to make sure it was thrown into the sea. However, when Byrne died at the age of twenty-two, Hunter bribed the fishermen (or undertaker's men) with £500 and took possession of the corpse. He kept the skeleton hidden in the museum for two years before putting it on display. It remains in the collection.

In 2011 an article in the *British Medical Journal* by Len Doyal, a professor of medical ethics at the University of London, and Thomas Muinzer, a lawyer at Queen's University in Belfast, called for Byrne's skeleton to finally be given a sea burial as he had wished. The authors argue that while important research has been carried out on the skeleton, the DNA that has already been extracted from the bones should be sufficient for further study, alongside a synthetic model of the skeleton. For their part, the Hunterian argues that the scientific value of keeping Byrne in the collection outweighs the benefits of honoring his last wish, in part because of ongoing research into individuals who share Byrne's condition.

The skeleton of one of the most notorious human spectacles of the nineteenth century, "Elephant Man" Joseph Merrick, has been dealt with somewhat differently. Merrick, who suffered in life from a rare disorder that caused extremely malformed bones and skin, was exhibited as a touring attraction before dying in 1890 at age twenty-seven (perhaps while accidentally dislocating his neck in his sleep). The Queen Mary University of London keeps his skeleton in a glass case at the School of Medicine and Dentistry's pathology museum, inside a locked room accessible only by medical professionals and students who have received permission from the curator.[40] A replica of his skeleton is on display elsewhere in the museum.

In June 2016 there were new calls for Merrick's burial from the granddaughter of one of his managers, who argued: "He was Christian

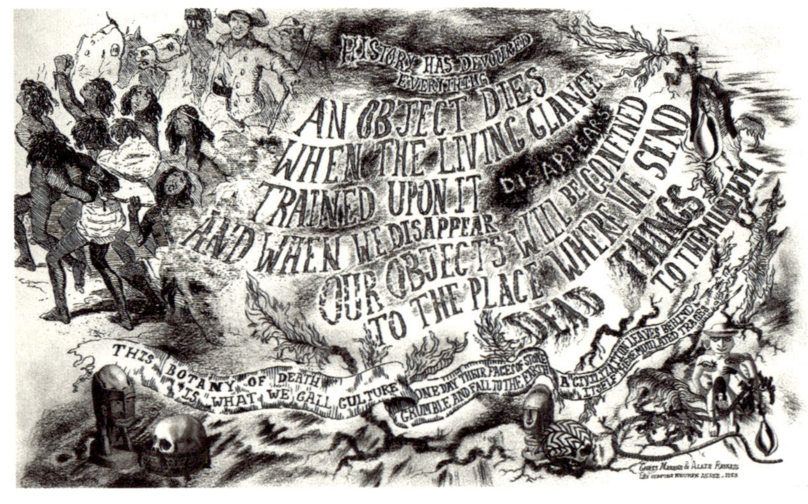

Erik Tlaseca, page from *La Extraordinaria Historia de Julia Pastrana,* zine no. 2, 2016; risograph

and would have expected a Christian burial." A group called the Friends of Joseph Carey Merrick has also repeatedly called for his reburial. The museum, however, says that viewing Merrick's real remains is an invaluable part of medical education, and notes that they regularly consult Merrick's living relatives over the display.[41]

The cases in this essay are different from each other, and from the life and afterlife led by Julia Pastrana. In the case of individuals exhibited because of truly rare medical conditions (and not simply because of their ethnicity), it's possible that compelling scientific reasons exist for preserving their bodies for research. However, such scientific justifications must be carefully weighed against the ethical imperative of providing death rituals and resting places in accordance with the deceased's wishes or expectations. This ethical imperative need not stem from any mystical concern for the soul. Ultimately the benefit is for us, not them. If we want to believe that our own wishes regarding the fates of our bodies will be respected, we must extend the same right to people of the past. A remove of several centuries is not an ethical excuse.

It should be added that display in a museum is not necessarily victimization—some have willed their bodies for such display—but the issue is one of agency. Having one's body stolen from the grave (or never buried in the first place) and exhibited in opposition to one's wishes is a violation. Whether or not they were exhibited in life, people of the past who expected a particular kind of burial in accordance with their religious beliefs should be afforded that dignity.

As we've seen with the cases of Julia Pastrana, Sara Baartman, and El Negro, such reburials often become healing rituals for an entire community. As a society, we need to know that we've moved beyond the day when those who looked different were paraded before the public as freaks, often without their consent and control. By burying these bodies, we symbolically lay to rest a deeply problematic period in European history—or so we can hope.

NOTES

1 The spellings "Sara" and "Sarah" are used interchangeably in various publications. Clifton Crais and Pamela Scully, *Sara Baartman and the Hottentot Venus* (Princeton: Princeton University Press, 2009), 7, and Susan Frith, "Searching for Sara Baartman," *John Hopkins Magazine*, June 2009, accessed June 2016, http://pages.jh.edu/~jhumag/0609web/sara.html.

2 Rachel Holmes, *African Queen: The Real Life of the Hottentot Venus* (New York: Random House, 2007), 72.

3 Holmes, *African Queen,* 113.

4 Frith, "Searching for Sara Baartman."

5 Crais and Scully, *Sara Baartman and the Hottentot Venus,* 27.

6 Ibid., 40.

7 Ibid., 48.

8 Frith, "Searching for Sara Baartman." Though many accounts pinpoint Baartman as being twenty-two at this point, the scholars Clifton Crais and Pamela Scully have shown that she was in her early thirties, and likely more world-wise than she is often given credit for.

9 Holmes, *African Queen,* 33.

10 Ibid., 43.

11 Crais and Scully, *Sara Baartman and the Hottentot Venus,* 116.

12 Holmes, *African Queen,* 82.

13 Ibid., 99.

14 Ibid., 103.

15 Ibid., 105.

16 Kenn Harper, *Give Me My Father's Body: The Life of Minik, the New York Eskimo* (New York: Pocket Books, 2001), 2.

17 Ibid., 29.

18 Ibid., 23.

19 Ibid., 25.

20 Michael T. Kaufman, "About New York: A Museum's Eskimo Skeletons and Its Own," *New York Times*, August 21, 1993, accessed May 2016, http://www.nytimes.com/1993 /08/21/nyregion/about-new-york-a-museum-s-eskimo-skeletons-and-its-own.html.

21 Harper, *Give Me My Father's Body*, 46.

22 Ibid., 92.

23 Ibid., 102.

24 Ibid., 96.

25 Ibid., 117.

26 Kaufman, "About New York."

27 Harper, *Give Me My Father's Body*, 209.

28 "El Negro of Banyoles," University of Botswana History Department, accessed May 2016, http://www.thuto.org/ubh/afhist/elnegro/eln0.htm.

29 Miquel Molina, "More Notes on the Verreaux Brothers," *Pula: Botswana Journal of African Studies* 16 (2002): 1, accessed May 2016, http://pdfproc.lib.msu.edu/?file=/DMC /African%20Journals/pdfs/PULA/pula016001/pula016001006.pdf and "El Negro/El Negre of Banyoles: Bushman from Bechuanaland, or Bechuana from Bushmanland?" University of Botswana History Department, accessed May 2016, http://www.thuto.org/ubh/afhist /elnegro/banyol3.htm.

30 Pat Morris, "Stuffed Humans," in *The Morbid Anatomy Anthology*, ed. Joanna Ebenstein and Colin Dickey (New York: Morbid Anatomy Press, 2014), 168–69.

31 "El Negro/El Negre of Banyoles."

32 Ibid.

33 Doug Cress, "'Bushman' to Stay for the Olympics," *New York Times*, May 22, 1992, accessed May 2016. http://www.nytimes.com/1992/05/22/sports/22iht-cres.html.

34 My account largely follows Dr. Wilfried Seipel, "Mummies and Ethics in the Museum," in *Human Mummies: A Global Survey of their Status and the Techniques of Conservation*, ed. Dr. Konrad Spindler et al. (Vienna: Springer, 1996), accessed May 2016, doi: 10.1007/978-3-7091-6565-2.

35 Heather Morrison, "Dressing Angelo Soliman," *Eighteenth-Century Studies* 44: 3 (Spring 2011) 361, doi: 10.1353/ecs.2011.0001.

36 Ibid.

37 Gaby Wood, *The Smallest of All Persons Mentioned in the Records of Littleness* (London: Profile Books, 1996).

38 Jan Bondeson, *A Cabinet of Medical Curiosities* (New York: W. W. Norton, 1999), 2011.

39 Ibid., 194.

40 Queen Mary University of London, "Our History," accessed June 2016, http://www.qmul .ac.uk/about/history/index.html and BBC News, "'Elephant Man' Joseph Merrick 'Should Be Buried in Leicester,'" June 9, 2016, accessed June 2016, http://www.bbc.com/news /uk-england-leicestershire-36478601.

41 BBC News, "Elephant Man."

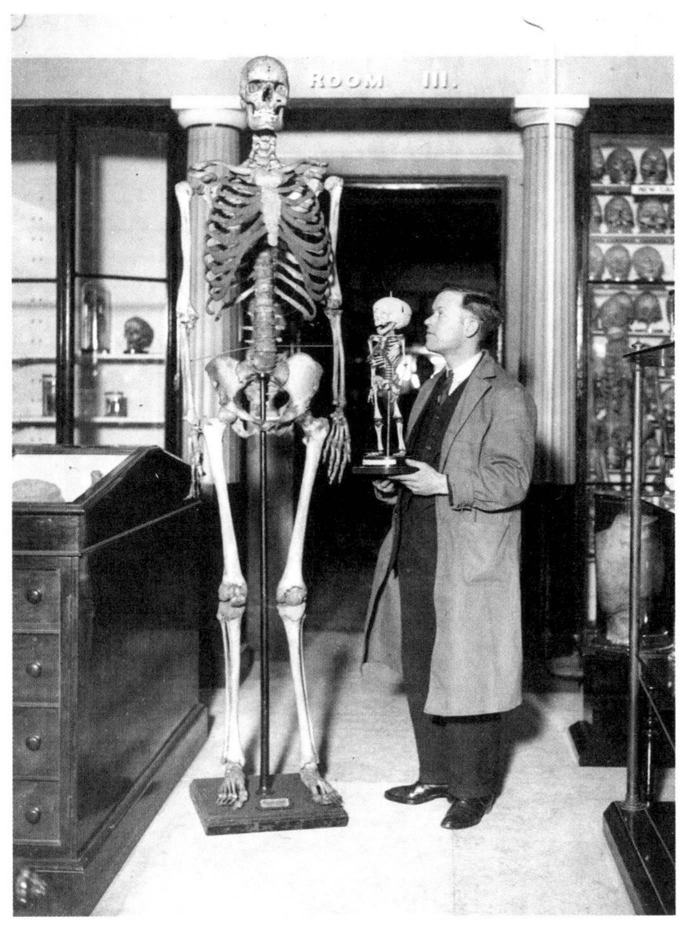

Museum attendant standing next to skeleton of Charles Byrne
and holding skeleton of Caroline Crachami, c. 1920s

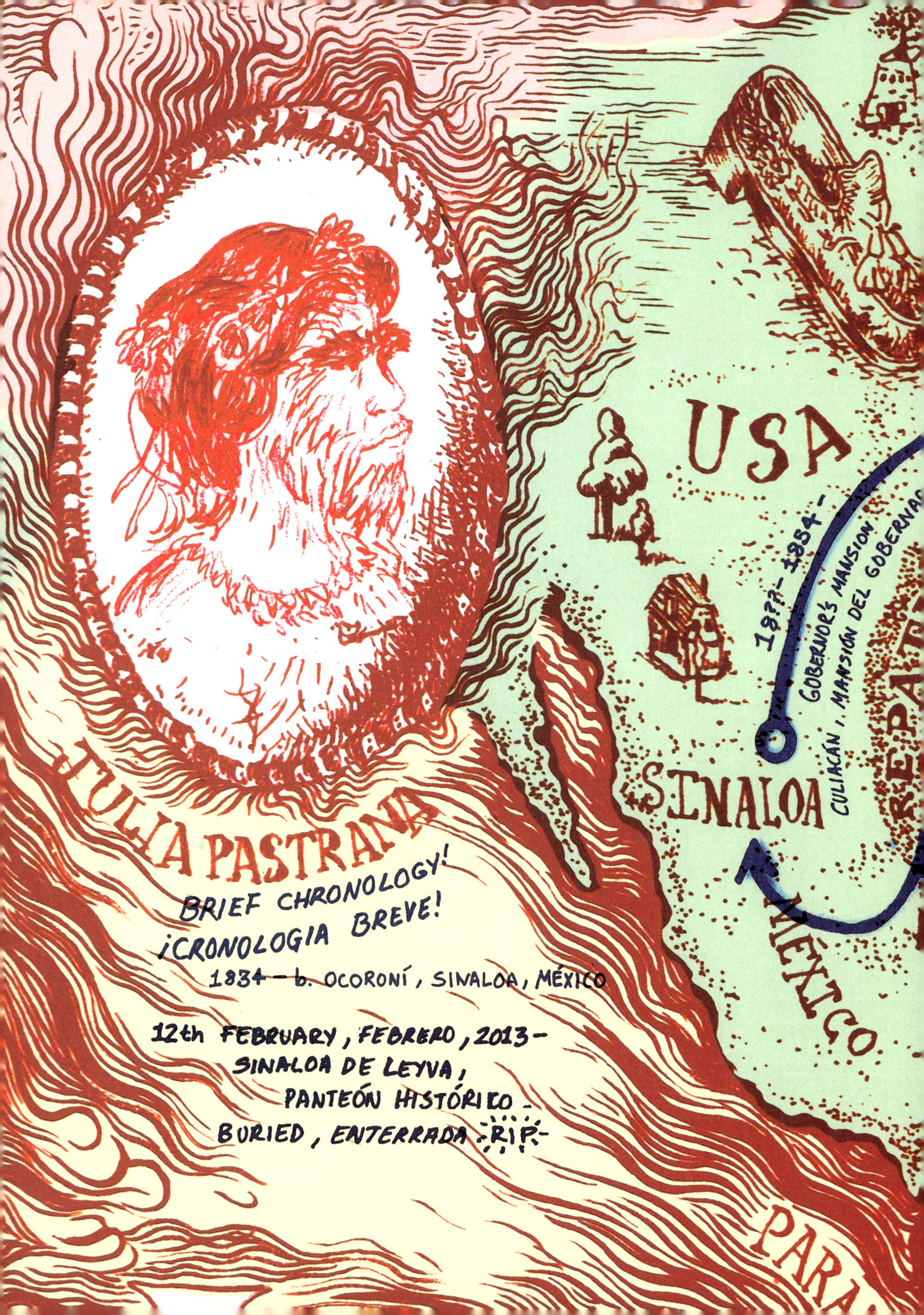

JULIA PASTRANA

BRIEF CHRONOLOGY!
¡CRONOLOGIA BREVE!
1834 — b. OCORONÍ, SINALOA, MÉXICO

12th FEBRUARY, FEBRERO, 2013 —
SINALOA DE LEYVA,
PANTEÓN HISTÓRICO —
BURIED, ENTERRADA -RIP-

USA

SINALOA

MÉXICO

1877 - 1854 -
GOBERNOR'S MANSION
CULIACÁN, MANSIÓN DEL GOBERNADOR

REPATR

PARA

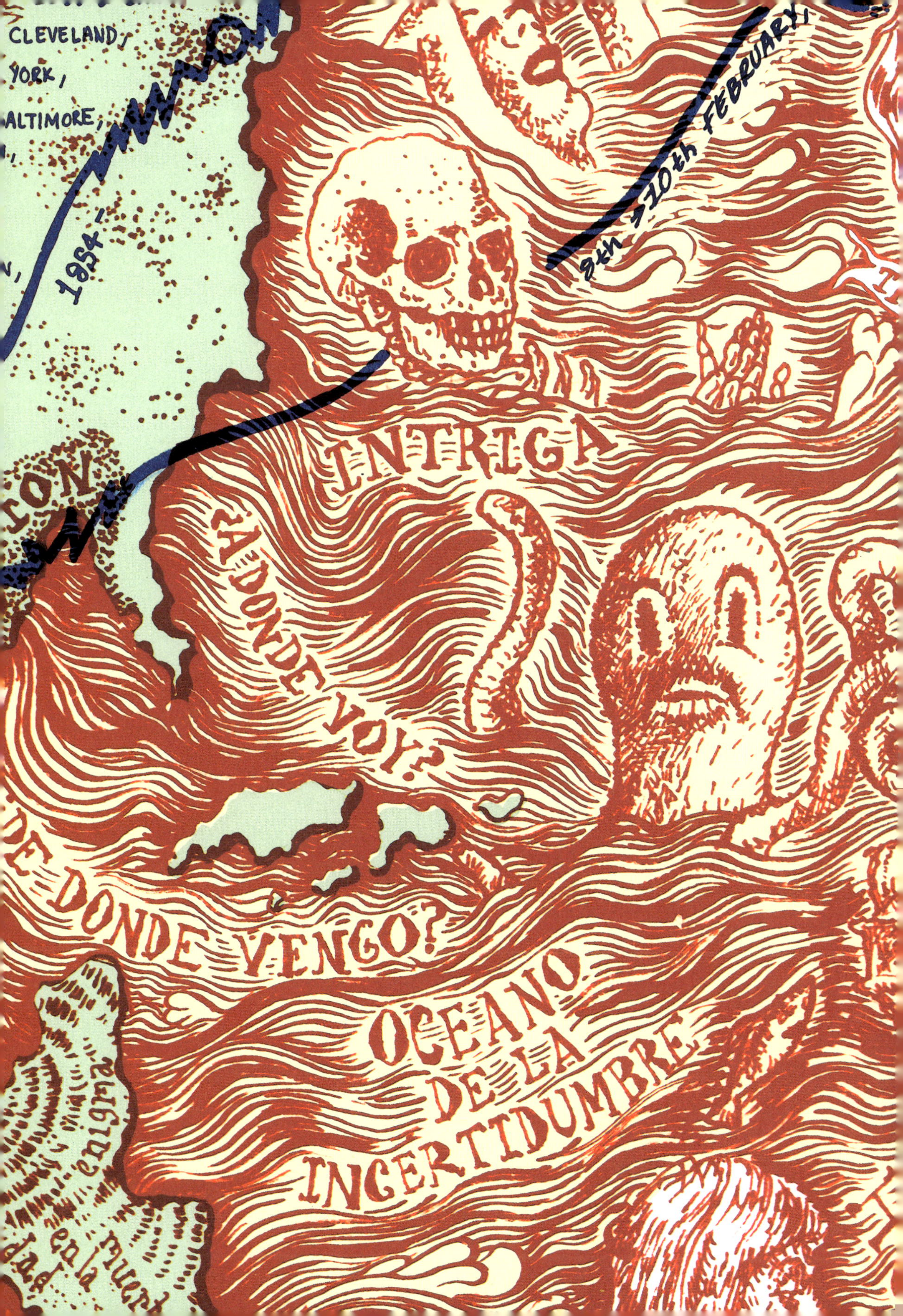

CLEVELAND,
YORK,
ALTIMORE,
1854
8th 10th FEBRUARY,
INTRIGA
¿A DONDE VOY?
¿DE DONDE VENGO?
OCEANO
DE LA
INCERTIDUMBRE

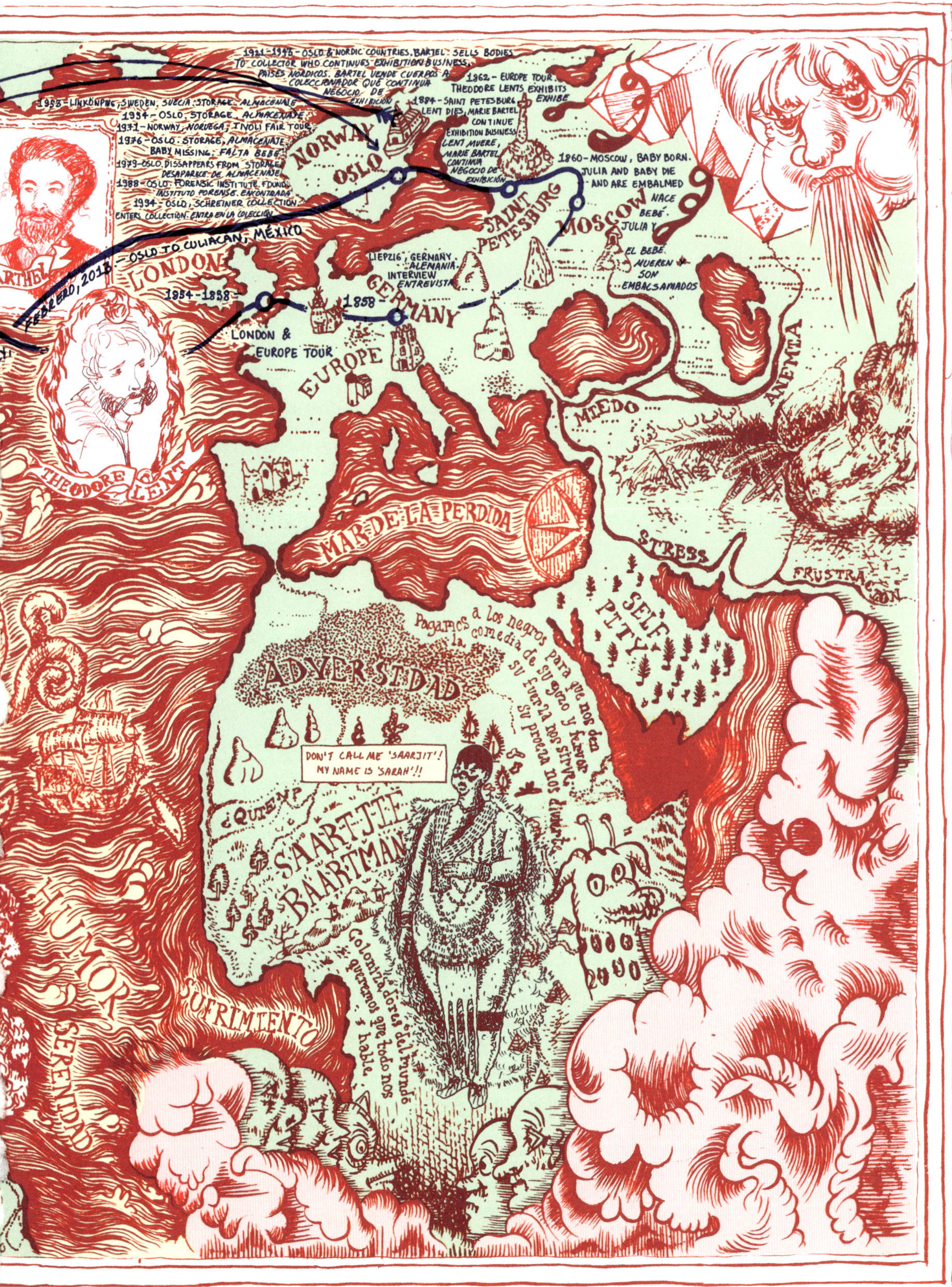

1921-1945 - OSLO & NORDIC COUNTRIES. BARTEL SELLS BODIES TO COLLECTOR WHO CONTINUES EXHIBITION BUSINESS. PAISES NORDICOS. BARTEL VENDE CUERPOS A COLECCIONADOR QUE CONTINUA NEGOCIO DE EXHIBICIÓN
1958 - LINKÖNPING, SWEDEN. SUECIA. STORAGE. ALMACENAJE
1954 - OSLO. STORAGE. ALMACENAJE
1971 - NORWAY, NORUEGA. TIVOLI FAIR TOUR.
1976 - OSLO. STORAGE. ALMACENAJE. BABY MISSING. FALTA BEBÉ.
1979 - OSLO. DISSAPPEARS FROM STORAGE. DESAPARECE DE ALMACENAJE.
1988 - OSLO. FORENSIC INSTITUTE. FOUND. INSTITUTO FORENSE. ENKONTRADA
1994 - OSLO. SCHREINER COLLECTION. ENTERS COLLECTION. ENTRA EN LA COLECCIÓN
1862 - EUROPE TOUR. THEODORE LENTS EXHIBITS. EXHIBE
1884 - SAINT PETESBURG. LENT DIES, MARIE BARTEL CONTINUE EXHIBITION BUSINESS. LENT MUERE, MARIE BARTEL CONTINUA NEGOCIO DE EXHIBICIÓN
1860 - MOSCOW. BABY BORN. JULIA AND BABY DIE AND ARE EMBALMED. NACE BEBÉ. JULIA Y EL BEBÉ MUEREN Y SON EMBALSAMADOS
OSLO TO CULIACAN, MÉXICO
FEBRERO, 2013
LONDON
1854 - 1858
LONDON & EUROPE TOUR
LIEPZIG, GERMANY. ALEMANIA. INTERVIEW. ENTREVISTA
1858
BARTHEL
THEODORE LENT
NORWAY
OSLO
SAINT PETESBURG
MOSCOW
GERMANY
EUROPE
ANEMIA
MIEDO
STRESS
FRUSTRACIÓN
SELF PITY
MAR DE LA PERDIDA
ADVERSIDAD
¿QUIEN?
SAARTJIE BAARTMAN
SUFRIMIENTO
HUMOR
SERENIDAD
DON'T CALL ME 'SAARJIT'! MY NAME IS 'SARAH'!!
Pagamos a los negros para que nos dan la comedia de su gozo y fervor. Su fuerza nos sirve. Su proeza nos divierte.
Colonizadores del mundo queremos que todo nos hable.

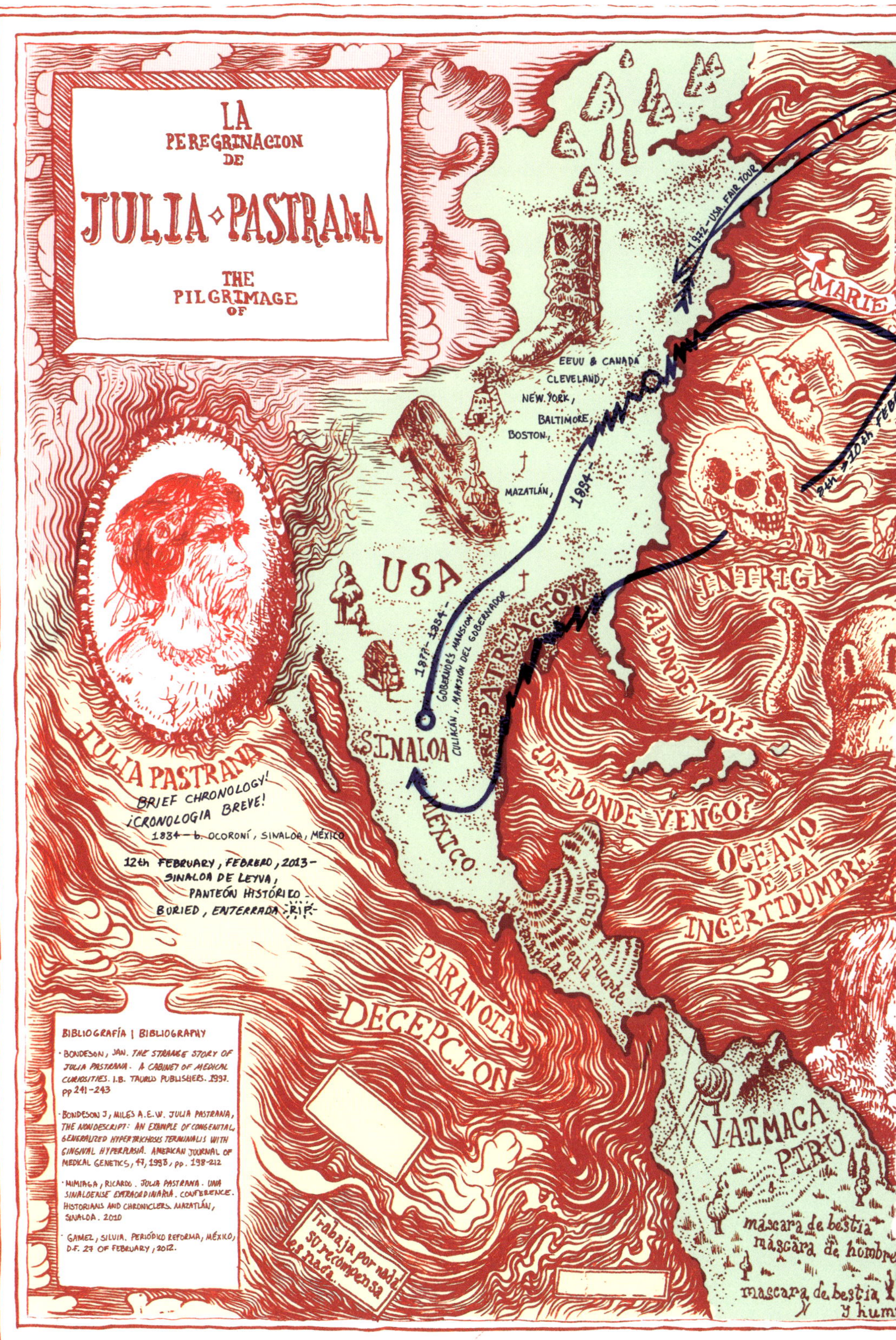

LA
PEREGRINACION
DE
JULIA · PASTRANA
THE
PILGRIMAGE
OF

JULIA PASTRANA
BRIEF CHRONOLOGY!
¡CRONOLOGIA BREVE!
1834 - b. OCORONÍ, SINALOA, MÉXICO

12th FEBRUARY, FEBRERO, 2013 -
SINALOA DE LEYVA,
PANTEÓN HISTÓRICO -
BURIED, ENTERRADA -RIP-

EEUU & CANADA
CLEVELAND,
NEW YORK,
BALTIMORE,
BOSTON.

MAZATLÁN

1854 -

1871 -

USA

GOBERNADOR
CULIACÁN - MANSIÓN DEL GOBERNADOR

SINALOA

MÉXICO

REPATRIACIÓN

1984

1854 - USA FAIR TOUR

MARIE

4th - 10th FEBRU

ENTREGA

¿A DONDE VOY?

¿DE DONDE VENGO?

OCEANO
DE LA
INCERTIDUMBRE

PARANOIA

DECEPCIÓN

VATMACA
PERU

máscara de bestia
máscara de hombre

máscara de bestia
y huma

BIBLIOGRAFÍA | BIBLIOGRAPHY

· BONDESON, JAN. THE STRANGE STORY OF
JULIA PASTRANA. A CABINET OF MEDICAL
CURIOSITIES. I.B. TAURUS PUBLISHERS. 1997.
pp 241-243

· BONDESON J, MILES A.E.W. JULIA PASTRANA,
THE NONDESCRIPT: AN EXAMPLE OF CONGENITAL,
GENERALIZED HYPERTRICHOSIS TERMINALIS WITH
GINGIVAL HYPERPLASIA. AMERICAN JOURNAL OF
MEDICAL GENETICS, 47, 1993, pp. 198-212

· MIMIAGA, RICARDO. JULIA PASTRANA. UNA
SINALOENSE EXTRAORDINARIA. CONFERENCE.
HISTORIANS AND CHRONICLERS. MAZATLÁN,
SINALOA. 2010

· GAMEZ, SILVIA. PERIÓDICO REFORMA, MÉXICO,
D.F. 27 OF FEBRUARY, 2012.

Trabaja por nada
su recompensa
es nada...

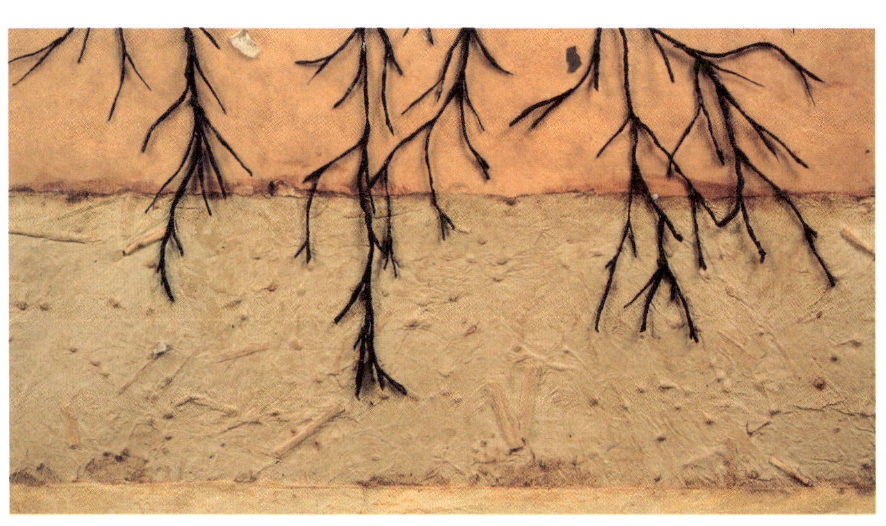

Julia Pastrana
Chronology

1834 Julia Pastrana is born in a small village in the western Sierra Madre region of the State of Sinaloa, Mexico. She has generalized hypertrichosis terminalis and severe gingival hyperplasia, which causes her to be covered with thick hair and have overdeveloped gums.

1834–185? The details of her life as a child are uncertain. According to Ricardo Mimiaga's oral history research, Julia's mother dies when she is very young; her uncle becomes her caretaker, and then sells her to a traveling circus.

18??–1854 Pastrana lives in Culiacán, in the home of Pedro Sanchez (the governor of Sinaloa from 1836 to 1837). We can assume that during this time she begins her training as a mezzo-soprano and dancer. She also learns English and French, languages in which she becomes fluent, in addition to Spanish and her native indigenous language, Cahita. Pastrana leaves the governor's house when she is sold to Francisco Sepulveda, the administrator of maritime customs of Mazatlán. According to accounts by Irineo Paz, Sepulveda partners with the governor of Sinaloa and an American businessman, Theodore Lent, to showcase Pastrana in the United States.

1854–1855 Pastrana performs in Guadalajara, Mexico. From evidence found in archival documents, it is possible that Pastrana travels from Veracruz to New Orleans with Sepulveda to meet Lent. Upon her arrival, Lent convinces Pastrana to marry him and becomes her manager. She is exhibited by Lent as they travel to New York, Cleveland, Baltimore, Boston, and Canada.

1854–1858 Lent bills Julia Pastrana as the Nondescript, the Hirsute, the Ape Woman, the Female Hybrid, the Wonderful Hybrid, Bear-woman, and Baboon Lady, among other sobriquets. They travel to London and throughout Europe, presenting shows in which Pastrana dances and sings opera arias. She is visited and examined by doctors, and is written about by Francis T. Buckland and Charles Darwin.

1858 An interview with Pastrana is published in *Gartenlaube* newspaper, Leipzig, Germany.

1859 Pastrana becomes pregnant by Lent.

1860 Pastrana and Lent travel to Moscow. On March 20, Julia gives birth to a boy who is diagnosed with the same condition as herself. The infant dies thirty-five hours later. Complications during childbirth keep Pastrana hospitalized, and Lent sells tickets to view her in her hospital bed. On March 25, she passes away from puerpereal metroperitonitis. Lent sells the bodies of his wife and child to Dr. Sokolov of the University of Moscow, who had developed embalming techniques.

1862 Lent visits the hospital of the University of Moscow. When he sees the results of Sokolov's work on Pastrana and her son, he demands that they be returned to him. The request is denied. Lent reaches out to the US Embassy to reclaim them, and with their intervention he is successful. He puts Pastrana and the child inside a glass case and begins to exhibit them throughout Europe. His commercial success is greater than when she was exhibited alive.

1864 Lent meets Marie Barthel, a young bearded woman from Karlsbad, Germany. He marries her and changes her name to Zenora Pastrana. Barthel becomes part of the exhibition, which presents Julia Pastrana and her baby as Zenora's sister and nephew. Lent's economic success continues.

1884 Theodore Lent dies in a psychiatric hospital in Saint Petersburg. Barthel inherits the bodies of Pastrana and the infant and continues to exhibit them.

1921 Marie Barthel sells Julia and her son to the Norwegian Håkon Jaeger Lund, who exhibits them in Oslo, Norway. Later, his son Hans Jaeger Lund takes the bodies on tour.

1943 Shortly before World War II, the German diplomat in charge of the medical department in Oslo orders that the bodies of Pastrana and her son be confiscated and sent to Berlin. Lund declines and takes them on tour through the Nordic countries.

1953 The bodies of Pastrana and her child are stored in Linköping, Sweden.

1954 Hans Jaeger Lund dies, and his son Bjørn inherits the bodies of Julia Pastrana and her child. They are stored in a warehouse in Oslo.

1971 Pastrana and her son are exhibited in Norway multiple times as part of the touring Tivoli Fair.

1971–1972 Pastrana and her son are transported to the US and exhibited in fairs.

1973 Sweden and Norway pass laws that prohibit the exhibition of human bodies. The bishop of Oslo requests that the bodies be confiscated and buried in a Catholic ceremony.

1976 Bjørn Lund puts Pastrana and her son in storage in Oslo. Thieves break into the warehouse and throw the mummified infant into a field, where it is eaten by rodents. Pastrana's arm is ripped from her body. Later, it is found in a dumpster and taken to the police.

1979 Lund's warehouse is vandalized again. Pastrana's body disappears.

1990 Jan Bondeson finds Pastrana's body in a janitorial closet in the basement of the Institute of Forensic Medicine at the Rikshospitalet in Oslo. The body is restored, and she is kept at the Institute.

1993–2005 Jan Bondeson, Rosemarie Garland-Thomson, and numerous other authors publish studies on Pastrana in Europe and the United States. In Mexico she is virtually unknown.

1994 The University of Oslo and other organizations discuss the future of Pastrana. Voting is in favor of burying Julia; only Per Holck, the director of the Schreiner Collection, is opposed. Shortly after the vote, the Royal Ministry of Health and Church Affairs orders that Julia Pastrana must remain in custody of the Schreiner Collection in the Department of Anatomy at the University of Oslo for research purposes.

2003 Laura Anderson Barbata becomes familiar with the life story of Julia Pastrana when her sister Kathleen Culebro invites her to collaborate on the costume design for a play based on Pastrana, produced by Amphibian Stage Productions. Culebro sends a letter to the Mexican Embassy in Norway requesting the repatriation and burial of Pastrana. She gathers hundreds of signatures in support. The letter is sent to Norway, but no reply is received.

2004 Barbata is invited to Oslo by the Office of Contemporary Art (OCA) to meet with Sami communities in northern Norway. She is in contact with institutions, academics, scholars, artists, politicians, and activists. She learns that the Schreiner Collection, where Pastrana is kept, has hundreds of Sami skulls that were questionably acquired.

2005 Barbata is awarded an artist residency in Norway by OCA. She proposes a project regarding Pastrana during her residency, and begins correspondence with the University of Oslo, Per Holck, anthropologists, sociologists, Sami scholars, intellectuals, historians, artists, and the ethics committee of the university. The National Committee for Research in the Social Sciences and the Humanities (NESH) tells Barbata that they are forming a new board to evaluate cases involving human remains. They agree that she can bring Julia Pastrana to the board as the first case for review.

2005 Barbata publishes an obituary for Julia Pastrana in the Oslo newspaper, which states that there will be a Catholic ceremony (the faith that Pastrana practiced during her life). With the aid of Christiane Erharter, Barbata organizes a mass in memory of Pastrana in St. Joseph Chapel in Oslo. It is the first humanitarian gesture toward Pastrana and is attended by hundreds of people; many are circus performers who bring flowers.

2005 The new Board for the Evaluation of Human Remains under NESH is officially formed, and Barbata requests their evaluation of the case for Julia Pastrana's repatriation and burial in Mexico.

2007 The committee informs Barbata that the case of Pastrana will be reopened. The official document stating this is lost by the US Postal Service, but is recovered and delivered to Barbata, damaged, one year later.

2007–2011 Barbata consults scientists specializing in genetics in an effort to find Julia Pastrana's relatives. After extensive research, it is clear that a moral and ethical argument is a more feasible justification for the repatriation than finding her relatives, since DNA samples are not available. Barbata meets Ricardo Mimiaga, a historian from Sinaloa who has researched the life of Pastrana. Together they search for related documents: certificates of birth, baptism, etc.

2011 Silvia Gámez, a reporter from *Reforma* newspaper in Mexico, discovers the story of Julia Pastrana and of Laura Anderson Barbata's involvement in her repatriation. Gámez begins correspondence with Barbata, the University of Oslo, and Norway's Ministry of Health, as well as scientists and historians in Mexico. She publishes her findings, and the story is picked up by hundreds of news sites around the world.

2012 The Ministry of Health recognizes that no investigation has been done on Pastrana's body, nor have they received any official requests for Pastrana to be buried. Barbata speaks with Remigio Mestas in Oaxaca to discuss the creation of a ceremonial pre-Hispanic *huipil* for Pastrana's burial. The *huipil* and *enredo* textiles are made by Francisca Palafox, a master weaver from Oaxaca, utilizing natural cotton, *coyuchi*, *caracol*, and human hair.

March 14, 2012 In Culiacán, Barbata has an audience with the secretary to the governor of Sinaloa to propose the repatriation of Julia Pastrana to her native state for burial.

April 16, 2012 Mario López Valdez, the governor of Sinaloa, joins Barbata's repatriation efforts, sending a letter to NESH petitioning for the return of Julia Pastrana's body. The governor's letter is accompanied by a letter from Barbata that includes the moral, ethical, and social justifications for Pastrana's return for burial.

May 8, 2012 In Oslo, NESH meets to evaluate the letters from Mexico requesting Julia Pastrana's repatriation.

June 4, 2012 NESH responds to the petition with a recommendation that Julia Pastrana be repatriated for burial in accordance with her religious faith. The recommendation is received by the University of Oslo and the Institute of Basic Medicine at the university, both of which agree to the repatriation.

June–December 2012 Barbata contacts the institutions that will be involved in the project: the Office of Foreign Affairs of Mexico, the Embassy of Mexico in Belgium that is responsible for Norway, the University of Oslo, the Ministry of Health of Norway, Albin International Repatriation Services Ltd., funerary services in Oslo, Mexico City, and Culiacán, the Institute of Culture of Sinaloa, and the office of the governor of Sinaloa.

January 2013 Barbata initiates "A Flower for Julia," an international call for flowers to symbolically welcome and give closure to Julia Pastrana's long journey home on the day of her burial.

February 7, 2013 Laura Anderson Barbata, along with forensic anthropologist Nicholas Márquez-Grant from the University of Oxford, act as witnesses that the body of Julia Pastrana is sealed in her coffin. In the chapel at Rikshospitalet, Oslo University Hospital, a private ceremony takes place for the transfer of custody of Pastrana to the Government of Mexico. Barbata represents the State of Sinaloa. Artists, academics, and activists attend the ceremony.

February 8–10, 2013 Julia Pastrana's coffin is transported from Oslo to Mexico in a sealed coffin. The body arrives in Culiacán, Sinaloa. Barbata verifies that Pastrana is in the coffin, and the coffin is not opened again.

February 12, 2013 The coffin of Julia Pastrana is transported from Culiacán to Sinaloa de Leyva. Pastrana is welcomed with official ceremonies and a funeral mass, then taken to the municipal cemetery, following local traditions. As music plays, Pastrana's coffin is covered in flowers and buried. Inside she wears pre-Hispanic ceremonial *huipil* garments and has a photograph of her child on her chest. Her tomb is completely covered in concrete and enclosed in walls that are more than a meter thick to protect it from being vandalized and to guarantee that she will never be removed from her resting place. The tomb is then covered with thousands of flowers that have arrived from all over the world.

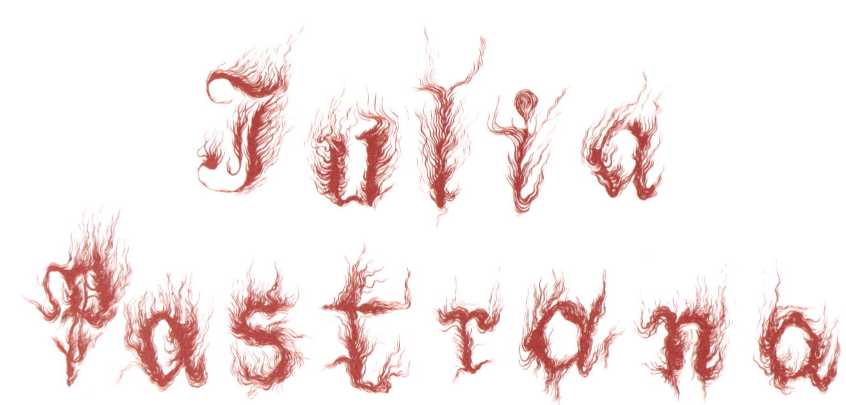

Julia
Pastrana

Born in Mexico City, LAURA ANDERSON BARBATA is a visual artist based in Brooklyn and Mexico City. Since 1992 she has worked primarily in the social realm, and has initiated projects in the Venezuelan Amazon, Trinidad and Tobago, Mexico, Norway, and the United States. Among them is her ongoing project *The Repatriation of Julia Pastrana*, begun in 2005, which resulted in the removal of Pastrana's body from the Schreiner Collection in Oslo and its successful repatriation and burial in Sinaloa, Mexico, Pastrana's birth state. The project continues with upcoming publications and performances.

Barbata is also known for her project *Transcommunality* (2001–ongoing), working with stilt walkers and artisans from Mexico, New York, and the Caribbean. This project has been presented at various museums, schools, and other venues, among them the Museum of Modern Art, New York; the Modern Art Museum of Fort Worth, Texas; BRIC Arts | Media House, Brooklyn; Rutgers University; University of Wisconsin, Madison; Museo Textil de Oaxaca, México: and Museo de la Ciudad de México.

Her work is in various private and public collections, including the Metropolitan Museum of Art, New York; el Museo de Arte Moderno, México D.F.; Landesbank Baden-Württemberg, Stuttgart, Germany; Colección Patricia Phelps de Cisneros; American Express Co., México; Museo Carrillo Gil, México; Museum of Contemporary Art, San Diego, California; Thyssen-Bornemisza Art Contemporary, Vienna, Austria; and Museo Jaureguía, Navarra, Spain.

Barbata was a recipient of the Anonymous Was a Woman 2016 Award; an honorary fellow of LACIS (the Latin American, Caribbean, and Iberian Studies Program), University of Wisconsin, Madison; and a fellow of the Thyssen Bornemisza Art Contemporary TBA21 The Current program. She was a professor at the Escuela Nacional de Escultura, Pintura y Grabado La Esmeralda of the Instituto Nacional de Bellas Artes from 2010 until 2015.

La Extraordinaria Historia de Julia Pastrana is a beneficiary of the National Fund for Culture and Arts through the National System of Arts Creators (2014–2017), México.

JAN BONDESON was born in Sweden in 1962 and attended Lund University, where he qualified as a doctor in 1988 and was awarded his PhD in 1996. He then moved to London to join the prestigious Kennedy Institute of Rheumatology as a research fellow, where he remained until 2001 when he was promoted to senior lecturer. He is an honorary senior research fellow at Cardiff University, Wales, and author of more than a hundred publications in refereed scientific journals. He is also the author of twenty-one books about the history of medicine, zoology, and cynology, and the history of crime, including *Cabinet of Medical Curiosities* (1997), *The Two-Headed Boy* (2000), *Buried Alive* (2001), and *The Pig-Faced Lady of Manchester Square* (2004). In 1990, he rediscovered the missing mummy of Julia Pastrana, and was the first to establish her correct diagnosis as congenital hypertrichosis with terminal hair, and associated gingival hyperplasia.

ROSEMARIE GARLAND-THOMSON is professor of English and bioethics and the founding codirector of the Disability Studies Initiative at Emory University. Her specialties are disability studies, American literature and culture, bioethics, and women's studies. Her work develops the field of critical disability studies in the health humanities, broadly understood, to bring forward disability access, equity, and identity to communities inside and outside of the academy. She is the author of *Staring: How We Look* among other publications. Her current book project is *Habitable Worlds: Disability, Technology, and Eugenics*.

GRANT KESTER is professor of art history in the Visual Arts Department at the University of California, San Diego, and the founding editor of *FIELD: A Journal of Socially Engaged Art Criticism*. His publications include *Art, Activism, and Oppositionality: Essays from Afterimage* (1998), *The One and the Many: Contemporary Collaborative Art in a Global Context* (2011), *Conversation Pieces: Community and Communication in Modern Art* (2013), and *Collective Situations: Dialogues in Contemporary Latin American Art 1995–2010*, an anthology of writings by art collectives working in Latin America, produced in collaboration with Bill Kelley Jr. (2017). He is currently completing work on a new book that develops a more detailed theoretical account of dialogical aesthetics.

BESS LOVEJOY is a writer and editor who lives in Brooklyn. She is the author of *Rest in Pieces: The Curious Fates of Famous Corpses* (2013) and currently an editor at *Mental Floss*. Previously, she was an editor at Smithsonian.com and on the Schott's Almanac series. Her writing has appeared in the *New York Times*, the *Wall Street Journal*, *Time*, *Atlas Obscura*, *The Believer*, *Lapham's Quarterly*, the *Boston Globe, Public Domain Review*, and elsewhere. She is passionate about telling stories from the overlooked corners of history. She is currently at work on a fiction project.

NICHOLAS MÁRQUEZ-GRANT is a lecturer in forensic anthropology and Course Director in Forensic Archaeology and Anthropology at Cranfield Forensic Institute, Cranfield University, Defence Academy of the United Kingdom. He is also a research associate of the School of Anthropology and Museum Ethnography at the University of Oxford. Previously he worked as an osteoarchaeologist and as a specialist forensic practitioner in anthropology and archaeology for a number of independent forensic science providers in the UK. He has considerable experience in the excavation and study of cremated and unburnt bone from prehistoric and present-day sites. Márquez-Grant has been teaching biological/physical anthropology at the University of Oxford since 2001, and has published numerous papers on archaeology and anthropology as well as reference texts in the field; among his interests are issues surrounding ethics and human remains.

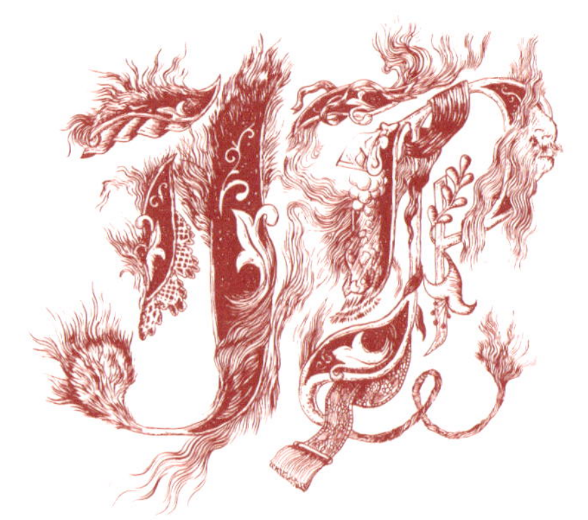

Acknowledgments

We are honored to have Lucia|Marquand as our publishers, and our sincerest thanks go to their outstanding team: Melissa Duffes, Leah Finger, Jeremy Linden, Meghann Ney, Ryan Polich, and Kestrel Rundle.

We wish to express our profound gratitude to:

Susan Kelly, this book's designer, who immersed herself in Julia Pastrana's story by researching archival and contemporary imagery in order to capture the essence of her life. Susan's commitment and sensitivity to her process resulted in this beautiful volume.

Thomas Frick, for his insightful editing of the texts.

Our contributing authors, for providing a unique look into the life and history of Julia Pastrana: Jan Bondeson, Rosemarie Garland-Thomson, Grant H. Kester, Bess Lovejoy, and Nicholas Márquez-Grant.

The photographers who generously shared their images for this book: Carlos Barrera, Thor Brødreskift, Dignicraft, Stefan Hagen, Michaela Klouda, Tor Einar Krogtoft-Jensen, Bjørn Lund, Alix Milne, Martha Patricia Montero, Marco Pacheco.

Jan Bondeson, who kindly shared images from his personal collection, and Erik Tlaseca for his extraordinary drawings.

Kathleen Godfrey for her research assistance. Her generosity in sharing her online project, Pastranaonline.com, fueled by her desire to communicate the truth about Julia Pastrana with great integrity, have enriched the contents of this book.

Ute Meta Bauer, Marc Joseph Berg, Kathleen Culebro, Magne Furuholmen, Clayton Kirking, Melissa Potter, and Alfonso Diaz Tovar; all are artists, friends, and collaborators who have been enthusiastic supporters of work related to Julia Pastrana, and who have provided ongoing guidance throughout this process.

And lastly, to the Sistema Nacional de Creadores de Arte and the National Fund for Culture and Arts of Mexico for generous support toward the making of this book.

We hope this tribute to Julia Pastrana will stand as a reminder that we must learn from the past to correct grave injustices and strive for a more humane and ethical future. We dedicate this book to her life and memory.

LAURA ANDERSON BARBATA **AND** DONNA WINGATE

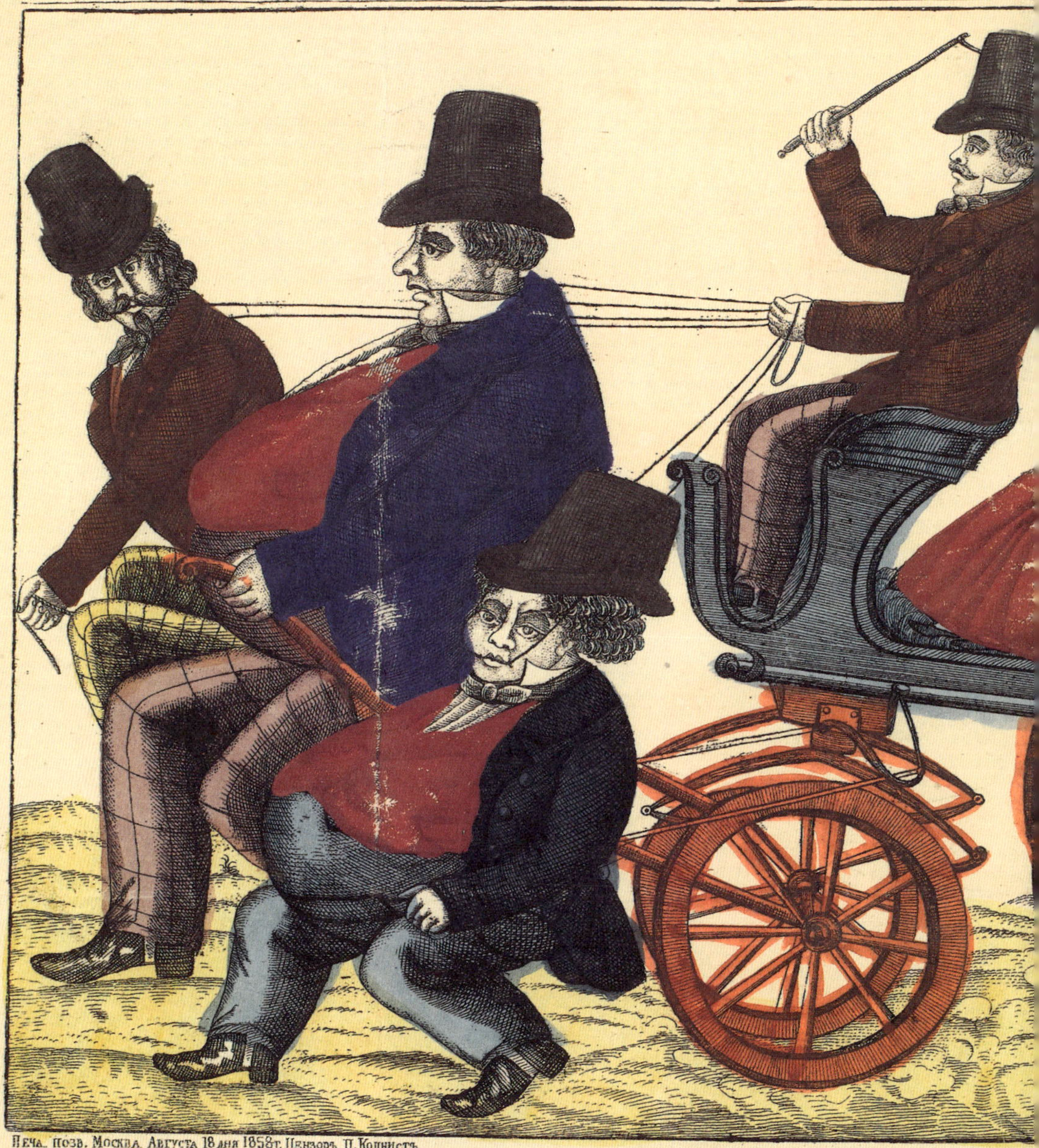

Печа. позв. Москва. Августа 18 дня 1858г. Цензоръ П. Кописть.

Отъѣздъ Дѣвицы Ю.

Вотъ Юлія уѣжаетъ,
Англію оставляетъ.
Она тамъ побыла,
Денегъ много набрала.
И многихъ прельстила,
Собой обворожила.
Занёй много гонялися,
На красу соблазнялися.
Руки добивалися,
Да съ носами всѣ осталися.
Но любовь не игрушка,
Говоритъ Петрушка.
Вишъ какъ ее обожали,
Проотъѣздъ женихи узнали,
Вмигъ кней прикатили,
Коней отложили.

Рожеримъ толстякъ,
Страшный добрякъ.
Въ оглобли впрегся,
Тащить Юлію взялся.
Онъ больно здаровъ,
Вѣсить 15ть пудовъ.
Брюшкомъ толстъ,
И огромный ростъ.
Хоть каго потащитъ,
И порядкомъ бѣжитъ.
Ганго Худано тожъ засуетился,
На право въ пристяжку пустился.
Ужасть какой худой,
Да рысистой такой,—
Въ часъ по 15ть верстъ катаетъ

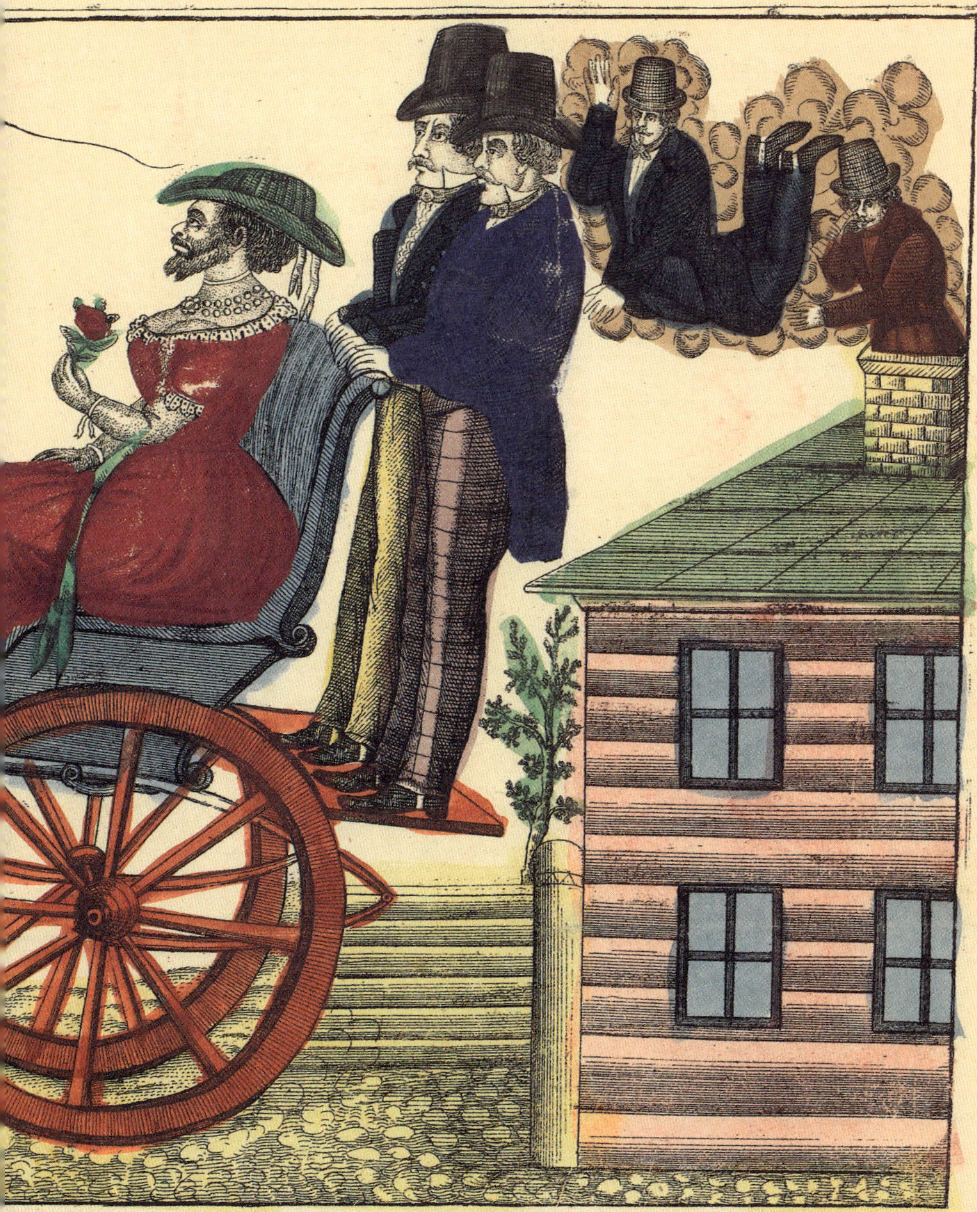

...СТРАНА ИЗЪ АНГЛІИ

...льшая,
...завитая.
...же изъ жениховъ постарался,
...кое мѣсто забраля.
...у взнуздалъ,
...мъ понукать сталъ.
...скакала,
...хотала.
...кряхтелъ,
...потѣлъ.
...ожъ сторался,
...тъ кнута сгибался.
...тонаетъ,
...поспѣваетъ.
...а жениха назапятки встали.

Что-бъ наней женится,
Да денженками разжится.
Все послѣдніе продавали,
И Юлію соблазняли.
Разные сюрпризы дарили,
И все съ себя спустили.
Юлію не добыли,
А въ трубу съ дымомъ укатили.
Ишъ хотятъ ее дагонять,
Назадъ подарки взять.
Да Рожеримъ такъ катитъ,
Что всѣхъ удивляетъ;
Отъ куда рысь берется.
Такъ изъ оглобель и рвется
И Худано съ Пузано неунываютъ

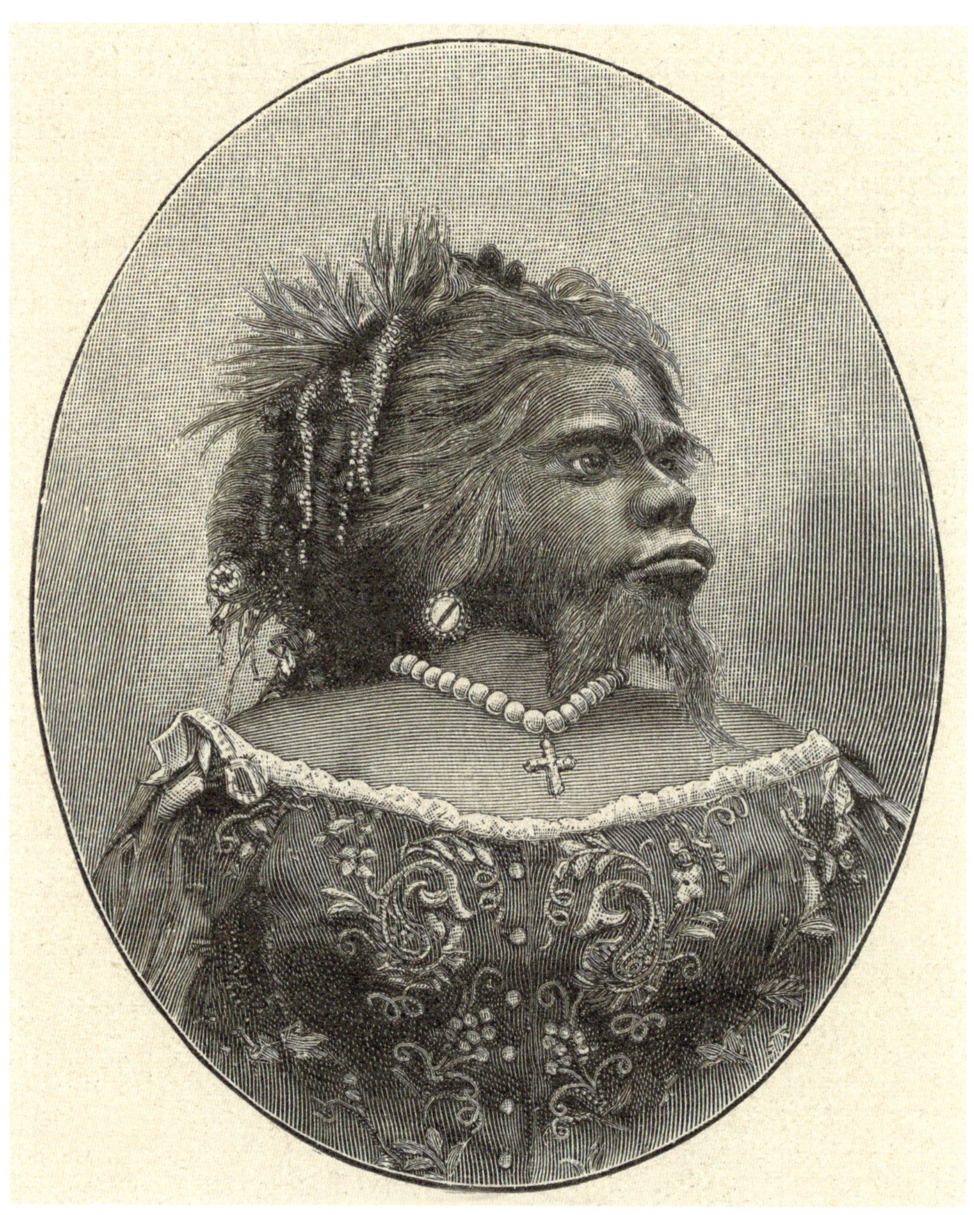

Portrait of Julia Pastrana embalmed, c. 1860–70

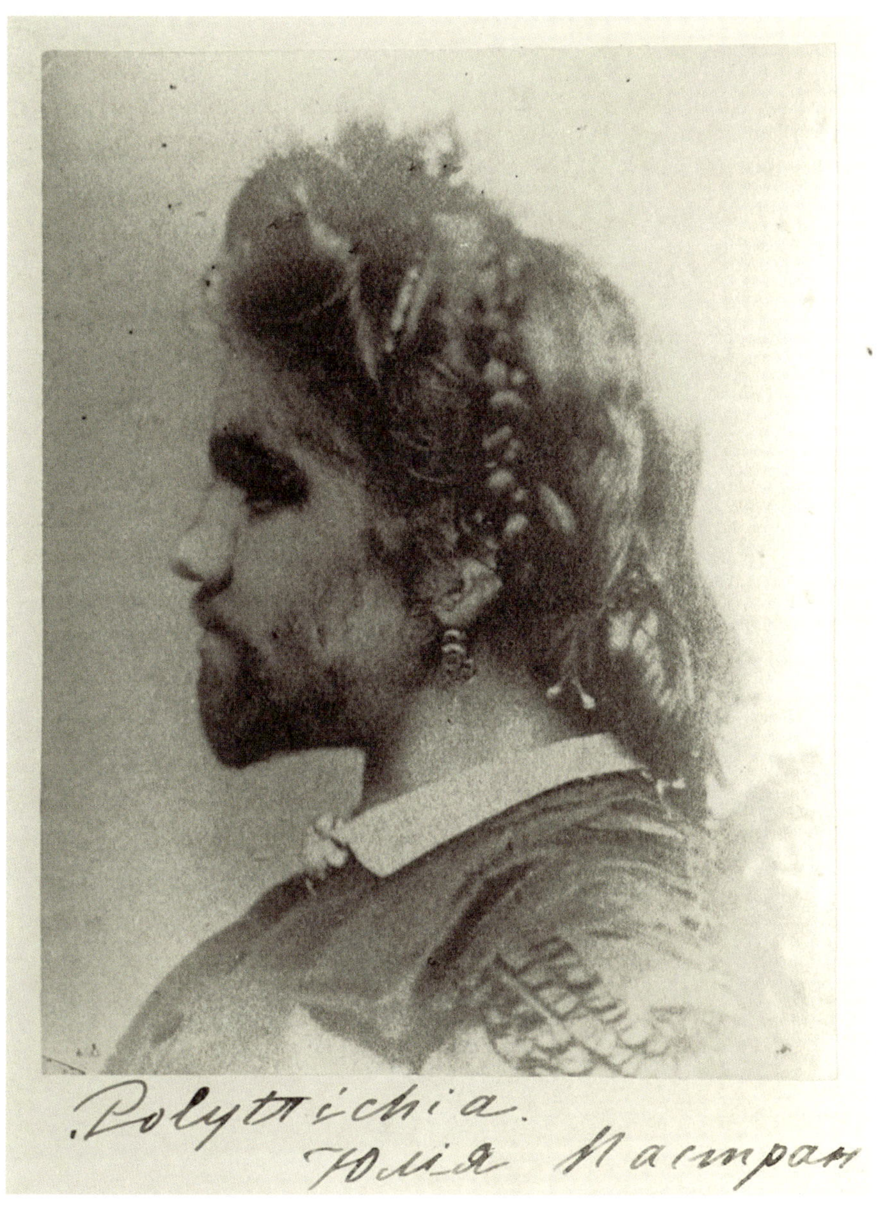

Possible photo of Julia Pastrana, with the caption "Iulia Pastrana" written by physician Nikolaĭ Mansurov in Cyrillic script

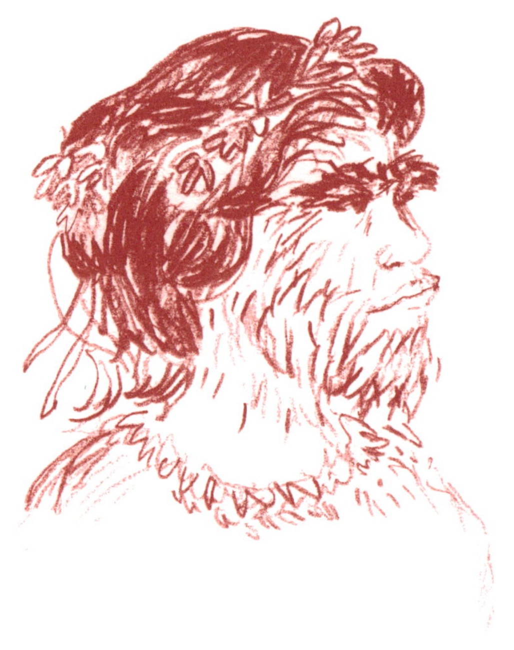

Additional captions

Cover and p. 2 Retouched daguerreotype portrait of Julia Pastrana, c. 1855–60

p. 6 Julia Pastrana exhibition in the United States, c. 1972

p. 28 Easter Week festivities, Mayo indigenous group, Tehueco, Sinaloa, Mexico, 2013

p. 64 Julia Pastrana's carriage in storage, c. 2013

p. 80 Entrance to the cemetery where Julia Pastrana is buried, 2013

p. 98 Lateral head radiograph of Julia Pastrana

p. 128 Julia Pastrana's coffin at the reception ceremony in Sinaloa de Leyva, Mexico, 2013

p. 152 Visitor studying skeleton displays of Charles Byrne and American giant Charles Freeman, Jonathan Wild, and Caroline Crachami, 1958

pp. 178–79, foldout Laura Anderson Barbata and Erik Tlaseca, pages from *La Extraordinaria Historia de Julia Pastrana*, zine no. 2, 2016; risograph

p. 180 Laura Anderson Barbata and Rafael Esquer, *Julia Pastrana, su vuelta y sus raíces*, 2013; animation still

pp. 194–95 Julia Pastrana leaves England, 1858; lithograph

198

Library of Congress Cataloging-in-Publication Data

Names: Anderson, Laura, 1958– author.

Title: The eye of the beholder : Julia Pastrana's long journey home / Laura Anderson Barbata, Jan Bondeson, Rosemarie Garland-Thomson, Grant H. Kester, Bess Lovejoy, Nicholas Māarquez-Grant ; edited by Laura Anderson Barbata.

Description: Seattle : Lucia|Marquand, [2017] | Includes bibliographical references.

Identifiers: LCCN 2017017438 | ISBN 9780692762189 (hardcover : alk. paper)

Subjects: LCSH: Pastrana, Julia, 1834-1860. | Hypertrichosis--Patients--Biography. | Freak shows--History--19th century.

Classification: LCC RL431 .A53 2017 | DDC 616.5/46--dc23

LC record available at https://lccn.loc.gov/2017017438

Published by Lucia|Marquand, Seattle
www.luciamarquand.com

Available through:
ARTBOOK | D.A.P.
75 Broad Street, Suite 630
New York, NY 10004
www.artbook.com

Edited by Laura Anderson Barbata and Donna Wingate
Copyedited by Thomas Frick
Designed by Susan E. Kelly
Typeset in Surveyor by Susan E. Kelly
Proofread by Ted Gilley
Color management by iocolor, Seattle
Printed and bound in China by C&C Offset Printing Co., Ltd.

Laura Anderson Barbata, Miembro del Sistema Nacional de Creadores de Arte. This book was made with support from the National Fund for Culture and Arts through the National System of Arts Creators, (2014–2017).

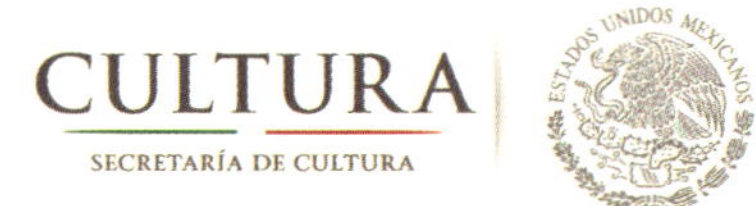

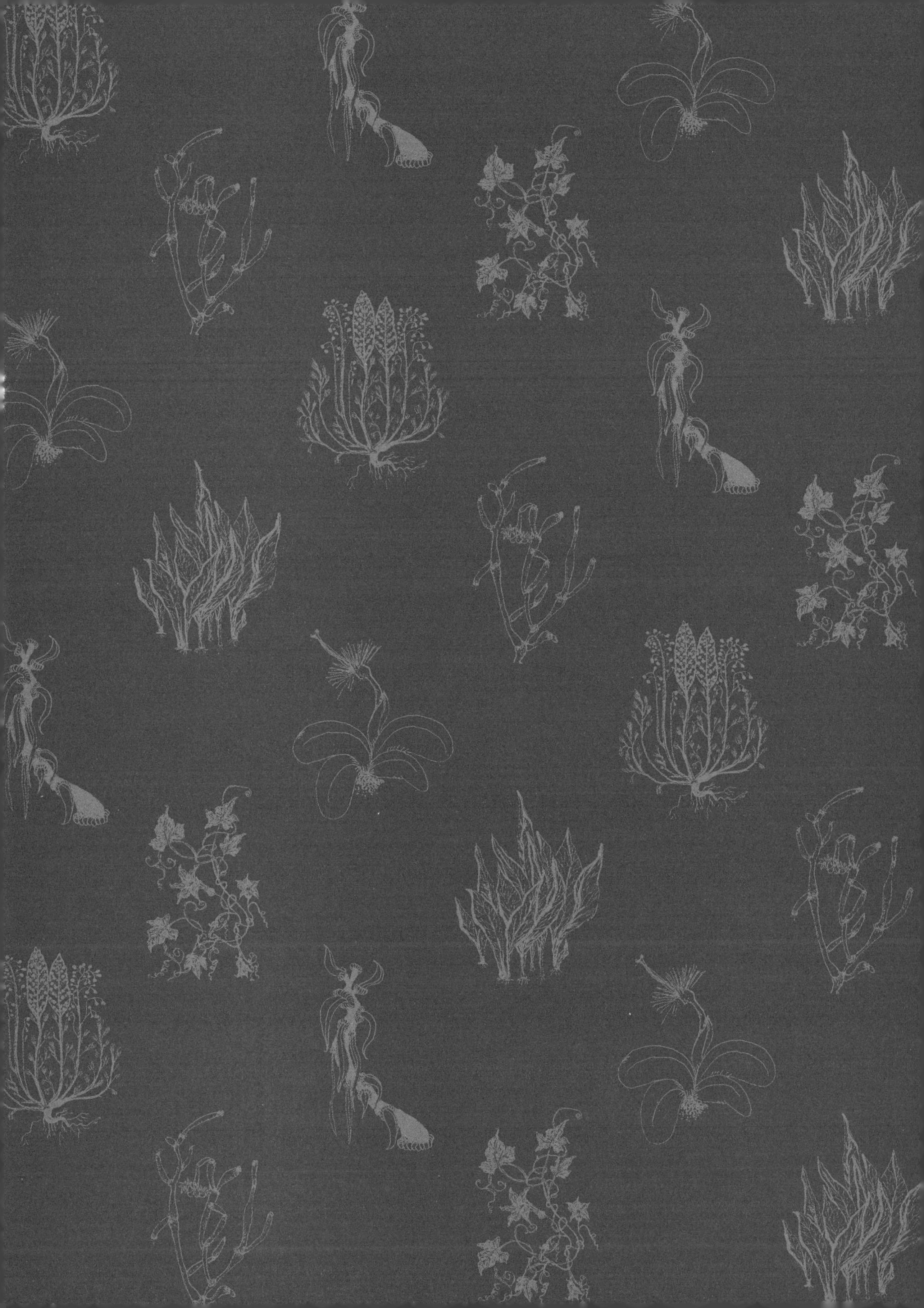